The Price of Loyalty

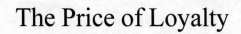

Vietnam: America in the War Years

Series Editor: David L. Anderson
California State University, Monterey Bay

The Vietnam War and the tumultuous internal upheavals in America that coincided with it marked a watershed era in U.S. history. These events profoundly challenged America's heroic self-image. During the 1950s the United States defined Southeast Asia as an area of vital strategic importance. In the 1960s this view produced a costly American military campaign that continued into the early 1970s. The Vietnam War ended with an unprecedented U.S. failure to achieve its stated objectives. Simultaneous with this frustrating military intervention and the domestic debate that it produced were other tensions created by student activism on campuses, the black struggle for civil rights, and the women's liberation movement. The books in this series explore the complex and controversial issues of the period from the mid-1950s to the mid-1970s in brief and engaging volumes. To facilitate continued and informed debate on these contested subjects, each book examines a military, political, or diplomatic issue; the role of a key individual; or one of the domestic changes in America during the war.

Titles in the Series

The Price of Loyalty

Hubert Humphrey's Vietnam Conflict

Andrew L. Johns

ROWMAN & LITTLEFIELD
Lanham • Boulder • New York • London

Published by Rowman & Littlefield
An imprint of The Rowman & Littlefield Publishing Group, Inc.
4501 Forbes Boulevard, Suite 200, Lanham, Maryland 20706
www.rowman.com

6 Tinworth Street, London SE11 5AL, United Kingdom

British Library Cataloguing in Publication Information available.

Library of Congress Cataloging-in-Publication Data Available

ISBN 9780742544529 (cloth : alk. paper)
ISBN 9780742544536 (electronic)

♾ ™ The paper used in this publication meets the minimum requirements of American National Standard for Information Sciences Permanence of Paper for Printed Library Materials, ANSI/NISO Z39.48-1992.

Contents

Introduction

"The Graveyard of Presidential Ambitions"

It's like being naked in the middle of a blizzard with no one to even offer you a match to keep you warm: that's the vice presidency.
—Hubert Humphrey

He who blinded by ambition raises himself to a position whence he cannot mount higher must thereafter fall with the greatest loss.
—Niccolò Machiavelli

The delegates assembled in the Miami Beach Convention Center cheered wildly as the newly crowned Democratic nominee raised his hands in triumph on stage. Standing next to Lyndon Johnson—who would serve longer in the White House (over nine years) than anyone except Franklin Delano Roosevelt and who had just finished introducing his presumptive successor as president—the former U.S. senator from Minnesota basked in the rapturous adulation of the crowd, equally exhausted by the long week of political maneuvering at the convention and energized by the prospect of running for president against Ronald Reagan in a battle of contrasting ideological prescriptions for the country's future. The conservative governor of California, who had narrowly lost his party's nomination four years earlier to Richard Nixon, had prevailed in the hard-fought GOP primaries against House minority leader Gerald Ford (R-MI), Governor Nelson Rockefeller (R-NY), and Governor George Romney (R-MI). Reagan's coronation as the Republican presidential candidate would take place four weeks later in the same building in which the vice president now stood on stage.

It had been a long and winding road to Miami for the Democratic standard-bearer. Over the past eight years, the Johnson administration had faced

1

complex challenges both at home and abroad: social upheaval, racial strife, congressional battles over domestic reforms, and the omnipresent Cold War, just to name a few. But the president's decision in February 1965 to disengage from Vietnam and allow the United Nations to oversee elections based on the 1954 Geneva Accords had not only prevented a potentially long and costly war but also made Johnson realize just how valuable the vice president's domestic political acumen and foreign policy experience could be. Their partnership since that decision, based on mutual respect and loyalty, defined the administration's legacy and contributed significantly to the success of Johnson's presidency. Now, at long last, the vice president's unwavering allegiance to LBJ had been rewarded with the president's full support in the primaries. Now his political dreams and ambitions had been realized, and he had unbridled optimism for the future of the United States. Now he would build on the domestic achievements of the Great Society and lead the country and the world into a new era of peace, prosperity, and justice, all shaped by his deeply held liberal principles. As Hubert Horatio Humphrey Jr. approached the podium to formally accept the 1972 Democratic presidential nomination, he was the personification of the politics of joy.

* * * * *

In reality, of course, history did not play out that way. Instead of following Hubert Humphrey's perspicacious advice in February 1965, Lyndon Johnson chose war in Vietnam and escalated the U.S. presence in Southeast Asia exponentially. That decision would lead not only to a disastrous conflict that wasted billions of dollars and resulted in millions of U.S. and Vietnamese lives lost but also to deep and lasting divisions in U.S. society. The Vietnam conflict would cripple the once-dominant U.S. economy, weaken the nation's diplomatic and moral influence, fundamentally alter the social and cultural fabric of the country, and cause permanent damage to U.S. political institutions. Moreover, it would cost LBJ and Richard Nixon their presidencies and would so undermine the public's faith in its government that it would never recover. The war in Vietnam also become the decisive factor in Humphrey's loss to Nixon in the 1968 presidential election, with Johnson's lack of support for his vice president playing a crucial role. In fact, the president repaid Humphrey's steadfast personal and political loyalty—which dated to their time in the Senate in the 1950s—with dismissal, disdain, and disrespect despite the vice president's outspoken defense of U.S. Vietnam policy in 1966 and 1967. Humphrey's inability to break with the Johnson administration acted as an albatross to his campaign and contributed significantly to the fractures that plagued the Democratic Party through most of 1968 and into the new decade. By the time the Minnesotan decided to return to and embrace his long-held principles and announce his opposition to the conflict, it was too late to save his candidacy. For Humphrey, and for so many other politicians who sought the White House, Vietnam was truly "the graveyard of presidential ambitions."[1]

Hubert Humphrey occupies an interesting place in the nation's historical memory. Many historians and pundits view him as a character from a Shakespearian tragedy, the protagonist who makes a difficult or impossible choice that then leads to problems from which he can never recover. Others consider him the lost progressive hope for America, the "conscience of the country," as his most recent biographer described him, who could have spared the United States the agony of the Nixon years, shortened the Vietnam War, avoided Watergate, and helped to achieve long-held liberal aspirations for the United States.[2] A few contrarians see him as an opportunist, a political vagabond whose views shifted according to the predilections of the moment and his own ambitions, a chameleon who does not deserve the approbation of history.[3] Yet most scholars see the former vice president in a generally positive light. For example, forty-five years after Humphrey lost the presidential election, political scientist Norman Ornstein recalled that the former vice president was a "force of nature, with the intellect, personal integrity, and personal force that transcended policy differences" in a way that moved colleagues and outsiders alike. He was "a remarkable and unique human being; he would have made a marvelous president."[4]

While opinions vary, two things are quite clear. First, the former Minnesota senator's long and largely distinguished political career had a profound influence on the trajectory of U.S. history for over four decades. Second, Humphrey is an absolutely essential figure for historians to understand and assess in order to achieve a panoptic view of the trajectory and historical implications of the U.S. experience in Vietnam, particularly in the crucial period after 1964. Why? Because the war had such devastating consequences for the former vice president's political fortunes. If Hubert Humphrey had a political Achilles' heel, it was his inability to grapple successfully with the Vietnam conflict from 1964 to 1968. That failure not only cost him the White House but also damaged his historical reputation. For Humphrey, that was a reality that was at once tragic and ironic given his political beliefs and his aspirations for his country. The mayor who fought discrimination and championed civil rights, the senator who sought peace and disarmament, and the vice president who preached social justice at home and abroad would see his legacy permanently tarnished by his association with the debacle in Southeast Asia. As David Halberstam, the journalist whose reporting on the then-emerging conflict in Southeast Asia won a Pulitzer Prize, wrote in the wake of the 1968 election, if "one wanted to do a study of what the war in Vietnam had done to a generation of older American liberals, Humphrey would have been exhibit A."[5]

Yet Humphrey's difficulties with the war predated the 1968 presidential campaign. From the moment he accepted LBJ's offer in the summer of 1964 to serve as vice president, the Vietnam conflict evolved from being simply another skirmish in Humphrey's long crusade against communism into the defining and ultimately destructive issue of his otherwise impressive political career. Edgar Berman, Humphrey's personal physician and confidant, wrote in 1979 that "Vietnam was the cause of the most harrowing and unproductive years of Humphrey's life: it ruined his relationship with the president, engendered accusations of warmongering by his best friends and beloved public, and eventually cost him the presidency itself." Part of the reason for this, Berman suggested, was that Humphrey's "true antiwar feelings were never made known to the public during his vice presidency." As a result, "It was especially agonizing for him that the public, which knew him from the very beginning as a man of peace . . . should turn him into a man of war. Even more disconcerting was that they would think his beliefs, always so consistent, could change so easily."[6] While Berman's apology for Humphrey's ambivalence on the war during his tenure as vice president may be overstated, it does encapsulate the fatal harm the conflict did to Humphrey's reputation—especially among his political allies on the left and in the antiwar movement—and to his presidential ambitions.

In his memoirs, the former vice president seemed to still be in denial about U.S. involvement in Vietnam, his role in the war's evolution, and the conflict's destructive impact on his political career. He recalled, "Though we involved ourselves in Indochina almost immediately after World War II, we never really had a Vietnam policy. . . . We edged up to it and finally slid in. Policy was never formalized, except in the most general terms. Our predecessors and we never resolved adequate, realistic short- or long-range objectives. Until early 1968," he observed, "with the 'A to Z' review, there never appeared to be any real measurement of the ultimate costs, what our presence entailed, what actual benefits could be expected."[7] The problems the Minnesotan identified were real; indeed, his perceptive February 1965 memorandum to LBJ, which advocated for disengagement from Vietnam based on domestic political calculations, highlighted many of them. Why, then, did Humphrey—renowned for his political instincts, foreign policy expertise, and intelligence—fail to recognize the danger inherent in linking himself inextricably to the administration's Vietnam policy after Johnson rejected his advice? The answer can be explained in three words that make up the primary themes in this book: loyalty, principle, and politics.

During a debate in the House of Commons in June 1976, British Labor leader Neil Kinnock said, "Loyalty is a fine quality, but in excess it fills political graveyards."[8] That sentiment neatly summarizes the effect that Humphrey's loyalty to Lyndon Johnson had on Humphrey's political destiny. The friendship between the two men dated back to their time in the U.S.

Senate, where Humphrey proved to be crucial to LBJ realizing his ambition to become Senate majority leader. As a leading northern liberal, Humphrey possessed political *bona fides* and could rally support from the left that Johnson desperately needed in order to achieve his goals.

The same scenario played out in the summer of 1964 during both the administration's efforts to pass the Civil Rights Act and the vice presidential selection process. LBJ needed Humphrey; the relationship was primarily (although not exclusively) transactional for Johnson. Nevertheless, Humphrey understood clearly what accepting the vice presidency meant, later saying, "Anyone who thinks that the vice president can take a position independent of his administration simply has no knowledge of politics or government. You are his choice in a political marriage, and he expects your absolute loyalty . . . could you imagine what would happen to a Vice President who publicly repudiated his Administration? Man, that's political suicide."[9]

But as laudable and understandable as Humphrey's allegiance to LBJ might have been in 1964, it ended up causing him insurmountable problems, both as vice president and presidential candidate, over the four years that followed. Why? Because that loyalty was never reciprocated by Johnson. Humphrey maintained his allegiance to LBJ long after it became clear that the relationship was essentially a one-way street. By doing so, the vice president allowed himself to be manipulated, used, and ultimately discarded. It forced him to advocate vociferously for a war about which he harbored serious doubts. It led him to waver endlessly about the conflict despite consistent and escalating pressure from his friends, advisers, and political allies. And it limited his ability to unite the polarized Democratic Party in 1968, which crippled his presidential campaign and contributed to his defeat. Loyalty may have defined Humphrey's political career, but it also irreparably damaged it.

While loyal to LBJ to a fault, Humphrey demonstrated less fealty to the principles and ideas that launched his political career. To be sure, Humphrey's support of the Great Society programs, civil rights, and other domestic initiatives animated his decisions on Vietnam and reflected the liberal beliefs that had brought him to national prominence as the firebrand progressive mayor of Minneapolis, as did his advocacy of the nonproliferation treaty and international development programs. As one of the founding members of Americans for Democratic Action and a political tsunami who boldly excoriated the 1948 Democratic convention for its failure to act on civil rights, Humphrey's liberal credentials could not be questioned. To be fair, Humphrey's fierce advocacy for the Great Society—both at home and abroad—harkened back to his reputation as a radical progressive. Yet when it came to the Vietnam conflict, Humphrey abandoned or ignored his principles out of a combination of political expediency, ambition, and allegiance to the president. Even as he faced cascading criticism from his liberal allies in 1966 and

1967, Humphrey privileged other considerations above his principles, leaving himself vulnerable to attacks from across the political spectrum on the issue of the war during the presidential campaign in 1968.

That truth is even more surprising given that Humphrey's long career in politics honed his political instincts to a razor-sharp edge. During his vice presidency (at least after February 1965) and presidential candidacy, however, those same instincts seemed to vanish or were pointedly ignored as Humphrey placed LBJ's political interests ahead of his own. Even when the obvious political calculation was to reject the administration's stance on the conflict, Humphrey hesitated. More generally, nothing could be more obvious than the fact that Vietnam was a political war, which makes Humphrey's choices even more perplexing. The U.S. decisions to support the Saigon regime from 1954 onward reflected the demands of anticommunism and the domestic political realities of U.S. presidential elections, the relationship between the conflict and the demands of the Great Society, and the personal political interests of John Kennedy, Lyndon Johnson, and Richard Nixon, among others. One cannot fully understand U.S. involvement in Vietnam without appreciating the degree to which decisions were made, delayed, or avoided due to domestic political considerations. That fact underscores the power that the nexus of domestic politics and foreign policy has had in the U.S. political context. That relationship, which played such a pivotal role during the entire U.S. involvement in Vietnam and would certainly have ramifications for Humphrey, represents a central theme in this book. [10]

* * * * *

While Humphrey looms large in U.S. political history due to his five terms in the Senate (1949–1964 and 1971–1978), his four years as vice president (1965–1969), and his 1968 presidential campaign against Richard Nixon, the scholarly literature on his life and career has been relatively sporadic for someone so influential in the events that played out during the Cold War. The three most detailed examinations of Humphrey's life are biographies by Dan Cohen, Carl Solberg, and Arnold Offner. [11] The vice president's memoirs, *The Education of a Public Man*, provide a retrospective of his career that is balanced, not overly self-congratulatory (unlike so many examples in the genre), and supported by historical documentation. [12] Additional personal and political details about Humphrey are recounted in memoirs by his friend and physician, Edgar Berman, and his adviser-cum-speechwriter, Ted Van Dyk. [13] Specific aspects of Humphrey's political career and his involvement with issues such as civil rights have been explored by Timothy Thurber and Robert Mann, among others. [14] His rise in politics in Minnesota and his initial tenure in the U.S. Senate, which are discussed briefly in chapter 1, have received a modest amount of attention, particularly in terms of his staunch anticommunism.[15] The 1968 presidential election, however, boasts its own cottage industry of analysis, with scores of titles examining the close Humphrey–Nixon–George Wallace race and the issues that defined the election, including Vietnam.[16]

As far as Humphrey's engagement with the Vietnam War, the historiography is even less complete. The Solberg and Offner biographies cover Humphrey and the war as a discrete part of the broader narrative of the vice president's life, with Offner's account being the more detailed and enlightening. The February 1965 memorandum Humphrey sent to Lyndon Johnson, which will be discussed in chapter 2, is referenced and assessed in numerous studies.[17] Humphrey's exile and redemption from 1965 to 1967, the subject of chapters 2 and 3, make cameo appearances in a number of histories of that period, but most of the attention paid to his struggle with the Vietnam conflict is devoted to his efforts to grapple with the issue during the 1968 presidential campaign, which will be assessed in chapters 4 and 5. But no academic study has attempted to examine Humphrey's positions on the war, his role in the Johnson administration, his Faustian relationship with LBJ, and his influence on the trajectory of U.S. policy over the course of the long U.S. involvement in Indochina in a comprehensive or holistic way until this book.

Of course, as significant as the Vietnam conflict was to Humphrey's career, his legacy goes far beyond the war. His involvement with a myriad of crucial issues during the Cold War—nuclear nonproliferation, civil rights, education, and domestic and international anticommunism, just to name a few—makes him one of the most prominent U.S. senators of the twentieth century. It is ironic, then, that the man who pushed so relentlessly for disarmament and fought so valiantly for liberal causes would become the prototypical apologist for U.S. involvement in the Vietnam War by 1966. How did that happen? What changed? This book explores how and why Vietnam loomed so large for Humphrey as vice president from 1964 through the 1968 election campaign against Richard Nixon. It assesses the price of Humphrey's loyalty to Lyndon Johnson, who emerges as the villain of the story in many ways, and how that allegiance would negatively affect Humphrey's political ambitions. And it engages the disconnect between Humphrey's principles and the intricate politics of his convoluted relationship with the president and his unsuccessful presidential campaign. It is a complex and frustrating narrative, the results of which would be tragic, not only for Humphrey's presidential aspirations but also for the war in Southeast Asia and the future of the United States.

Chapter One

The Happy (Cold) Warrior

Foreign policy is really domestic policy with its hat on.
—Hubert Humphrey

We cannot attribute to fortune or virtue that which is achieved without either.
—Niccolò Machiavelli

Brilliant. Gregarious. Optimistic. Eloquent. Ambitious. Emotional. Loyal. Inquisitive. Loquacious. Empathetic. Driven. These are just a few of the adjectives that have been used by contemporary observers, friends, political allies, and historians to describe Hubert Humphrey. The Minnesotan was a political polymath, interested in a wide range of domestic and international issues and willing to fight with passion and commitment for causes in which he believed. Like any politician, he had his share of successes and failures throughout his career, all of which were magnified by his national reputation and stature. He lost his first mayoral race in Minneapolis, suffered through being passed over by the Democratic convention to be Adlai Stevenson's running mate in 1956, and tearfully lost the 1960 presidential nomination to John F. Kennedy after a poor showing in the West Virginia primary. But almost every time he faced an obstacle or lost a political engagement, he jumped back into the fray, working harder and more diligently than ever to see his vision of the country realized. The one issue on which he failed and from which he would not recover would be the war in Vietnam.

That Humphrey would grapple futilely with the Vietnam conflict as he ran for president may not be surprising in retrospect, but in real time it could be considered an anomaly in an otherwise impressive career of public service. Hubert Humphrey was one of the most intelligent men to ever serve in the U.S. Senate. Few senators have ever tackled such a broad spectrum of domestic and international issues and still managed to achieve the understanding and level of detailed engagement that he did. He excelled as "a stand-up, hip-pocket diplomatist" in the Senate, "a technician in the wooing and wheedling and all-around negotiation with which majorities are put together."[1] Only a few twentieth-century politicians accomplished as much of lasting significance as did Humphrey. He played perhaps the crucial and decisive role in the complex parliamentary maneuvering as the Democratic whip in the Senate that resulted in the passage of the landmark Civil Rights Act of 1964. Humphrey, not JFK, first proposed the Peace Corps. It was Humphrey who was responsible for the ideas that led to the Food for Peace program in the 1950s and Medicare as part of the Great Society, and he was an early proponent of federal aid for education. Internationally, Humphrey advocated for the negotiation of a nuclear test-ban treaty years before it was consummated and supported foreign aid and economic development programs across the globe. A champion of scores of liberal causes, he was virtually without peer in the Senate during the early Cold War. As Lyndon Johnson once said, "Most Senators are minnows. Hubert Humphrey is among the whales."[2]

In addition to his legislative prowess, Humphrey in many ways personified the Cold War consensus. He burst onto the national political scene as a fire-breathing liberal zealot, "the aboriginal New Dealer," whose impassioned speech electrified the 1948 Democratic convention and persuaded the delegates to adopt a tough civil rights platform without regard for the Dixiecrat political secessionists.[3] He was a founder of Americans for Democratic Action (ADA), served as its chairman in 1949, and was a perennial vice chairman until 1964.[4] Throughout his years in the Senate, he focused on issues of social welfare, fair employment, and civil rights and displayed an idealism that earned him a devoted following among those on the left. To be sure, Humphrey was a political animal, a partisan Democrat who loved a good fight. After the 1956 election, for example, he declared that Democrats would be "digging their own graves" if they did not adopt a militantly liberal position—this despite his willingness to work closely with the Southern leadership of Lyndon Johnson in the Senate to work out a "middle way." That approach had cost him at least some of his progressive following, which complained that Humphrey was "induced into compromises regarded as treasonable by strong left-wingers."[5] Yet he gained widespread respect on both sides of the aisle for his forceful advocacy for the issues he embraced, his integrity, and his (often-long-winded, rapid-fire) eloquence. His consistently cheerful demeanor garnered him the nickname "The Happy Warrior."[6]

Humphrey's loquaciousness was legendary. In a single week in February 1958, for example, he spoke on the Senate floor on (among other topics) disarmament and the recession (repeatedly), dairy supports, disaster loans, trade development, antitrust laws, British and French politics, international civil aviation, Lithuanian independence, North African policy, regulatory agencies, unemployment, Adlai Stevenson, Soviet-American cultural exchanges, space exploration, and the federal reserve system. One newspaper account of his extensive remarks that month noted that he spent more time speaking in the Senate than most of his Democratic colleagues combined—an astonishing statistic. His rhetorical excesses also led to many good-natured jokes. Henry Kissinger, for example, would often describe how when Humphrey began speaking at the dedication of a grove of trees named in his honor in Israel, the trees were only knee-high. By the time he finished, however, he was speaking in the shade. [7]

At the same time, Humphrey's ardent anticommunism rivaled that of anyone on the right. In fact, opposition to communism would become one of Humphrey's defining political positions throughout his career and would actually cause problems for him with some of his supporters on the left. As mayor of Minneapolis from 1945 to 1948, he led the successful fight to drive communists out of the Democratic Farmer-Labor Party that had elected him. Like several other liberal internationalist senators in the Democratic Party, Humphrey occasionally went "overboard in trumpeting [his] strong opposition to communism." His sponsorship of the Communist Control Act in August 1954 is a prime example. Humphrey supported an amendment to the McCarran Internal Security Act of 1950 to outlaw the Communist Party in the United States as the agent of a hostile foreign power. His position on the bill dismayed many of his liberal friends, who characterized the legislation as a "low grade partisan maneuver" that would "widen the witch hunt." The senator's goal was "to thwart the Republican attempt to seize the high political ground on anti-Communism" since he was "tired of reading headlines about being 'soft' toward communism."[8] Humphrey most assuredly was not. Rather, the Minnesotan was "as immersed in the politics and ideology of the Cold War as any Democrat," a committed cold warrior who hounded communists at home and abroad. [9]

Given Humphrey's unyielding opposition to both domestic and international communism, it is not surprising that Vietnam was far from the first foreign policy issue on which he had an interest and influence. Even before he won election to public office, Humphrey displayed a keen interest in international affairs. As he rose to prominence in Minnesota, he spoke to a wide variety of audiences about the importance of the League of Nations, collective security, and taking a strong stand for democracy against fascism. [10] He overcame an initial reluctance to go overseas—rooted in his concern for his political reputation in Minnesota—and traveled extensively in the search for solutions to U.S. foreign policy dilemmas, turning himself into a nationally and internationally recognized figure. During the early Cold War, he became perhaps the leading Democratic spokesperson in the Senate on a wide range of international issues during the Truman and Eisenhower administrations.

As a member of the Senate Foreign Relations Committee (SFRC), Humphrey not only employed his expertise in international affairs but also served as his party's primary counterpoint to the incendiary rhetoric and brinksmanship of Republican Secretary of State John Foster Dulles.[11] In an interview in 1971, Humphrey recalled that Lyndon Johnson had asked him to serve on the SFRC after the 1952 election. According to Humphrey, LBJ "said the reason he wanted us over there—he was going to put Mansfield and myself—he said he wanted some new young blood on the committee. Secondly, he said that he was worried about John Foster Dulles becoming Secretary of State, and he wanted to have some good scrappers, battlers, over on that committee."[12] The senator challenged Dulles consistently throughout the 1950s, which only enhanced Humphrey's national profile on foreign policy issues. Humphrey's prodigious intellect and interests led him to engage with a wide range of policies, such as arguing for Ukrainian independence, pushing for a foreign aid agreement with Sri Lanka, and championing self-determination for the nations behind the Iron Curtain.

Humphrey also seized on opportunities to engage world leaders, utilizing his experience, position, and personality to further U.S. policy goals and his own political fortunes. An incident in 1958 is both instructive and indicative of Humphrey's international acumen. A "torrential talker," he spent over eight hours in an interview with Soviet premier Nikita Khrushchev in December 1958 that "left interpreters reeling."[13] In the meeting, Humphrey sparred with the Soviet leader on a variety of topics related to Soviet-American relations and the Cold War. At one point, the Soviet leader asked Humphrey where his hometown was. When Humphrey replied Minneapolis, Khrushchev drew a thick blue circle around the city on a map and said, "I will have to remember to have that city spared when the missiles start flying." The senator reciprocated, asking Khrushchev where he was from. When the premier answered Moscow, Humphrey quickly retorted, "Sorry, Mr. Khrushchev, but I can't do the same for you. We can't spare Moscow." Both laughed loudly.[14] The next day, Humphrey dictated a long memorandum for the Department of State; upon his return to Washington, D.C., he briefed Undersecretary of State Christian Herter, CIA Director Allen Dulles, and other officials on Khrushchev's comments and desire for a summit meeting with Eisenhower.[15] The publicity and notoriety that Humphrey gained from this conversation with the Soviet leader helped pave the way for his candidacy for the Democratic presidential nomination in 1960.

Humphrey's steadfast anticommunism, uncommon even among the most ardent cold warriors in the Democratic Party, informed his approach to international issues. Yet if one looks beneath the surface, it is easy to discern a duality in Humphrey's approach to foreign affairs. While he supported the Truman and Eisenhower Doctrines and the Marshall Plan as part of U.S. containment strategy, he believed strongly in peace and the brotherhood of man. He supported Truman's decision to fight in Korea but did so primarily because the president chose to act through the auspices of the United Nations, an organization whose *raison d'être* he avidly promoted. Humphrey supported the ratification of the North Atlantic Treaty Organization (NATO), but he also lobbied for Point Four and Public Law 480 funds for underdeveloped areas around the world and championed the Alliance for Progress.[16] He never voted against a military budget appropriation, yet he also helped to create the U.S. Arms Control and Disarmament Agency in 1961 and led the fight for the ratification of the 1963 Nuclear Test Ban Treaty. In fact, in a speech at Yale University in December 1959, Humphrey asserted, "Disarmament should be the core of American foreign policy."[17] Humphrey's liberal and anticommunist principles remained consistent throughout his career. The disconnect arose when those two impulses clashed or when other political imperatives interceded. When that occurred, the resulting decisions and rhetoric could make him appear to have adopted contradictory positions. Nowhere would this be more apparent than in dealing with Vietnam.

Humphrey's anticommunism and U.S. policy in Southeast Asia would collide in the 1950s. Given his visceral opposition to communism worldwide, Humphrey predictably backed U.S. policy in Indochina from the outset and consistently warned against the cost of losing ground to communism in the region in speeches on the Senate floor. On January 5, 1950, for instance, he said, "I want to stop communism, and I say that if we lose the south part of Asia, if we lose Burma, if we lose India, we shall have lost every hope that we ever had of being able to maintain free institutions in any part of the eastern world." When Harry Truman decided to increase U.S. aid to Indochina in the wake of the invasion of South Korea, he was supported by both sides of the political divide. Humphrey called it a "most encouraging" decision on the part of the administration. Humphrey wanted to protect Indochina from "the Communist onslaught," believing as did many in Congress that a communist victory in Vietnam would lead to the conquest of the entire region.[18]

Yet Humphrey would exhibit uncertainty about the proper course of action in Vietnam. He embraced the idea of an independent Indochina while vocally opposing those within the Eisenhower administration who suggested using nuclear weapons to aid the French in 1954. Although he refrained from publicly criticizing the administration on Indochina, Humphrey did express some reservations about U.S. policy privately. In February 1954, for example, he complained to John Foster Dulles that "it is patently obvious that we just do not have any plan." When the senator asked what the United States would do in the event that France abandoned Indochina, Dulles responded that the administration still had faith in the Navarre Plan: "I feel that the program upon which we are now embarked will probably hold the situation in Indochina." Humphrey was not wholly convinced.[19] On March 31, 1954,

Humphrey declared that "the loss of Indochina would be a tragedy for the free world . . . [and] would mean the loss of all Asia and probably the subcontinent." In April, following newspaper reports that the administration was considering deployment of U.S. troops to Indochina in the event of a French withdrawal, Humphrey and Senator Bourke Hickenlooper (R-IA) complained about the administration's lack of consultation with Congress, suggesting that this proposal went far beyond U.S. policy as they understood it.[20]

In the midst of the siege at Dien Bien Phu, Humphrey opined that he did not think that "anybody seems to have any plans whatsoever about Indochina" and that the odds of "getting anything very constructive toward the cause of the free nations" at the Geneva Conference was "very, very limited." The senator also worried that the administration did not have any contingencies in place in the event that the French decided to withdraw from Indochina. Given the importance of the region, he argued, "we just do not have any plan."[21] On April 19, 1954, Humphrey asserted that losing Indochina "is unthinkable. It cannot happen. It will not happen."[22] Yet it did happen. The French withdrew from Southeast Asia, the international agreement reached at the Geneva conference effectively created two states in Indochina, and the United States quickly committed itself to the task of maintaining a Western-oriented, noncommunist government in Vietnam irrespective of the language of the accords.[23]

As U.S. involvement in Southeast Asia entered a new phase, Humphrey continued to support efforts to oppose communism in the region. In 1955, it was Humphrey who made the motion that led to Senate ratification of the Manila Pact, more commonly referred to as the Southeast Asia Treaty Organization (SEATO), by a vote of 85–1. That agreement would be used by many in Washington to justify an expanded presence in South Vietnam. But Humphrey—along with several of his Senate colleagues, including J. William Fulbright (D-AK), Mike Mansfield (D-MT), and John F. Kennedy (D-MA)—viewed the Eisenhower-Dulles approach in Vietnam somewhat skeptically. While they agreed about the need to construct a bulwark against communist expansion and supported the Diem government, they were not completely satisfied with the administration's policy priorities. Humphrey later recalled, "When I spoke out in the fifties against what we were doing, mine was a relatively lonely voice. We narrowly avoided joining the French in the death throes of their Southeast Asian colonialism. This seemed absurd."[24] Hoping to prevent a recurrence of the French experience in Indochina, in September 1958 the senators asked the president to give more economic aid and less military assistance to the Diem regime in order to stimulate development and to bolster South Vietnam's social stability.[25]

During the Kennedy administration, Humphrey generally supported JFK's policy on Vietnam but also urged caution in terms of expanding U.S.

commitment. He told the Senate in 1962 that the United States should limit its participation in Vietnam to "military assistance, to supplies, and to military training" but remained steadfast in his commitment to preventing the spread of communism. Humphrey praised the administration's efforts to develop counterinsurgency programs, stating that "in recent months, the tide may well have turned for the forces of freedom against the Communist guerrillas of the north," and urged additional weapons and supplies to "put out these brush fires" in Vietnam.[26] But as things got progressively worse in Southeast Asia, it became clear to Humphrey that different solutions would be required to achieve U.S. goals.

As the United States faced increasingly difficult and limited choices in South Vietnam, Humphrey's views on U.S. involvement in Vietnam were shaped by General Edward Lansdale, the counterinsurgency expert who had been Ramon Magsaysay's chief adviser in the Philippines in the 1950s and who later became a special assistant to the U.S. ambassador to South Vietnam, Henry Cabot Lodge Jr. After Kennedy's assassination, Humphrey "tried to educate myself on Vietnam. I turned to Colonel (later General) Edward Lansdale . . . [who] urged a political approach. . . . After the election I became a conduit for his ideas to President Johnson."[27] Lansdale's theory, which Humphrey came to support enthusiastically, was that conventional military techniques were useless against a rural-based communist insurgency and that the only way to succeed would be to adopt similar tactics and demonstrate the potential benefits of democratic government through a rural reconstruction program. Humphrey embraced Lansdale's ideas in 1964, even sending LBJ a memorandum in the spring recommending against withdrawal of the 16,000 U.S. advisers in Vietnam but arguing that "direct U.S. action against North Vietnam, American assumption of command roles, or participation in combat of U.S. troop units are unnecessary and undesirable."[28] What is clear is that by early 1964, while Humphrey remained committed to opposing communism in Vietnam, he did not support the idea of a major escalation of U.S. military presence on the ground. That reluctance would inform Humphrey's advice to LBJ in the months of decision that followed.

The relationship that Humphrey had with Lyndon Johnson looms as a significant and indispensable part of the story. The two had been friends since the early 1950s. Johnson had mentored Humphrey in their early years in the Senate, helping to transform and legitimize Humphrey from an impulsive liberal zealot into a seasoned and effective legislator who understood that politics is the "art of the possible." Yet the relationship could not be described as balanced. Humphrey, for his part, considered Johnson to be a close friend and confidant. The Minnesota senator was a big fan of LBJ and defended him to other Senate liberals in the 1950s. In fact, Humphrey thought Johnson was "a lot more liberal" than he appeared, telling his allies, "On minimum wage he's with us; on health measures . . . he's with us; on agriculture measures he's with us; on all the public works programs he's with us; on public employment measures when we had recessions he was with us." It helped that the two men shared a common background. Both were from small-town rural communities, both had worked as teachers, and both came from impoverished backgrounds that left them suspicious of the far-off power of financial elites. [29]

Johnson, on the other hand, was friends with Humphrey "the same way a grave digger is friends with his shovel." Although they got along well personally, the friendship might be best described as superficial—if genuine—because it was grounded largely in what Humphrey could do for Johnson politically. Politics took precedence in everything in LBJ's life; indeed, lurking just beneath the veneer of his civility was Johnson's penchant for instinctive and visceral political calculation. Ambitiously aiming to be king of the Senate, Johnson "systematically manipulated Humphrey to make the Minnesotan believe he was the Texan's friend and would deliver the northern liberal Senate votes" the majority leader needed. While LBJ rewarded Humphrey's support with seats on the Senate Foreign Relations Committee and other important committees, the fact remains that Johnson trusted his colleague "no more, and probably a good deal less, than he did other northern liberals."[30] Humphrey's impeccable progressive credentials would serve the same purpose in 1964 when the president asked the Minnesota senator to join him on the Democratic ticket, but when Humphrey ran afoul of liberals due to his staunch defense of administration policies in Vietnam over the next four years, LBJ found that he had little use for his vice president and essentially cast him aside—especially during the 1968 presidential campaign.

It is worth taking a moment to pause and explore Johnson's personality further, as it is central not just to understanding his decisions that led to the Americanization of the war in Vietnam but also to appreciating his relationship with Humphrey. David Halberstam provides one of the most insightful descriptions of LBJ in his magisterial, albeit imperfect, account of the origins of U.S. involvement in Vietnam, *The Best and the Brightest*. For Halberstam, Johnson was "a relentless man who pushed himself and all others with the same severity and demanded, above all other qualities, total loyalty." That loyalty had to be "first and foremost to Lyndon Johnson. Then Lyndon Johnson would become the arbiter of any larger loyalty. Those who passed the loyalty test could have whatever they wanted." LBJ, Halberstam continued, "was ill at ease with abstract loyalty, loyalty to issue, to concept, to cause, which might lead one to occasional dissent, a broader view, and might mean that a man was caught between loyalty to civil rights and loyalty to Lyndon Johnson." But unlike others, Johnson demanded loyalty out of insecurity. Why was LBJ, who had risen to the heights of political power in the United States, insecure? According to Halberstam, it was Johnson's sense that he was an outsider—he was not part of the Eastern establishment, he lacked an Ivy League pedigree, and he was not among the country's financial elite. That sense of not belonging was only magnified by the fact that those cohorts were so prominent in the Kennedy administration. That feeling "was a profound part of him. . . . He was haunted by regional prejudice, and even the attainment of the Presidency did not temper his feelings."[31]

Complicating matters was Johnson's experience as JFK's vice president. Kennedy kept the former Senate majority leader—who was accustomed to power, control, and prestige after dominating the legislative process on Capitol Hill for so many years—busy with a series of seemingly insignificant, although traditionally vice-presidential, tasks.[32] LBJ never forgot his own miserable years spent one heartbeat away from the presidency, later admitting that he "detested every minute of it."[33] That helps to explain why Johnson, who did not speak up in cabinet meetings about civil rights despite his strong feelings on the issue, probably wondered why Humphrey spoke up so forcefully on Vietnam early in his tenure as vice president and treated him poorly as a result. Indeed, that attitude comes through clearly in the interactions between the two men. Early in 1965, LBJ told Humphrey, "I had none [power], 'cause Kennedy wouldn't give me any. He didn't just assign it to me. . . . Kennedy felt if I did it . . . they'd say I was the 'Master Craftsman' and so forth."[34] President Johnson would show Humphrey even less consideration over the next four years than he had received from JFK.

Given that perspective, and despite the fact that Humphrey shared Johnson's outsider background, LBJ's treatment of Humphrey becomes more understandable, if not excusable. Johnson had "always viewed Hubert Humphrey as something of a convenience, to be used at times for his own and the country's greater good," but the Texan never held the kind of respect for Humphrey that he did for people like Richard Russell. Humphrey was "too prone to talk instead of act, not a person that other *men* would respect in a room when it got down to the hard cutting." The relationship was "almost completely one-sided, Johnson using Humphrey on Johnson's terms," whether on civil rights, the Great Society, or the conflict in Vietnam.[35] Understanding this dynamic on both a personal and institutional level is absolutely vital to grasping how the LBJ–Humphrey relationship influenced Humphrey on the issue of Vietnam during his vice presidency.

While Vietnam loomed large for the new president, Lyndon Johnson also had to focus on the impending 1964 presidential campaign and the question of who he would select as his vice president. Although he vetted several possibilities, Hubert Humphrey stood out in Johnson's calculations because Humphrey possessed a number of potential campaign assets: the senator was a Northerner, an intellectual, and a certified liberal, all electoral weaknesses for a Southern Democrat like Johnson. Those qualities made for a tempting set of ticket-balancing credentials for LBJ. It helped that Humphrey and Johnson worked well together, their unequal relationship notwithstanding. In his memoirs, Johnson characterized Humphrey as "a strong contender" along with Senator Eugene McCarthy (D-MN) for the vice presidency but eventually concluded that Humphrey "was the best choice in the light of all the circumstances."[36] Still, the president continued to have reservations about Humphrey throughout the first half of 1964. At one point, LBJ told White House aide Bill Moyers, "I would have lots of problems with him. He's so exuberant, so enthusiastic; he'd get off the reservation all the time"—not exactly what Johnson was looking for in a vice president.[37]

The president's concerns may have been exaggerated and certainly betrayed LBJ's insecurities. The reality is that after nearly two decades in the Senate, Humphrey's sharp liberal edges had been softened. While still energetic, garrulous, and firmly committed to his causes, he had learned to be "a half-a-loaf pragmatist instead of an all-or-nothing martyr." Even though the Minnesota senator still possessed the "instincts of a brawler," he was no longer brash, and he understood the etiquette demands of the Senate to be "no less pointed but far more genteel."[38] To his arsenal of rhetoric and passion, Humphrey added the quiet skills of conciliation and negotiation that allowed him to become effective in coalition building, compromise, and political maneuvering, the critical components of legislative success. That being said, Humphrey still spoke truth to power and advocated for his causes, but he did so in a more mature and measured way. Of course, speaking one's mind as a member of the Senate is one thing; it would be entirely another to be candid as vice president—especially to Lyndon Johnson.

Nevertheless, according to journalist Kenneth Crawford, Humphrey possessed the most important qualification to be vice president: "he is essentially a contented man" who would "not be chafed by subordination to the President or by the degree of anonymity this imposes. He already has adjusted gracefully." Crawford also observed that Humphrey understood the ground rules of the relationship with LBJ most importantly that Humphrey would "speak for the President only when the President specifically authorizes him to do so," despite the fact that Humphrey "has never been one to sit quietly for long in a back seat." Crawford believed that the two men shared a "mutual respect and understanding and finally trust and affection."[39] It was an optimistic perspective but a mostly accurate assessment in mid-1964. Unfortunately for Humphrey, those bonds would fracture over the next four years.

After Humphrey agreed to serve as vice president, Johnson warned him—presciently, as it would turn out—that the requirements and realities of their new working relationship would probably ruin their long-standing friendship. "There is something about the jobs and responsibilities that seem to get in the way of those friendships and understandings," LBJ told Humphrey, speaking from his own experience. "You have to understand that this is like a marriage with no chance of divorce. I need complete and unswerving loyalty." Humphrey assured Johnson that he accepted the parameters of the job, and the deal was done. Humphrey fully understood that his role as vice president would be, in his words, "what the President wants it to be."[40] The loyalty on which LBJ adamantly insisted and that Humphrey willingly proffered is an integral part of the story of Humphrey's struggles with the Vietnam conflict. Humphrey's conception of the role of the vice president, his personal fealty to Johnson, and the resulting compromises Humphrey would make with his principles for political reasons over the next four years would have far-reaching ramifications for his political ambitions, U.S. Vietnam policy, and the country's future.

Humphrey's defenders have argued that he was trapped by his position as vice president and that he only supported the war because of his misguided loyalty to Lyndon Johnson. Scholars have long recognized that roles can shape, influence, or even determine rhetoric for leaders in the U.S. political system, and perhaps nowhere is that observation more accurate than with the vice presidency.[41] One of Humphrey's oldest friends, civil rights attorney Joseph Rauh, suggested that "Hubert just had blinkers on. I said to him once, 'If you were President, we'd be out of this war in ninety days.' He said, 'No.' He really thought the war was right. But he was only thinking it through from A to B because of those blinkers he'd put on out of loyalty to Lyndon Johnson. If he'd let himself think it through, he'd have been against the war." But, Rauh continued, "as it was, you have to say that he stayed and out-Johnsoned Johnson. You have to have forgiveness, though, because he is a really fine and noble man, and it was loyalty that made him do it." Other observers suggest that such a conclusion is "untenable." They point out that Humphrey's rhetoric on the war in 1966 and 1967—which was passionate and overzealous, sometimes bordering on the fanatical—transcended what solidarity with the administration required. As one pundit commented, "One should do him the credit of believing him."[42] The truth, however, is that, regardless of his true beliefs, Humphrey never managed to deal successfully with the war from a political standpoint, regardless of what his loyalty or principles may have dictated.

Throughout the summer of 1964, the situation in Vietnam continued to deteriorate as the Johnson administration devoted its energy to avoiding any decisions that might undermine the president's electoral prospects that fall. Meanwhile, Humphrey continued to express doubts about the trajectory of U.S. policy in Southeast Asia. In June, for example, Humphrey spoke out in support of his colleague Senator Frank Church (D-ID), who suggested that the Vietnam conflict should be put before the United Nations and articulated his strong opposition to escalating the war. "What is needed in Vietnam," Humphrey noted, "is a cause for which to fight, some sort of inspiration for the people of South Vietnam to live for and die for." Shortly thereafter, he privately told LBJ, "No amount of additional military involvement can be successful" without providing "some hope" around which the Vietnamese people could rally. Military action against North Vietnam or intervention with U.S. combat troops, he argued, was "unnecessary and undesirable."[43]

Humphrey was being cautious. LBJ had asked him for his views on Vietnam, but John Rielly, Humphrey's thirty-five-year-old Harvard University and London School of Economics–trained foreign policy adviser, had urged the senator to avoid discussing Vietnam with the president or becoming one of the administration's spokesmen on the conflict. Rielly told Humphrey, "(1) Do not make any speech on the subject of Vietnam. (2) Do not present to the President any memoranda on Vietnam. (3) Do not permit yourself, if at all possible, to be maneuvered into the position by the President where you become the principal defender of the Administration's policy in the Senate against critics like Mansfield, Church, Morse, Gruening and others." That said, Rielly advised Humphrey to "raise certain questions" with the president about "the implications of certain alternative lines of actions." Rielly argued that the United States had become "overcommitted" in Southeast Asia and counseled Humphrey that, while it had been "a mistake to intervene" in Vietnam in 1954, "our prestige is so committed that there can be no justification of an immediate pull out." Yet a withdrawal achieved "gradually and gracefully" that would not leave South Vietnam vulnerable to domination by the North would be in the country's best interest. He cautioned against introducing U.S. ground troops, arguing that "Once we land troops in a country, it is difficult to get them out. We find it difficult to disengage—and usually end up becoming more involved than ever." Rielly did admit that in an election year, "it is politically dangerous to talk about any scheme for 'neutralizing the area'" but argued that "a political settlement is our ultimate goal. You may not care to emphasize this at the present time (i.e., before November 1964)."[44] Rielly's advice would prove to be astute; the confrontation between Johnson and Humphrey in February 1965 would demonstrate just how accurate Rielly's predictions and prescriptions had been.

That counsel notwithstanding, Humphrey did reply to LBJ's request in a memorandum—which was prepared with significant input from Edward Lansdale and Rufus Phillips, Lansdale's protégé and a former CIA officer— in which he counseled restraint in U.S. policy toward Vietnam. Humphrey argued that the Vietnamese "must be skillfully and firmly guided, but it is they (not we) who must win their war." Playing the domestic political card that the president understood so well, Humphrey went on to point out that a "political base is needed to support all other actions. . . . No amount of additional military involvement can be successful without accomplishing this task." Indeed, Humphrey concluded that direct U.S. military action or assumption of control in Vietnam would be "unnecessary and undesirable." Any U.S. involvement should be confined to supporting counterinsurgency efforts rather than airstrikes or other conventional responses. Humphrey recommended that a team of U.S. counterinsurgency experts be dispatched to Vietnam. Johnson's military aide, Major General Chester V. Clifton Jr., responded to Humphrey's suggestions negatively, and LBJ took Clifton's advice.[45] Clearly, Humphrey and Johnson did not share the same opinion on what approach to follow in Southeast Asia.

While the questions of how, when, and to what extent the United States should act in Vietnam remained fluid, the fall election campaign between Johnson and Senator Barry Goldwater (R-AZ) took priority. Although Humphrey seemed to be a lock for the vice-presidential slot, the Democratic convention would not be held until the end of August 1964, and LBJ's decision had not yet been finalized. In fact, Humphrey's nomination was nearly derailed in the wake of the Gulf of Tonkin attacks.[46] On August 4, the president spoke with former campaign manager James Rowe in the middle of the crisis. He complained that Humphrey's "garrulousness" was endangering national security. "Our friend Hubert is just destroying himself with his big mouth," LBJ complained. "Every responsible person gets frightened when they see him. . . . Yesterday morning, he went on TV and . . . just blabbed everything that he had heard in a briefing." Johnson called him a "damned fool" who "just ought to keep his goddamned big mouth shut on foreign affairs, at least until the election is over. . . . He's hurting *us*!" The president concluded by telling Rowe that if Humphrey did not stop, he might reconsider the Minnesota senator as his running mate.[47]

Johnson's disapproval failed to prevent Humphrey from addressing the situation in Southeast Asia. During the truncated debate that preceded the overwhelming passage of the Gulf of Tonkin Resolution, Humphrey said "the aggressor seeks to bite off piece by piece the areas of freedom . . . our objective is to achieve stability in the area so that we can then go to the conference table. But we ought to make it clear to the world that we do not intend to sit at the conference table with a Communist gun at our heads."[48] Humphrey made it clear he supported the administration's request for authorization to retaliate for the attacks and defend both U.S. interests and South Vietnam. "It is my view that the minute we back away from commitments we have made in the defense of freedom, where the Communist powers are guilty of outright subversion and aggression, on that day the strength, the freedom, and the honor of the United States starts to be eroded." He returned to his familiar anticommunist rhetoric and argued that he was "of the opinion that what is going on in Southeast Asia is a persistent attack on the part of the Communist forces to nibble away at certain areas in Southeast Asia which we can call free and independent, to take them one by one." There was no question in Humphrey's mind that the United States had to act. "A great power must be an honorable power," he said. "A great nation must be willing at times to make great and difficult decisions. I would be the last to say that this decision did not have within it the possibilities of even greater troubles ahead. But I do not believe that we can duck these troubles. I do not believe that we can avoid them by pretending they are not there."[49]

The approval of the Gulf of Tonkin Resolution effectively neutralized Vietnam as a campaign issue in the fall, but it did not stop Humphrey from expounding on his prescription for U.S. policy.[50] At a town hall meeting in Los Angeles on August 17, 1964, he laid out what he saw as the goals for U.S. involvement in Vietnam: "We must stay in Vietnam—until the security of the South Vietnamese people has been established. We will not be driven out . . . the primary responsibility for preserving independence and achieving peace in Vietnam remains with the Vietnamese people and their Government. We should not attempt to 'take over' the war."[51] In addition to being consistent with his long-standing views on the Vietnam conflict, Humphrey's statement fit perfectly with the administration's focus on avoiding the question of potential escalation during the presidential election. Moreover, it was sufficiently restrained as to ease the president's anxiety over the prospect of Humphrey as his vice president.

The Democratic convention in Atlantic City, New Jersey, nominated LBJ unanimously, and the president quickly selected Humphrey to join him on the ticket. After Johnson announced that he would officially choose Humphrey as his running mate, calling him the "best-qualified man to assume the office of the President," Humphrey was nominated by acclamation.[52] In Humphrey's acceptance speech at the convention, he attacked Goldwater on foreign policy, suggesting that the GOP candidate had failed to learn that "politics should stop at the water's edge."[53] It was an enthusiastic, inspiring, and powerful speech, a sharp contrast to Johnson's remarks that "had neither vitality nor a memorable phrase and left television viewers in their late-night lethargy."[54] The contrast between the dour LBJ and the charismatic Humphrey underscored Johnson's insecurities and would influence the way the president treated his running mate throughout the campaign.

The election energized Humphrey, who did most of the national campaigning for the ticket, as Johnson largely spoke from the White House in an effort to appear presidential and above the political fray. Conservatives saw Humphrey as "a decoy for the GOP's firepower, an ideological magnet by which Johnson hopes to draw abuse away from his Person, and so remain above the battle. . . . One look at Hubert, or so LBJ probably supposes, and they'll be turned to stone."[55] In mid-September, Humphrey evinced his concern about the Democratic campaign strategy, worrying that it had become simply "anti-Goldwater." Humphrey wanted to deliver a "thoughtful and substantive speech" on key topics like the Alliance for Progress and world peace. He believed that the Johnson-Humphrey campaign needed "to develop some substantive matter, to proclaim this administration, to show that we know what we are doing" if the administration hoped to take advantage of an electoral victory in November.[56]

Humphrey's reluctance to be the ideological attack dog—the traditional role for a vice presidential candidate—can partially be explained by his evolution as a politician during his senatorial career. His status as a fire-breathing liberal icon had, by 1964, shifted to that of a pragmatist who was satisfied to win what he could rather than to go down to defeat in an uncompromising, all-or-nothing mentality. "I am not a theologian; I'm a politician."[57] But despite his reluctance, he was effective. In October 1964, Richard Reston of the *Los Angeles Times* described how LBJ (primarily through Humphrey) had used foreign policy in "a conscious political effort to isolate the more aggressive stand" of Goldwater. By celebrating bipartisanship and linking the policies of Eisenhower and Dulles to his administration while simultaneously highlighting Goldwater's extreme view on the use of nuclear weapons, Johnson hoped to marginalize Goldwater as disconnected from mainstream foreign policy thinking. On October 26, Humphrey spoke in Wisconsin and told the crowd that a vote for Goldwater was a vote for war: "The 'solutions' he offers are not solutions at all. They are instead a sure path to widening conflict—and, ultimately, to a terrible holocaust."[58] Robert David Johnson suggests that as a result, foreign policy emerged as the president's "most potent political weapon" in the campaign.[59] While Humphrey may not have enjoyed his role, he was effective and contributed to the success of the campaign.

With Johnson's landslide victory over Barry Goldwater in the 1964 presidential election, Humphrey became vice president. It was a new and substantially different role for the long-time legislator, but he considered it a singular honor to assume the country's second-highest elected office, not to mention that it put him one step closer to his ultimate political ambition. As a senator, Humphrey had traveled extensively and had forged a strong reputation for foreign policy expertise. Thus, it is not surprising that *U.S. News & World Report* suggested shortly after the election, "It is considered likely, therefore, that President Johnson will consult his Vice President closely on foreign policy."[60] That assumption would prove to be misguided. Humphrey would have little input or influence on foreign policy questions generally or on Vietnam specifically in the Johnson administration. This would be especially true once the decision for escalation occurred in early 1965 and LBJ ignored Humphrey's advice on the trajectory of U.S. policy on the Vietnam conflict.

Moreover, while Humphrey had agreed to the boundaries regarding their relationship set by the president the previous August, in the aftermath of the election, the vice president "was brutally reminded by Johnson himself how completely—how abjectly—dependent on the president he was." LBJ consistently demeaned and marginalized Humphrey in an effort to demonstrate his dominance.[61] Part of the ritualized humiliation was simply the president's way of interacting with subordinates, a component of the infamous "Johnson treatment." But it also reflected LBJ's insecurities. In short, Johnson expected Humphrey to quietly stand by and give his full support to the administration's policies, avoiding comment on issues unless directed by the White House and fulfilling those constitutional and traditional duties of a vice president—presiding over the Senate and attending state funerals—that Johnson himself had performed during his tenure in the nation's second-highest office. With the new responsibilities came the recognition that Humphrey no longer served the people of Minnesota; he served the needs and whims of the president, and Lyndon Johnson had an undeniably specific job description in mind for his former colleague.

Despite his willingness to sublimate his views to those of the president in public, however, Humphrey shared the concerns of many of his fellow senators over the trajectory of U.S. involvement in Vietnam in late 1964. While Congress—including then-Senator Humphrey—had voted overwhelmingly to approve the Gulf of Tonkin Resolution in August, many members on both sides of the aisle expressed doubts about the direction in which the administration was heading in Southeast Asia. For example, when Frank Church spoke out against increasing U.S. presence in South Vietnam in an interview with *Ramparts* in December 1964, Humphrey wrote him and said, "You have performed a great service for American foreign policy."[62] Yet the vice president–elect was not ready to speak out publicly against the burgeoning conflict, which separated him from opponents of escalation such as Church, Senator Wayne Morse (D-OR), and Senator John Sherman Cooper (R-KY). In addition, although Humphrey was "somewhat removed" from the inner circle of administration foreign policy in late 1964, he was worried about the optics of escalation. National Security Council staffer James Thomson, who had been "on loan" to Humphrey during the campaign, recalled that the incoming vice president did not believe that the administration would begin bombing due in larger measure to the possibility of an "adverse public reaction." Humphrey, according to Undersecretary of State George Ball, expressed opposition to bombing in meetings with the president and other advisers in "forceful and frank" terms.[63] Humphrey understood LBJ's preoccupation with domestic political considerations better than anyone; indeed, it would be this line of reasoning that would influence the memorandum that would irreversibly fracture the Johnson-Humphrey relationship in early 1965.

Unfortunately, the gradual disintegration of their friendship had already started. Although Humphrey may not have been totally aware of it, Johnson was "irritated by the way Humphrey communicated with him, which Johnson thought was inappropriate for any vice president." Of course, the president's views had been shaped by his experience as Kennedy's vice president: "I . . . had a general policy of never speaking unless I was spoken to and never differing with him in public. Frequently, he and I would talk, and I would say, 'We have this difference, and here is my viewpoint.' But I never thought it would be appropriate or desirable to debate differences of opinion in open meetings with others." Ted Van Dyk, one of Humphrey's aides, stated, "Johnson had talked to him at great length before he took office, saying he didn't want Humphrey disagreeing with him at meetings and that they should discuss their differences privately. And right at the start Humphrey breached this. I'm sure this angered the hell out of Johnson—maybe even more than the fact that Humphrey disagreed with him."[64]

As the inauguration approached in January 1965, Humphrey's concerns over Vietnam placed him in a difficult and contrarian position *vis-à-vis* the president and most of the administration's key foreign policy advisers. Throughout 1964, the administration had recognized that the deteriorating situation in Vietnam would require additional U.S. efforts—including, perhaps, the introduction of combat troops to supplement the 16,000 "advisers" on the ground. Detailed plans for such an escalation had been discussed and developed for months, with the domestic political implications of the election in November 1964 standing as the only barrier to a decision from the White House.[65] Humphrey's reluctance to follow the conventional wisdom in the administration on Vietnam derived from his fervent belief that escalation would be a serious mistake. Acting on that conviction would lead to his exile from LBJ's inner circle for most of the year that followed. But it would be his loyalty to Johnson that would trump Humphrey's principles and subsequently lead him to mount a full-throated defense of the administration's policies in Southeast Asia and begin a sequence of events that would end with the vice president's loss in the 1968 presidential election.

Chapter Two

No Good Deed Goes Unpunished

Anyone who thinks that the vice-president can take a position independent of his administration simply has no knowledge of politics or government. You are his choice in a political marriage, and he expects your absolute loyalty.
—Hubert Humphrey

There is no other way for securing yourself against flatteries except that men understand that they do not offend you by telling you the truth; but when everybody can tell you the truth, you fail to get respect.
—Niccolò Machiavelli

From the moment that Hubert Humphrey took the oath of office as the thirty-eighth vice president of the United States on January 29, 1965, he made it clear to anyone who would listen that he was the president's man. "A Vice President," he would later assert, "will be and is what the President wants him to be, and above all, a Vice President must be loyal."[1] During the weeks that followed, the loyalty that Humphrey valued and that Lyndon Johnson demanded placed the vice president in an impossible position when it came to the burgeoning crisis in Vietnam. Indeed, in an effort to demonstrate his fealty to the president by charting a course out of the quagmire in Southeast Asia, Humphrey would irreparably damage his relationship with LBJ and diminish any influence he might have exerted on the administration's decision-making process just when the United States was dramatically escalating its presence in Vietnam. Ironically, if LBJ had listened to Humphrey's advice, it is likely that the choice would have led not only to fundamental change in U.S. policy in Vietnam and in Johnson's political fortunes but also would have unquestionably altered the trajectory of U.S. history. This chapter focuses on one of the most significant, if underappreciated, documents of the entire war—Humphrey's February 1965 memorandum to Lyndon John-

son urging him to settle the conflict rather than escalate—and the consequences that followed for the vice president and for U.S. policy in Vietnam.

Perhaps the most pressing issue facing the administration after the 1964
election was Vietnam. Having postponed major decisions on U.S. policy
during the campaign, Johnson and his advisers now had the opportunity to
address the deteriorating situation on the ground in Southeast Asia without
worrying about domestic reactions or electoral considerations—at least in the
short term. Yet from a domestic political standpoint, LBJ had considerable
room to maneuver. William Bundy, Johnson's assistant secretary of state for
East Asian and Pacific Affairs, argues correctly that the president could have
carried public opinion with him "on whatever course he chose" with respect
to Vietnam in the wake of his landslide victory over Goldwater. It is also
clear that any political heat generated from GOP hawks like Nixon and
Goldwater for abandoning Vietnam would not have been debilitating and
certainly would have caused less consternation for Johnson in the years that
followed than what actually ensued. And, of course, Vietnam was not a
deeply divisive issue at this point. Opposition to the conflict remained em-
bryonic, and no real consensus existed in Congress or in the country on what
to do. For LBJ, however, the pathological fear of a "who-lost-Vietnam"
debate dominated his thinking, and any consideration of withdrawal or disengagement failed to register as a realistic option. [2]

It is easy to paint a monochromatic portrait of Johnson's approach to
Vietnam, particularly given the decisions he made that led to the massive
escalation of U.S. involvement in the war. Yet it should be noted that LBJ did
not want war and did realize, at least on some level, that Americanization of
the conflict could easily lead to a disastrous outcome. He did have doubts;
the extensive documentary record from 1964 and even early 1965 demonstrate that fact clearly. In a conversation with McGeorge Bundy on March 2,
1964, for example, LBJ said, "But I don't know what we can do if there is. I
guess that we just. . . . What alternatives do we have then? We're not going to
send our troops in there—are we?" [3] But those concerns, which Humphrey
shared, were ultimately overridden by domestic political considerations as
the president privileged his commitment to the Great Society—along with his
worry about attacks from the political right—over any thought of withdrawal, negotiation, or disengagement in the wake of Johnson's electoral victory
over Goldwater.

This was the situation Hubert Humphrey encountered as he prepared to
transition from the Senate to his new responsibilities as vice president. His
long support for U.S. anticommunist efforts in Southeast Asia would be
tested as he recognized the difficult choices facing the United States in Vietnam and began to appreciate that his constituency now consisted of one man,
Lyndon Johnson. Shortly after the election, John Rielly cautioned Humphrey
to "listen and learn" at National Security Council meetings and not to partici-

pate in discussions to avoid what he characterized as the "great risk" of disagreeing with Johnson. Rielly also counseled that any attempt to influence LBJ should be limited to contacts "before and after" formal meetings and that Humphrey needed to be "as independent as possible and as compliant as the President thinks necessary."[4] Once again, Rielly's shrewd advice—and Humphrey's failure to heed it—would be a portent of developments during the early weeks of 1965. It is worth pondering what degree of influence Humphrey might have exercised on the crucial decisions made by the administration in the months that followed had he done so.

Instead, Humphrey embraced his new role with his accustomed enthusiasm and little regard for Rielly's counsel. The vice president always believed that his oratorical skills and intellect would be sufficient to convince LBJ (or anyone, for that matter) of the merits of his arguments. In early January 1965, Humphrey arranged for General Edward Lansdale, with whom he had established a close relationship, to meet with Senators J. William Fulbright and John J. Sparkman (D-AL)—the chair and ranking Democratic member of the SFRC, respectively—in order to discuss Lansdale's perspective on the conflict in Vietnam. Lansdale favored a political solution in South Vietnam, and Humphrey agreed with the general's assessment. Humphrey told Fulbright and Sparkman, "Everybody says we have to improve the political situation. But in the meantime they say you can't improve the political situation until you win the military situation. You know, it is just hopeless if you keep talking like that."[5] After the meeting concluded, all three senators expressed support for Lansdale's position and agreed that they should talk to the president and urge him to rethink his approach to the conflict. Humphrey said, "It is just a tragedy to think we are losing when we don't need to. I know some of the decisions . . . that are being made as we sit here and talk right now. I feel that maybe we are going to make some decisions that will be disastrous." Yet when Humphrey and his colleagues—along with the ranking Republican on the SFRC, Bourke Hickenlooper—met with LBJ, they "got a very cool reception."[6] Johnson clearly believed that a military solution represented the administration's only realistic option to salvage the situation in South Vietnam.

Humphrey tried valiantly to push back against the growing consensus in support of escalation. At a dinner on January 18, 1965, Humphrey spoke with James Thomson about the war. Thomson expressed concern about the administration's intentions in Vietnam, telling Humphrey, "I am very fearful that plans are going ahead to expand the war to bring Hanoi to its knees." With his characteristic optimism, Humphrey replied, "I know exactly what you're talking about, but it'll never happen. Before it does, a neutralist government will come to power and ask us to leave." Given the state of affairs in early 1965, this was "a provocative prediction and a perfectly reasonable one."[7] What the incoming vice president did not realize—but what the documentary record makes clear—is that Lyndon Johnson was willing to do whatever it took to prevent defeat and avoid the domestic and international consequences of failure.

On January 27, 1965, only a week after the inauguration, national security adviser McGeorge Bundy told Johnson that current U.S. policy in Vietnam "can only lead to disastrous defeat." LBJ would have to choose between two alternative policies: either "to use our military power in the Far East and to force a change in Communist policy" or "deploy all our resources along a track of negotiation, aimed at salvaging what little can be preserved with no major addition to our present military risks."[8] Both Bundy and Secretary of Defense Robert McNamara supported the former course of action, as did Johnson; in fact, according to William Bundy, the memorandum "summed up all the feelings of all us at that moment" except for Secretary of State Dean Rusk.[9] While Humphrey did not attend this meeting—and would have dissented from the consensus if he had—he did continue to consult with his former Senate colleagues about the conflict, now with the benefit of information available to him as vice president. Frank Church wrote to Humphrey on January 29, "Many thanks for sending me the memorandum on Viet Nam. I read it with interest and profit. In the high councils which will direct our course in Viet Nam during the critical months ahead, it is reassuring for me to know that your voice will be heard."[10]

Church's expectation that Humphrey's concerns about the war would be included in administration debates about the path forward would be premature. Not only would Humphrey's actions limit his involvement, but the discussions about the situation on the ground in Vietnam had been ongoing for a year, and the blueprints for Americanization of the conflict already existed. It is important to realize, however, that while momentum for escalation overwhelmed any thought of negotiation or withdrawal at this juncture, most in the administration understood the potential dangers those courses of action would bring. And while the decision to expand the U.S. presence in Vietnam had essentially been made, even the most hawkish of Johnson's advisers understood that a provocation on the part of the enemy would be necessary before proceeding further down the path to a substantial increase in U.S. involvement.

The pretext for action would happen swiftly. On February 6, 1965, the U.S. helicopter base at Pleiku was attacked, resulting in eight U.S. servicemen killed and sixty more wounded. Hawks within the administration—most notably McGeorge Bundy, who was in Saigon at the time meeting with General William Westmoreland and U.S. ambassador to South Vietnam Maxwell Taylor—strongly urged LBJ to retaliate against the North Vietnamese. The Pleiku attack gave the administration, in the words of NSC staffer Chester Cooper, "an opportunity to put into motion a policy which they had already decided upon but needed a fairly conspicuous threshold before they could implement."[11] Humphrey had been in Minnesota during the attack and was not called back to Washington to attend the NSC meetings held on February 6 through 8. In his absence, the administration—including Undersecretary of State George Ball—approved launching air attacks on North Vietnamese targets by an overwhelming margin; only Senate Majority Leader Mike Mansfield (D-MT), who sat in on the meetings and urged negotiations, dissented.

By the time that Humphrey was back in Washington, the Viet Cong had attacked the U.S. barracks at Qui Nohn on February 10. Prior to the NSC meeting convened to deal with the latest attack, Humphrey spoke to several administration officials regarding the retaliatory strikes and the rapidly evolving situation in Vietnam. Humphrey later noted, "I talked with several of the President's most intimate advisers, expressing my opposition [to the bombing]. One explicitly said he agreed with me; others implied concurrence." Yet when Johnson began to question those at the table, starting with Dean Rusk, "Rusk said he thought we should bomb. Then he turned to me: 'Hubert, what do you think?'" Although he had been a staunch supporter of the U.S. presence in Southeast Asia since the 1950s, Humphrey had serious doubts about the effectiveness of a sustained bombing campaign. That belief clashed with his role as vice president, however, since when Humphrey had accepted the offer to join the Democratic ticket in 1964, he had pledged his complete loyalty to LBJ. While free to express his views in private, Humphrey understood that the president demanded absolute allegiance when in public; after all, that was the role that Johnson had been forced to play for John Kennedy.

But in this instance, Humphrey stood firm on his principles rather than defaulting to his loyalty to the president. Humphrey told Johnson, "'I don't think we should.' Then Johnson turned to McNamara, who agreed with Rusk that we should. I ended up the only dissenting vote. My prelunch allies had disappeared." George Ball had his doubts as well but remained silent. "Faced with an unanimous view, I saw no option but to go along," Ball reflected in his memoirs, although in an effort to defer the decision, he and former U.S. ambassador to the Soviet Union Llewellyn Thompson counseled that the raids be postponed until Soviet premier Alexei Kosygin left Vietnam in order to avoid any potential problems with Moscow. Humphrey went on to note that "Presidential advisers too often simply try to anticipate the President's decision, telling him not what he ought to hear but what they think he wants to hear. As the war went on, there was a clear tendency on the part of the men around Johnson to do that."[12]

Convinced that bombing North Vietnam was a terrible idea, and perhaps oblivious to the reality that LBJ was seeking support rather than actual advice, Humphrey naïvely spoke his mind. He asserted that the administration should not pursue retaliatory strikes immediately, agreeing with Ball and

Thompson that waiting until Kosygin departed from Hanoi would be advisable. Humphrey later recalled that his arguments "fell before the weight of the others, and I ended my first significant meetings on Vietnam as part of a rejected minority . . . and my views frequently not particularly welcome." Johnson fumed at the vice president's public disagreement, and despite Humphrey's dissent and Ball's temporizing, the strikes proceeded. But the damage had been done. As Curtis Solberg noted, at the "first important occasion of their partnership, Humphrey had broken his pledge."[13]

Hoping to rectify his well-intentioned yet disastrous exchange with Johnson in the NSC meeting, Humphrey agreed to join Ball on February 11 to approach the president about the potential dangers that loomed in an expanded Vietnamese conflict. Later that same day, Humphrey told John Rielly to "keep a good file on Vietnam" since he intended to sit down with Johnson, Rusk, and others soon to discuss U.S. policy in Southeast Asia "in all its implications." Rielly had to tell the vice president that he had learned that LBJ was meeting with the NSC already—without notifying Humphrey.[14] As a result of his failure to stand loyally with the president, Humphrey would not be invited to the NSC meeting two days later and would soon find himself on the outside of the decision-making process looking in, already stripped of any meaningful influence with the president and his key Vietnam advisers for his heresy. Unfortunately for Humphrey, that would only be the beginning of a banishment that would last for an entire year.

The proximate cause of Humphrey's exile dates to February 13, 1965. Humphrey received a phone call from Thomas L. Hughes, his former legal counsel and at the time the director of the Bureau of Intelligence and Research at the State Department. Hughes, who knew that Humphrey "had become very nervous about expanding the war," shared the vice president's skepticism about the escalation of U.S. presence in Vietnam and a potential sustained bombing campaign.[15] Hughes had spoken to George Ball earlier that day after the NSC meeting from which Humphrey had been excluded. Ball, who opposed the bombing reprisals and the possibility of the commitment of U.S. ground forces in Vietnam, saw Humphrey as an ally in the effort to dissuade the president from escalation and instructed Hughes to bring the vice president up-to-date on the administration's intentions in Vietnam. Parenthetically, this indirect method of communication would become a frequently used back channel for Humphrey on Vietnam as time went on and he remained isolated from Johnson and his closest advisers.

Hughes told Humphrey that the "die is cast"—the administration had decided to expand the U.S. role in the war, and any attempt to deter the president from that course of action would need to take place immediately. At the vice president's invitation, the next day Hughes flew to Georgia, where Humphrey had gone to shoot quail. The two men spent the weekend analyzing the latest cables and memoranda on Vietnam in order to determine how best to approach Johnson about their concerns. Ultimately, they agreed that Humphrey needed to spell out explicitly his concerns in a memorandum to the president. "I can only talk to him," Humphrey told Hughes, "as a long-standing political ally."[16] With Hughes's input, the vice president drafted a document that detailed his fears over the pending escalation of the war and the reason why he believed that terminating the U.S. role in Vietnam would be possible in domestic political terms.

Whereas other advisers such as Ball and James Thomson were more concerned with the international implications of escalation, Humphrey focused on the domestic political ramifications of an expanded U.S. presence in Vietnam. If the administration proved unable to limit the U.S. military commitment to Saigon, the vice president argued, the country would find itself "embroiled deeper in fighting in Vietnam over the next few months." If that occurred, the administration would face serious political trouble. "American wars," Humphrey pointed out, "have to be politically understandable by the American public. There has to be a cogent, convincing case if we are to enjoy sustained public support. In World Wars I and II we had this. In Korea we were moving under United Nations auspices to South Korea against dramatic, across-the-border, conventional aggression."

The situation in Vietnam, however, was starkly different. Humphrey argued that the U.S. public was confused by the complexities of the conflict and by the administration's constantly changing rationale for U.S. involvement. The perpetual instability in Saigon, moreover, only enhanced the lack of understanding of the conflict while concurrently undermining political support for the administration. The American people "simply can't understand why we would run grave risks to support a country which is totally unable to put its house in order." Humphrey concluded that the best solution was for Johnson to de-escalate the U.S. commitment rather than expand the country's role in a war that few in the United States understood. The vice president insisted that such a move would be politically feasible. The administration, he contended, "is in a stronger position to do so now than any administration in this century. Nineteen-sixty-five is the year of minimum political risk for the Johnson administration. Indeed, it is the first year when we can face the Vietnam problem without being preoccupied with the political repercussions from the Republican right."[17] To underscore his position, Humphrey reminded the president that "we stressed not enlarging the war" in the presidential campaign and won by a landslide.

Humphrey's argument hinged on three pivotal factors. First, he pointed out that by escalating the conflict through an expansion of bombing and the introduction of U.S. ground troops into Vietnam, the administration was essentially adopting Goldwater's policy. Why should the administration do that, Humphrey asked, in the wake of the overwhelming electoral victory the previous November? Given the scope of the mandate Johnson received, early

1965 was the perfect time to seek an alternative. Second, Humphrey expressed skepticism that the proposed escalation would be "politically understandable to the American public." Third, Humphrey recognized that escalation could lead to problems for the administration: "Political opposition will mount steadily," not just from the GOP but also from "Democratic liberals, independents, labor," all of which would be key constituencies for a potential LBJ reelection campaign in 1968.

Thus, Humphrey urged that Johnson should take advantage of the unique political moment in which the administration found itself. While politically strong and nearly four years away from facing the electorate again, LBJ should cut U.S. losses in Southeast Asia and divest the United States of its commitment to the Saigon regime. He supported this conclusion by flattering the president, writing that "President Johnson is personally identified with, and greatly admired for, political ingenuity. People will be counting on him to use on the world scene his unrivaled talents as a politician." For Johnson and the country, the "best possible outcome a year from now would be a Vietnamese settlement which turns out to be better than was in the cards because LBJ's political talent for the first time came to grips with a world crisis and did so successfully."[18]

According to vice presidential aide Ted Van Dyk, Humphrey "just argued out of political intuition and visceral reaction against the bombing. . . . Johnson had talked to him at great length before he took office, saying he didn't want Humphrey disagreeing with him at meetings. . . . And right at the start Humphrey breached this. I'm sure this angered the hell out of Johnson—maybe even more than the fact that Humphrey disagreed with him."[19] In a similar vein, Edgar Berman recalled, "this memo was as prescient about the war as anything ever put down on paper, either in or out of the Administration. Meant only to help Johnson, it could hardly be construed as a flaunting of authority or a confrontation of power."[20] Leaving aside the foresight displayed by the vice president's memorandum for the moment, it should be seen as prototypical Humphrey: He understood LBJ, considered the big picture, and—from Humphrey's perspective—acted out of loyalty, the key attribute for a vice president. His goal, at least in part, was ensuring a second full term for LBJ, along with trying to avoid the looming disaster in Vietnam. But even at this early moment, it was too late. Johnson had already essentially chosen war even before what many scholars consider the most important week of the entire U.S. engagement in Vietnam. Humphrey's astute political analysis could not derail the decision that had essentially been made when the president consciously decided to intertwine his presidency and credibility with success in Southeast Asia.

The memorandum bore all of the hallmarks of Hubert Humphrey: it was a penetrating, panoptic, thoughtful, and well-informed document that was grounded in practical realities rather than ideology, "one political heavyweight speaking to another."[21] Fredrik Logevall accurately describes it as "a tour de force . . . that must rank as one of the most incisive and prescient memos ever written on the prospect of an Americanized war in Vietnam."[22] To be sure, it is a remarkable historical document. It offers a glimpse at the road not taken in Vietnam at a moment when the path to war had not yet been irrevocably chosen. In light of the advice it contained, Michael Cohen suggests that while LBJ is "today generally considered to be a political wizard . . . Humphrey's analysis suggests he possessed the sharper political antenna . . . [and] showed himself to be the far more unsentimental of the two men."[23] Given LBJ's personal investment of his credibility and political future in the conflict's outcome, perhaps we should not be shocked by Cohen's thought-provoking insight.

Humphrey's strategy to sway the president's position can only be characterized as incisive political calculation combined with a shrewd understanding of his audience. Rather than trying to make his case from a military, strategic, or diplomatic perspective—since those approaches had been constantly debated and largely adjudicated over the past year without his input—Humphrey tried to convince LBJ using the most potent weapons available to him: by asserting his loyalty to the president and by stressing a rationale that they both understood intuitively domestic political considerations. He discussed the potential damage that an expanded war could do to Johnson's Great Society programs, to the administration's broader foreign policy agenda, and to the image and credibility of both the country and Johnson himself. Moreover, he argued that because the administration had not framed the escalation in terms of U.S. national interest, a wider war "would not make sense to the American people." Humphrey also appealed to LBJ's concerns about dissent from within his own party, pointing out correctly that "in Washington and across the country, the opposition is more Democratic than Republican." This point would have resonated with the president, who needed support from the Democrats in Congress to further his Great Society agenda.[24]

Humphrey sent Johnson the final draft of the memorandum through Bill Moyers, who was LBJ's informal chief of staff. There is no explicit account of Johnson's reaction to the document. It does not appear in his memoirs, and there is nothing in the archival record that reflects the president's specific response, although Moyers recalled making the "mistake" of giving it to Johnson, which led to a "harsh attack on Humphrey."[25] But on the heels of Humphrey's comments in the February 10 meeting, it definitely confirmed the president's decision to exclude the vice president from subsequent meetings. At the same time, however, it would have been at once persuasive and perturbing to the president. Although Humphrey had put the dilemma in the political terms most familiar to the president, Johnson was still displeased with the vice president. That would have made the memo a hard sell, but despite Humphrey's rapidly disintegrating influence and the president's fear that Humphrey had written the memo in order to leak it later, it is clear that LBJ took Humphrey's warnings seriously.

Johnson could not ignore the political calculus and realities that Humphrey identified. In fact, the president's enthusiasm for the bombing campaign had waned somewhat, in part due to the possibility of domestic opposition in the United States. He told McNamara, "bombers won't bring 'em [the North Vietnamese] to their knees—unless we do something we wouldn't do. We'll be called warmongers—elsewhere, and here in the U.S. that'll be more pronounced. Peacemakers'll be after us." Yet ultimately Humphrey's memo seemed only to "strengthen the president's resolve not to disclose the operation," since, as McGeorge Bundy pointed out, "you do not want to give a loud public signal of a major change in policy right now."[26] The secrecy and dissembling reflected in this approach would be endemic to the Johnson administration throughout the entire conflict.

Despite his lingering concerns, LBJ believed that withdrawal as outlined by Humphrey was not a realistic option. In his mind, it would be a political humiliation similar to what Truman had experienced after 1949 with China, which would limit his effectiveness both domestically and internationally. And since the status quo had proven to be ineffective, the only other viable choice was to escalate the conflict.[27] But Johnson's reservations were tempered after a meeting with former president Dwight D. Eisenhower—coincidentally held on February 17, the same day as Humphrey's memorandum. Eisenhower had become an ardent hawk on the war and enthusiastically supported the notion of expanded bombing. "We cannot let the Indochinese peninsula go," Eisenhower asserted, and if that meant expanded bombing or even the commitment of U.S. ground troops, then "so be it." Johnson was convinced—especially with the prospect of politically advantageous support from Eisenhower—and any residual uncertainty over escalation that lingered from Humphrey's memo evaporated.[28] Within two weeks, what became known as Operation ROLLING THUNDER commenced.

Perhaps realizing the risk of challenging LBJ on the direction in which U.S. policy was moving, Humphrey had ended his memorandum with a clear statement of loyalty to the president: "I intend to support the Administration whatever the president's decision." And, indeed, he honored that promise, never again disagreeing publicly with the president in Vietnam-related meetings—a sharp contrast to the actions of an increasing number of Democrats in the Senate.[29] Yet that did not stop him from making another effort to change LBJ's mind. Humphrey, who apparently did not fully comprehend the depth of Johnson's ire, gave the president another cautionary memorandum two weeks later, suggesting that the president reconsider the "dangerous" bombing policy, avoid the introduction of combat troops, and seek "every direct means of sounding out weaknesses on the other side that might lead to negotiations." Johnson reacted predictably and dismissively, angrily yelling at Humphrey, "We do not need all these memos!" and later telling others, "in a choice between Humphrey and General Taylor as our major strategist, I am disposed toward Taylor."[30]

Interestingly, just the week before the February 17 memorandum, *Time* had observed that Johnson kept Humphrey "on a close leash, wants to know at all times where he is, what he is doing and, most important, what he is saying or planning to say."[31] In this instance, LBJ's control over his vice president was clearly less complete than he expected. As a result, Humphrey's apostasy damaged the relationship between LBJ and his vice president, perhaps irrevocably. Even when Johnson relented and allowed Humphrey to return to favor in 1966—with the vice president eagerly providing a full-throated defense of administration policy—LBJ remained suspicious of Humphrey, his motives, and his allegiance. So fractured was their previously close partnership that LBJ's lingering concerns about Humphrey's loyalty would lead him to refuse to support his vice president fully throughout the 1968 presidential campaign, even in the final weeks when Nixon's electoral shenanigans with the South Vietnamese became apparent. Johnson's anger was obvious to his vice president. Humphrey told Hughes that the document on which they had collaborated had only "infuriated" LBJ and poisoned their relationship further.[32] But despite LBJ's palpable anger and frustration, in February 1965 Humphrey seemed "blithely unaware that Johnson was about to cast him into purgatory," an exile that would last a year and have profound ramifications for Humphrey and the country.[33]

One of the most intriguing counterfactual questions of the entire U.S. experience in Vietnam is what might have happened if LBJ had heeded Humphrey's advice and pursued an alternate strategy in early 1965. Counterfactual analysis can be a useful tool for understanding both decisions that were made and options that were discarded, provided that it does not go too far in recasting historical events.[34] Assuming that Johnson followed Humphrey's roadmap, not only would the massive escalation in July 1965 not have occurred, but the 500,000 troops that followed over the next three years would never have gone to Southeast Asia. The Great Society programs, many of which Congress passed with a flourish but then allowed to wither into a state of permanent ambiguity, would not have been starved of funds, and the backlash against LBJ's reform agenda could have been largely avoided. The Democratic Party would not have splintered over the war in 1968, which would have had profound consequences for both the party and for U.S. presidential politics in the years that followed.

More significantly, most of the 58,000 U.S. combat deaths and millions of Vietnamese deaths that occurred over the next eight years would have been avoided. Politically, in the absence of the Vietnam conflict, Johnson would have been in a much stronger position to run for reelection in 1968. In

terms of the U.S. economy, the massive expenditures in Vietnam led directly
to the economic woes of the 1970s. The social upheaval of the 1960s and
1970s, while not wholly derived from the antiwar sentiment that emerged
after 1965, could have been mitigated. Perhaps the pace and timing of U.S.
diplomacy with regard to the Soviet Union and People's Republic of China
would have accelerated in the absence of Americanization of the war. And
while projecting too far into the future is problematic, the lack of an expanded Vietnam conflict certainly could have prevented a Nixon presidency,
Watergate, and much of the national pathos of the 1970s. Clearly, then, the
decisions made in February 1965 in the wake of LBJ's rejection of Humphrey's advice represent a profoundly significant moment and critical turning
point in the Vietnam War.

Humphrey "paid a stiff price" for his outspokenness in February 1965.
The president believed that Humphrey had "violated their pre-election ar-
rangement regarding the absolute allegiance that Johnson expected from his
vice president." As a result, for "one agonizing year" Humphrey was excluded from Johnson's inner circle, specifically "banished from foreign policy discussions." LBJ's retaliation was both petulant and all-inclusive. Because of his resentment about Humphrey's positive press, he would not allow
the vice president to invite reporters on out-of-town trips. The president
restricted the size of Humphrey's staff, made him submit all speech drafts to
the White House, and even refused to let Humphrey use government aircraft
without permission. In preparation for a speech at a United Nations conference, for example, Johnson forced Humphrey to allow McGeorge Bundy to
vet his comments. Bundy deleted three sections from the speech, including a
proposal for negotiations to resolve the conflict. After Humphrey gave the
speech, one of his friends told him it was "the worst speech I have ever heard
you give" because of its innocuous language that essentially parroted the
State Department's press releases on the conflict. [35]

Johnson's paranoia about Humphrey extended to his obsessive concern
about potential leaks. In particular, the president worried that if too many
doubts about administration policy were committed to paper, they would
inevitably be made public and damage his presidency. Complicating matters
for LBJ were the close relationships the gregarious Humphrey had with
members of the Washington, D.C., media. Speechwriter John Roche recalled,
"Johnson once said about ways of getting information around Washington:
'Telephone, telegraph, or tell Hubert.' . . . Johnson had the utmost regard for
Humphrey, thought very highly of his wisdom and judgment, but didn't tell
him things because Humphrey told his staff who leaked to the press." From
Johnson's perspective, "Humphrey really was, in effect, a security risk. . . . It
wasn't that Johnson was mad at Humphrey for his views substantively; it was
that Johnson had a passion for keeping things quiet." [36] Given Johnson's
penchant for secrecy, the idea that Humphrey could be the source of leaks

about administration policy on an issue as inflammatory as Vietnam infuriated the president. As Edgar Berman recalled, "Johnson blamed Humphrey for almost every leak that ever came from the White House and would rant, 'Hubert runs his mouth ninety miles an hour without thinking.' Lack of real evidence never deterred those accusations. . . . It was as if Johnson needed a scapegoat for his failing war policies and he chose Humphrey, who represented all of the 'fuzzy-headed' liberal community LBJ now hated more than ever." Humphrey "became a pariah in his own White House," and word spread quickly that the vice president had lost Johnson's confidence.[37]

Notwithstanding his status as an outcast, Humphrey did attend NSC meetings and did talk to Johnson privately, although Humphrey suggests it was "more to say what was on his [the president's] mind than to listen to what was on mine." Technically, Humphrey could not be excluded from NSC meetings: the vice president is a statutory member, and Humphrey would in fact continue to attend even after Johnson's dismissal. Yet those meetings would not carry much significance going forward, as LBJ chose to make the most important decisions on the war in his Tuesday luncheons with Rusk, McNamara, McGeorge Bundy, CIA Director John McCone, and General Earl Wheeler, chairman of the Joint Chiefs of Staff. As a result, Humphrey would not be involved in the pivotal decisions over the next several months that culminated in the introduction of over 125,000 combat troops in Vietnam by the end of July 1965. Humphrey recalled that in the wake of the memo, his "participation in Vietnam discussions had ended for 1965. No one ever said, 'You're out, and here are the reasons why.' In the brief span of my vice presidency, I had spoken my mind on Vietnam only in the councils of government, yet the President, in addition, apparently thought I had leaked something about the meetings. I had not, but that became irrelevant. I served on the National Security Council as a matter of law, but Johnson held fewer of those regular meetings and began to discuss Vietnam in the informal sessions he preferred."[38]

Humphrey's exclusion from Vietnam strategy sessions did not, however, "extend to matters relating to the impact of the war on the domestic front. Johnson still expected him to help quiet the rising criticism touched off by the escalation of the war, particularly among Humphrey's former colleagues in the Senate."[39] This new role originally emerged shortly after the decision to initiate ROLLING THUNDER. The president sent McGeorge Bundy to Humphrey's office at the Capitol in late March to talk with five key liberal senators who were critical of the administration and who were all good friends of the vice president: Frank Church, George McGovern (D-SD), Eugene McCarthy, Gaylord Nelson (D-WI), and Stephen Young (D-OH). Bundy "lectured the five senators on the need for unified support for the president's Vietnam policies," taking them to task for their statements in the

Congressional Record that gave the impression that they did not stand 100 percent behind the administration.

Nelson later recalled, "It was a very strange thing, and it irritated us all." Humphrey sat silently at his desk during Bundy's lecture, and the meeting actually had the opposite effect—all five left the briefing even more skeptical about the situation.[40] Nelson rode home with Humphrey and expressed surprise at the discussion he heard from other members of Congress about committing U.S. ground troops to Vietnam. He told the vice president, "My God, Hubert, if we put ground troops in there, we're going to get into a hell of a big war." Humphrey acknowledged the pressure on Johnson to increase the U.S. commitment and told Nelson, "there are people in the Pentagon and the State Department who want to send in three hundred thousand troops," but he reassured his former colleague of his faith in LBJ's judgment. "The president will never get sucked into that," Humphrey asserted somewhat disingenuously.[41]

As his comment to Nelson demonstrates, despite being ostracized, the vice president committed himself to defending the administration's policies—both at home and abroad—in an effort to reestablish his loyalty to the president. Yet obstacles existed there as well, as Humphrey's exile extended beyond the Oval Office. In an effort to create a conduit to the president and regain some semblance of influence on Vietnam policy, Humphrey sought out a closer alliance with George Ball. Humphrey recalls that Ball "had continued to send memoranda to the President that expounded his dissenting views and then met with Johnson to expand on them." Humphrey tried to use John Rielly as a go-between with Ball's staff to keep communication open informally, but "Ball's people clearly wanted to keep a safe distance from me, and they did. I could not blame them. There was the unmistakable possibility that he would have joined me in limbo, his access to the President limited, his counsel less welcome."[42]

As a result, Humphrey kept any doubts about the involvement in Vietnam to himself, hidden from the president, the press, and his liberal friends. To be sure, this would come back to haunt him, especially during the 1968 campaign. But it would provide him with opportunities to assist others in their efforts to work with Johnson. When asked by British Prime Minister Harold Wilson for advice on how to get on the president's good side, for example, Humphrey responded by telling him that the best strategy would be to offer "unquestioned support" for the Vietnam conflict—a tough challenge for Wilson given the British domestic opposition to the war, especially in his Labor Party.[43] Whenever Humphrey made a public appearance that included engagement with the press, he responded to questions about Vietnam with the administration's official position, loyally supporting the president.[44] That Humphrey would allow his fealty to the president override his principles on

Vietnam remains one of the most remarkable developments of the entire Vietnam saga.

The crucial question, of course, is what happened to transform the public Humphrey from a skeptic who argued that the United States should cut its losses in Vietnam and disengage in February 1965 into the staunchest defender of administration policy by the end of the year. Could the vice president have changed his mind and become an advocate for an escalated war? Possibly. But as Michael Cohen argues, the more logical explanation is that "he came to believe that being a strong public supporter of the war—and an unfaltering endorser of the president's policies—was a better political position than contrarianism."[45] Humphrey made a conscious decision to subordinate his principles, which dictated that he continue to express his misgivings on the war, to his commitment to serving Johnson loyally as vice president and privileging political considerations over his instincts about the conflict. The catastrophic situation created by this decision for both Humphrey and the country would not be fully realized until 1968.

Even with the vice president's exile, some advisers believed that Humphrey could still be useful to the administration. McGeorge Bundy suggested to LBJ in a memorandum on April 14 that the president might consider sending Humphrey to Saigon. While acknowledging that "you have been very reluctant to use him in foreign affairs, and for excellent reasons," Bundy argued that "there is no doubt that such a mission would give us a great chance for public attention to the real problems." Humphrey could "emphasize the pacification program, the forgiveness for defectors, the search for peace, and other such noises, all within the framework of Johnsonian firmness." The upside would be that the vice president would "collect a number of brickbats, which would do him some good here at home. But do you want to use him this way?" Alternatively, Bundy suggested that LBJ could make a statement in which the president could "sharpen the point that what is at stake is the future of South Vietnam and the hopes of its own people." Johnson chose the second option.[46]

Despite being marginalized by the president and notwithstanding his own reservations about the situation in Vietnam, Humphrey continued to speak publicly in support of administration policy and echoed his previous anticommunist rhetoric. In a speech in Norfolk, Virginia, in late April, he said that unless the United States had the "patience to work and bleed and die five thousand miles from home," the Communists would take over the world "bit by bit." Two days later, he spoke at Duke University and asserted that the administration "will not sacrifice small nations in the false hope of saving ourselves."[47] But such comments did not redeem the vice president in Johnson's eyes. On the heels of Humphrey's memorandum, the president was acutely aware of any divergence from administration policy by the vice president. Following Humphrey's Norfolk speech, LBJ spoke to McGeorge

Bundy on the phone to complain about Humphrey raising the possibility of negotiations over Vietnam. Johnson said, "I see he's got a good deal of negotiation in it. . . . I don't want anybody, while I'm President, talking about it until we have some indication that some of them *might* be willing to." The president referenced an article in the *Baltimore Sun* that opined that Humphrey's remarks "obviously have been cleared" by LBJ, thus signaling "an American diplomatic offensive." The president was perturbed and told Rusk, "Let's just watch him very carefully." He went on to say, "Hubert just talks and keeps the ball in the air and jumps around."[48]

Humphrey, of course, was not alone in his doubts about the trajectory of U.S. policy in Vietnam. In April 1965, George Ball and Bill Moyers began to work on potential alternatives to escalation in Vietnam. The two "apostles of restraint" were working with LBJ's blessing and began to enlist the support of a "diverse and formerly silent gaggle of dissenters." Ball thus became a symbol of dissent, particularly for the press.[49] One of the people who worked with Ball was State Department analyst Allen Whiting. Whiting also briefed Humphrey on Vietnam occasionally throughout the spring of 1965 at Ball's behest, because Ball was concerned that if he and the vice president held face-to-face discussions on Vietnam, they might both be "rudely ostracized" by Johnson—as Humphrey was. Ironically, contrary to his political convictions and personal affection for Humphrey, Ball found himself inadvertently contributing to the vice president's isolation. Ball compared LBJ's treatment of Humphrey to "hazing of a college freshman." Thus Ball was cautious in his contacts with Humphrey to avoid a similar fate. Indeed, by the time the spring deliberations on Vietnam had begun, as David DiLeo has observed, "the clouds of discord between LBJ and Humphrey were obvious for all to see, and the deficient relationship between the president and vice president in turn had a demonstrable effect on how information was processed at the top reaches of the government." Ball even went so far as to decline opportunities to deliver reports to Humphrey due to the president's sensitivity. Humphrey recognized and understood the position in which Ball found himself, even if it would cause him additional problems in terms of getting back on LBJ's good side.[50]

Another effort to get Humphrey reintegrated into the administration's foreign policy occurred on May 25, 1965. Chester Bowles, U.S. ambassador to India, asked Dean Rusk to have Humphrey tour Southeast Asia. Humphrey's staff, "eager to find a role for their boss," had made an effort to get LBJ to agree to send him. LBJ was not happy; he told Rusk, "I thought I had made it abundantly clear to you my view some time ago on the Vice President's going out of the United States. . . . [I] don't desire to make available the Vice President right now."[51] Nevertheless, Humphrey would strongly advocate for the administration's policies at every possible opportunity. Humphrey told Johnson on May 4, 1965, that he had recently "defended our

Vietnamese policy before student audiences of Louisiana State University, Duke University, Columbia University and the University of California, as well as before many gatherings of business and labor leaders." He urged the president that "we hit the Congress before the Memorial Day recess and line up our best people to get on the stump to carry the world of your policy to the people."[52]

Yet, behind the scenes, the vice president remained skeptical of burgeoning U.S. involvement in Vietnam and did everything in his power to dissuade Johnson from continuing down the road to escalation. Humphrey sent LBJ a memorandum on May 10, 1965, to give the president his "frank opinion concerning the beachhead-enclave approach." While granting that the idea had "obvious military merit," Humphrey expressed concern that "the plan will go forward hell-bent-for-leather without being geared and meshed into a total political plan for the area. Judging from past experience, I doubt that a political equivalent exists."[53] Once again, Johnson failed to heed the vice president's advice, ignoring Humphrey in favor of staying the course.

Humphrey's relationship with the president was the subject of an article by James Deakin in *New Republic* in May 1965. Deakin referred to Humphrey as "the Administration's faithful hussar, its mobile light cavalry" who had already traveled more than thirty thousand miles in 1965. Recognizing that the vice president was no longer the unvarnished firebrand he had been earlier in his career, the article noted that "there is no doubt that Humphrey at least finds living in the land of the consensus easier today than he would have in 1948." But the most interesting part of the essay was where Deakin noted that "The most intriguing questions about the Johnson-Humphrey relationship are in foreign affairs. Watching the awesome spectacle of Lyndon Johnson making foreign policy, some have wondered whether Humphrey could or would interpose objections or counsel restraint." What Deakin knew, however, is that Humphrey had tried and failed to do so and would likely not repeat the effort. As Deakin concluded, "Humphrey's loyalty is impeccable. He has gone down the line for the Administration on Vietnam. . . . Nevertheless, Humphrey's role in foreign affairs is not pronounced" since "Humphrey is not a member of the small group that is formulating day-to-day policy in the Vietnam and Dominican crises." What that meant for Humphrey was clear: While "proper Vice Presidential behavior," it was also "prudent politics"; Humphrey would "be in the clear if there is responsibility to be assigned later for foreign policy fiascos."[54] Here we see a keen observer of the administration crediting Humphrey for making concessions and rationalizing a compromising of his principles to politics and loyalty considerations.

As summer began and the situation in Southeast Asia remained problematic, Humphrey continued to speak in defense of U.S. Vietnam policy to audiences across the country. In a speech at Michigan State University on June 1, for example, he said, "the United States has continued to be challenged to match deeds with words in opposing aggression and defending the freedom of a friendly nation. We have met that challenge. Our firm and decisive response to naked aggression against South Vietnam has demonstrated to our friends that our power remains preeminent and our devotion to freedom firm—and to our foes that the United States is no paper tiger." He made it clear that, "In the face of armed conflict, in the face of continued aggression, we will not withdraw; we will not abandon the people of Vietnam. We shall keep our word." But he also asserted, "Recognizing that a political solution of the conflict is essential, we stand ready to engage in 'unconditional discussions.' We have no desire for further military escalation of the war. We stand ready to consider any solution which would bring peace and justice to all of Vietnam." He warned that "Our stakes in Southeast Asia are too high for the recklessness either of withdrawal or of general conflagration. We need not choose between inglorious retreat or unlimited retaliation. The stakes can be secured through a wise multiple strategy if we but sustain our national determination to see the job through to success."[55]

Humphrey's concerns over an "unlimited retaliation" would be validated by the military. Humphrey spoke with General Wallace Greene, commandant of the Marine Corps, who told the vice president, "You must understand that it will take no less than five hundred thousand troops on the ground to do what we must do to carry out our mission and bring an end in Vietnam." Shocked, Humphrey asked if Greene was serious and believed that estimate was accurate. The general replied, "Indeed I do, Mr. Vice President. You should have no illusions."[56] Shortly thereafter, Humphrey—in a speech not vetted by the White House—told a Detroit audience that "the United States must be prepared for a long, ugly, costly war," inadvertently revealing the true nature of the war to which LBJ was committing the country. Johnson was predictably apoplectic. LBJ told Moyers that "Hubert could not be trusted and we weren't to tell him anything" on Vietnam.[57]

In the aftermath, Humphrey did his best to mend fences with LBJ by enhancing his advocacy of administration policy. He told the president that the July 27 announcement ordering the First Cavalry Division and supporting forces to Vietnam was "tremendous" and that he could not have been "happier if Christmas came every day." Humphrey also criticized Senator Wayne Morse (D-OR), one of the two votes against the Gulf of Tonkin Resolution the previous August, for his assertion that sending additional troops meant "sliding into the morass of war" and calling for negotiations at the United Nations. Humphrey told Johnson that he could not understand Morse's attacks on the president since "you are using every opportunity to achieve meaningful negotiations."[58] But none of this had much of an effect on the president's displeasure and Humphrey's distance from decision-making.

As 1965 went on, however, Johnson grew increasingly concerned about his diminishing support from the left wing of the Democratic Party as a result of the war. Specifically, he worried about getting his antipoverty legislation passed and the rising popularity of Robert Kennedy, who had been elected to the Senate from New York in 1964 and was "gradually appropriating Humphrey's old liberal constituency as a result of his opposition to the war."[59] As a result, Johnson would look to the vice president to help shore up his flagging support among liberals in the coming months. It should not be surprising that political considerations featured prominently in LBJ's slowly changing attitude toward Humphrey—after all, Humphrey's liberal credentials had played an integral role in his becoming vice president in the first place. The president understood that he needed Humphrey's cache with the party's left flank to help persuade Senate liberals to moderate their attacks on the administration's policies.

Although his association with Johnson had undermined his reputation with this cohort of Democrats to an extent, the vice president understood that LBJ "needed bridges over those troubled waters." This would be Humphrey's ticket back into the inner councils of the administration.[60] In this case, politics overcame Johnson's annoyance with Humphrey. Yet the tension between the political realities created by the war and Johnson's inflexible demands for loyalty continued to cause problems for Humphrey. In assessing potential Democratic successors to LBJ, *National Review Bulletin* posited in June 1965 that "the fissure opened up in Democratic ranks by the President's acts in Vietnam" had accelerated the process. It also suggested that Humphrey had "little room for maneuver" and, "verily, must go all the way with LBJ. But his all-out defense of Johnsonian policy . . . forces him into sharpening clashes with his past constituency, the orthodox Liberals," who were "so bitterly opposed to the President's foreign policies that it may become hard for them to remain in the same party."[61] For conservatives and the GOP, still reeling from the Goldwater debacle the previous fall, the specter of a divided Democratic party in 1968 must have been enticing.

In the wake of the major escalation in July, Humphrey hammered opponents of the war on college campuses and in other venues around the country. At Washington University in St. Louis, he said that those who protested the war should instead "do something for those who suffer rather than proclaim themselves experts on matters of national security and foreign policy." He prided himself in being able to change the minds of those in his audiences. Humphrey told White House aide Jack Valenti after a speech in San Diego that several dissenters applauded him; "in other words," Humphrey boasted, "they confessed their sins and were saved." And after a speech at West Virginia State College, the vice president sent Johnson a declaration of support signed by more than half of the undergraduates on campus and said that the president should be encouraged by the "rising tide of support for your policy in Vietnam among college students."[62] In November, Humphrey met with Sweden's prime minister, Tage Erlander, a staunch opponent of the administration's policies. In the face of outspoken criticism of U.S. involvement in Vietnam, the vice president made an impassioned defense of administration policies. When learning of Humphrey's efforts, the president wrote, "There are few matters more important than making our position in Southeast Asia crystal clear to our friends and allies. As a result of your report, I am most optimistic about the success of your endeavors in this direction."[63]

These and other pro-administration efforts would pay dividends as 1965 came to a conclusion and the icy relationship between LBJ and Humphrey began to thaw. The change occurred in part because Humphrey "went overboard, doing many things that helped Johnson and even drew the president's begrudging commendation."[64] Yet Humphrey did have something that Johnson needed—indeed, something on which LBJ had relied for more than a decade: a good relationship with Senate liberals who were increasingly "the nucleus of the quickly expanding domestic opposition to the war in Vietnam." As the new year approached, however, Humphrey remained on the outside. In retrospect, he absolved Johnson to a degree, suggesting that the president "never intended for me to have any greater role in foreign-policy formulation than he himself had had during the Kennedy years. And there is good reason for that. . . . There can be only one foreign policy for the country. A Vice President cannot sustain a dissenting position. He can express his views firmly if discreetly. But on matters of high policy, once his views have been heard and rejected, he must accommodate to the limited scope of his role. Thereafter, criticism must come from the Congress or the public."[65]

Yet as 1965 drew to a close, a rapprochement between Humphrey and Johnson had begun to emerge. When an aide brought the text of a proposed speech to the White House for vetting, McGeorge Bundy relayed the president's instructions: Humphrey was free to say whatever he pleased whenever he pleased, and the White House staff were not to approve or censor anything he wanted to say.[66] On December 2, 1965, Humphrey sent a memorandum to LBJ reporting on a meeting he had with leaders of the antiwar protest movement, including Dr. Benjamin Spock, executive director of the National Committee for a Sane Nuclear Policy, Sanford Gottlieb, and pacifist and social activist Homer Jack. He told them that he would be happy to listen to and report on their proposals and criticisms of U.S. Vietnam policy—"even if I disagreed, which I told them I did with many of their suggestions"—and that "the President was deeply committed to the cause of peace." Humphrey's description of the meeting's tone, his recommendations to the critics, and his defense of Johnson and administration policy were clearly framed in an effort to curry favor with LBJ and preemptively show the president that Humphrey was not going behind his back to plot against the administration with opponents of its policies.[67]

Despite having spent most of his tenure as vice president on the outside looking in with regard to Vietnam, Humphrey managed to work his way back into relevance. He did so by transforming himself from a skeptic and critic of administration policy into a vocal advocate for the war. Only through that demonstration of loyalty and commitment to Lyndon Johnson could Humphrey redeem himself in LBJ's eyes and be allowed to end his exile. But in privileging allegiance to the president over all other considerations, Humphrey would sow the seeds of tragedy for his own political ambitions during his presidential campaign in 1968. For the immediate future, however, his strident defense of U.S. involvement in Vietnam—while politically advantageous for Humphrey in his relationship with LBJ—would help create the fissures within the Democratic Party and the political left that would have serious consequences for both in the years that followed.

Chapter Three

The Recruiting Sergeant

*The test we must set for ourselves is not to march alone but to march in such a
way that others will wish to join us.*
—Hubert Humphrey

Success or failure lies in conforming to the times.
—Niccolò Machiavelli

By the end of 1965, Lyndon Johnson freed Hubert Humphrey from the
presidential purgatory to which he had been banished since February. What
followed was, in the words of Humphrey biographer Carl Solberg, "the most
startling chapter in Humphrey's life."[1] In what can only be characterized as a
triumph of loyalty and politics over principle, Humphrey became the Johnson administration's leading spokesman for U.S. Vietnam policy in 1966 and
1967. As historian Michael Brenes has noted, "Humphrey convinced himself
of the truth he wanted to believe: Vietnam was winnable; it was a war for
democracy; it represented a global mission for peace and prosperity."[2] For
two years, Hubert Humphrey's unrelenting advocacy of the administration's
Vietnam policies both at home and abroad would not only define his role as
vice president but also have serious ramifications for Humphrey, for the
other candidates for the Democratic presidential nomination, and for the
country in 1968. By the eve of the presidential election year, the vice president's views on Vietnam would be nearly unrecognizable compared to his
opposition to escalation in early 1965. This chapter highlights Humphrey's
redemption and subsequent role as the champion of the administration's
Vietnam policy, examines the problems that the vice president's defense of
the conflict caused with his liberal friends and supporters, and foreshadows
the struggles with the war issue that Humphrey would have in his presidential campaign.

In a somewhat surprising turn of events, LBJ began treating his vice president "a little differently, a little better," as 1965 came to a close. This occurred for two reasons: first, Humphrey's efforts over the previous year to rehabilitate himself in Johnson's eyes and demonstrate his loyalty to the president began to gain traction, and second—and perhaps more significantly, at least from LBJ's perspective—because, as Arnold Offner observes, the "liberal community was deeply unhappy with Johnson and Vietnam policy. And while [Humphrey's] own reputation with the liberals was bruised, [the president] needed bridges over those troubled waters." Thus, Johnson's political needs overcame his lingering frustration with Humphrey's February 1965 transgressions. One indication of LBJ's newfound faith in Humphrey was the fact that he instructed McGeorge Bundy not to review or censor the vice president's speeches any longer. Of course, it helped that a recent Gallup poll showed that 58 percent of the public did not want Humphrey to become president, which helped to reassure the insecure Johnson that he did not need to worry about the vice president challenging him for the nomination in 1968.[3]

Meanwhile, Humphrey displayed remarkable loyalty to the president and his agenda. Given his desire to return to and remain in Johnson's good graces, Humphrey set aside any doubts he had about the wisdom of U.S. intervention and escalation in Vietnam and committed himself to supporting the president as vocally and as completely as possible. As he later wrote, the experience of being exiled in 1965 "had taught me that Vice Presidents don't make foreign policy and . . . to do what Johnson wanted."[4] LBJ had noticed and appreciated Humphrey's allegiance. One year after the fateful NSC meeting in which the bombing campaign had begun over Humphrey's objections, Johnson wrote to the vice president, "Your latest statements about our two-fisted war to defeat not only aggression but misery and unrest are coming through loud and clear. . . . Let me compliment you on such a good statement, and on your quick response to our concerns here."[5] LBJ's praise would soon be followed by a new assignment.

Hoping to use Humphrey's *bona fides* with liberals and his foreign policy expertise to overcome the growing discontent with the war, Johnson hinted that he might want Humphrey to travel to Asia in mid-December to rally support for the administration's policies. This move clearly indicated that there might be a path back to relevance on the war for the vice president. It also reflected the fact that the president believed that Humphrey's international experience would make him highly effective in cajoling foreign leaders. Yet when word of the impending trip leaked, Johnson reacted with predictable fury. Believing that Humphrey had been the source of the leak, the president abruptly canceled the trip. But this would only prove to be a minor setback for the vice president once Johnson realized that Secretary of

Agriculture Orville Freeman, not Humphrey, had inadvertently tipped off the press.

Shortly thereafter, LBJ chose Humphrey to represent the administration at the inauguration of the newly elected president of the Philippines, Ferdinand Marcos, who had agreed to send two thousand troops to Vietnam. This trip had a second purpose as well: it was part of a broader diplomatic initiative by Johnson to emphasize U.S. willingness to negotiate with the North Vietnamese during the Christmas bombing pause that had been implemented and would last through February 1966. Interestingly, in a conversation overheard by Jack Valenti, the president framed the pause this way: "We're going to try Hubert's way now." Johnson dispatched Humphrey to the Philippines, Taiwan, Japan, and South Korea and sent other administration representatives—including ambassador-at-large Averell Harriman, U.S. Information Agency director Leonard Marks, and McGeorge Bundy—to meet with thirty other foreign governments around the world in an effort to shore up support for U.S. policy in Southeast Asia.[6] It was a bold strategy, especially in light of the generally negative international perception of the U.S. involvement in Vietnam.

Back in Washington on January 3, 1966, Humphrey briefed the president on his trip and later told reporters that he had not seen any sign that North Vietnam wanted a peaceful settlement. He did say that he had assured each of the foreign leaders with whom he had met that the United States would not "sell out" South Vietnam. Johnson declared Humphrey's mission a success and said that it demonstrated the vice president's "capacity for leadership in foreign policy." At an NSC meeting two days later, Humphrey provided a more detailed and nuanced report in the absence of media scrutiny. He said that U.S. diplomatic efforts were being supported but doubted that they would produce the results the administration hoped. The other envoys at the meeting made similar comments. Secretary of State Dean Rusk opined that if the administration resumed bombing, "we will lose the support of almost all those who now support us."[7]

That conclusion troubled the administration, not just on its face but also as a symptom of the broader problems that had emerged with regard to the lengthening conflict. Disillusionment with the war had mounted as thousands of U.S. combat troops continued to be deployed to Southeast Asia in the new year. Not only did Johnson face the prospect of a growing number of defections among Democrats in Congress and an increasingly restless public, but the additional resources being expended in Southeast Asia had not made a noticeable difference, either in the fighting or in the tumultuous political situation in South Vietnam. In his State of the Union message on January 12, 1966, the president tried to put the best spin possible on the situation. The war "just must be the center of our concerns," he announced. The United States was strong enough, he insisted, to both fight the war and build the

Great Society, although LBJ reluctantly admitted that because of the war, "we cannot do all that we should or all that we would like to do." He bracingly asserted that "There is no cause to doubt the American commitment. . . . We will stay until aggression has stopped."[8] Yet the official optimism blurred the reality of the burgeoning concerns about the lack of progress on the war, both at home and abroad.

Indeed, the domestic political situation would become even more complicated for Johnson when J. William Fulbright launched public hearings into the war in the Senate Foreign Relations Committee. On January 28, Rusk appeared before the committee to speak in support of a request for supplemental funding for foreign economic aid. Yet his testimony quickly devolved into a confrontational exchange with members of the SFRC on the U.S. commitment to Vietnam. Fulbright told Rusk at the outset, "I need not tell you many of us are deeply troubled about our involvement in Vietnam," citing Senator John Stennis's (D-MS) comments the previous day that the United States might need to send up to seven hundred thousand troops to Vietnam. Fulbright also pointed to the expanding protests against the war, arguing that "something is wrong or there would not be such great dissent." Rusk pushed back against Fulbright's attacks, strongly defending the administration's decisions since the Gulf of Tonkin Resolution.

In the aftermath of Rusk's appearance, Fulbright was, according to Robert Mann, "strangely dissatisfied and eager for a more complete airing of the administration's Vietnam policies." For several weeks, he and his allies on the committee had considered holding public hearings on the war, an idea originally broached by Senator Jacob Javits (R-NY) and Frank Church in the summer of 1965 as a way to reassert the Senate's foreign policy prerogatives and avoid being marginalized as simply a "Presidential echo." The increasing unrest on college campuses, which SFRC aide Seth Tillman attributed to "the absence of significant debate on United States foreign policy," contributed to the demand for an open and frank discussion of the conflict. After LBJ decided to resume bombing, Fulbright was convinced that the hearings were necessary in order to "produce a true national debate and sufficient public pressure to contain the war within manageable limits and to induce a negotiated settlement." On February 3, the SFRC met in closed session and agreed to hold the public hearings beginning the following day, leaving the selection of the witness list to Fulbright and the ranking Republican on the committee, Bourke Hickenlooper.[9]

As the hearings got underway, however, LBJ announced that he would be leaving the next day to meet with the South Vietnamese leadership in Honolulu. This was an obvious effort by the president to draw public attention away from the committee's inquiry, underscoring yet again the pivotal relationship between domestic politics and foreign policy. As Johnson prepared to meet with South Vietnamese President Nguyen Van Thieu and Prime

Minister Nguyen Cao Ky, he warned Humphrey to be ready to travel, saying, "Keep your schedule loose." At the conclusion of the bilateral consultations in Hawaii, the two sides issued a U.S.-drafted "Declaration of Honolulu," which emphasized the need for economic, political, and social reform in South Vietnam; reiterated the importance of holding elections; stressed non-military programs; and made a clear commitment to a policy of pacification. Unfortunately, the upbeat statement served only to obscure the fact that the Thieu-Ky team, in the words of William Bundy, "seemed to all of us . . . absolutely the bottom of the barrel," as Ky in particular was less interested in reform than flashy uniforms, drinking, gambling, womanizing, and using U.S. Air Force resources for his own benefit. [10]

In the wake of the Honolulu summit, LBJ decided to send Humphrey to Saigon with Thieu and Ky and subsequently dispatched him on a nine-nation tour of Asia to explain the developments at the conference to U.S. allies. Humphrey later wrote, "After a year, more of isolation than participation, I was about to embark on a major trip in a delicate area, with no time for specific preparation, no briefing papers reviewed ahead of time, no time for study in depth." Yet this was exactly the kind of assignment that Humphrey had craved, and he embraced the opportunity to justify Johnson's newfound trust in him wholeheartedly. [11] Humphrey and LBJ met in Los Angeles on Air Force One on the president's way back from Honolulu, where Johnson sketched out what he expected the vice president to accomplish over the next two weeks. Humphrey's main task would be to champion public and allied support for the U.S. military effort while also encouraging social and economic reform and regional cooperation by and with the Saigon regime. In addition, the president "intended that [Humphrey's] trip both dramatize and publicize 'the other war'—what [the administration was] doing in a non-military way." [12] Traveling with Humphrey would be a sizeable entourage of administration officials, including McGeorge Bundy, Edward Lansdale, Jack Valenti, and Averell Harriman, along with much of the White House press corps. The inclusion of the media was notable, as the press rarely traveled with the vice president due to Johnson's concerns about Humphrey's close relationship to a number of journalists and the president's fear of potential leaks. But LBJ wanted the media on the trip to chronicle Humphrey's efforts on behalf of the administration.

While the trip signaled to observers both within and outside the administration that the vice president was back in favor, LBJ's actions made it apparent that the president did not have complete confidence in him. Before the delegation departed, Johnson instructed Valenti to report directly back to him on a daily basis about Humphrey's actions and statements, the fact of which Humphrey was not aware until he inadvertently saw one of Valenti's cables to the White House. But Humphrey knew well before that discovery that Valenti's inclusion on the trip represented "an indication that Johnson didn't trust me to be alone, that Valenti was a Johnson spy in our presence."[13] The blatant mistrust notwithstanding, given Humphrey's desire to demonstrate his loyalty to the president and his eagerness to undertake this diplomatic mission, he did not allow LBJ's lingering doubts or Valenti's presence on the trip to prevent him from performing his role on behalf of the president.

The administration may have thought the trip to be warranted, but skepticism about Humphrey's excursion to Asia and its implications for the war effort proliferated in the press. For example, the *New York Times* questioned whether the vice president's multicountry excursion was necessary. The editors suggested that Humphrey was "going to say many things that need to be said, including emphasis on the theme that is at the heart of President Johnson's Vietnam policy. This is the sincere desire for peace and for negotiations"; however, he was "also selling a product that cannot be quickly delivered."[14] More generously, *Newsweek* described Humphrey's mission on the trip in political terms. "As a longtime liberal and champion of economic uplift, it was logical, so they said, for the Vice President to spread the Honolulu summit doctrine that henceforth the U.S. approach to Asia would be more concerned with social justice than with military might."[15] This made Humphrey the perfect representative for the administration's new approach.

During his whirlwind two-day tour of South Vietnam, Humphrey did his best to win the hearts of the Vietnamese people and advocate for U.S. policy. After visiting an understaffed provincial hospital, for example, he promised more doctors, nurses, and equipment, as well as his intention to "raise unshirted hell." Later, he confidently proclaimed that the wars in Vietnam—against the Viet Cong and the "battle for progress"—would be won.[16] While in Saigon, Humphrey met with the U.S. military leadership and the diplomatic team at the embassy, had discussions with U.S. soldiers and civilians, and met with Vietnamese military leaders and government officials, including Ky, with whom Humphrey commiserated about the disappointments associated with being vice president. He also spent a significant amount of time with the press, selling the administration's policy. Humphrey was determined not to let LBJ down by challenging the president's public position on the war and made it clear that everything he saw confirmed his belief that the war could be won.

In fact, Humphrey's "hard-line rhetoric became more pronounced as the trip progressed." By the time he reached his final stops in Australia, New Zealand, South Korea, and the Philippines, "he was talking like an out-and-out hawk." In Australia, for example, he "lambasted U.S. critics of the war," including Fulbright, and told the Australians to send more men and supplies to Vietnam because they "stood only a few falling dominoes away from the threat of a Communist invasion." The vice president had convinced himself to frame Vietnam as "part of a much bigger battle—a massive struggle for

Asia comparable in every way to that [which] America undertook after 1945 when Communism took half of Europe but was stopped in its bid for the rest." Indeed, as he began to sketch the report he would give to LBJ on his return, the vice president told his staff, "The big picture must be shown, the big picture that Mansfield, Fulbright, Morse all missed. The Vietnam situation is a dramatized, concentrated example of what the Communists intend to do elsewhere." Recalling his fierce opposition to communism that dated back to his early days in politics in Minnesota, Humphrey characterized the situation in Southeast Asia as part of "a master plan, a designed conspiracy . . . an epidemic, and we must stop that epidemic. . . . We must lift the whole thing out of the quagmire in Saigon." But Humphrey's advocacy did not impress everyone. His speech in support of the war in Australia was characterized by his aide John Rielly as "just another hard-line harangue," demonstrating the growing gap between the neohawkish Humphrey and many of his political acolytes.[17]

In the midst of the trip, White House reporters who were traveling with Humphrey asked the vice president to react to Senator Robert Kennedy's (D-NY) latest comments on the war. Since leaving the attorney general's office and being elected to the Senate in November 1964, RFK had begun to take positions on the war that appealed to the disenchanted liberal wing of the Democratic Party that was feeling abandoned by Johnson and Humphrey. Kennedy's statement suggested that the Viet Cong be included in a coalition government in South Vietnam as a way toward peacefully resolving the conflict. LBJ thought the former attorney general's "switch" on Vietnam was "cynical, hypocritical, and dangerous," a move rooted in RFK's personal ambition, so the president ordered his team to attack.

Humphrey's response to the reporters demonstrated just how stridently he had come to support the administration's policies. The vice president dismissed Kennedy's remarks, suggesting that "Putting the Viet Cong in the Vietnamese government would be like putting a fox in the chicken coop" or "an arsonist in the fire department." The United States was "in Vietnam to see to it that the people of Vietnam have a chance for a free choice of their government. . . . We are not going to permit the VC to shoot their way into power." As Carl Solberg has written, "Probably nothing ever said about the Vietnam war . . . ever shocked American liberal opinion as much" as the vice president's comment, which "haunted Humphrey for the rest of his life." One liberal publication went so far as to describe the vice president as LBJ's "hatchet man" and to assert that he had become "more royalist than the crown," implicitly recognizing that RFK had unofficially succeeded Humphrey as the darling of the political left.[18] This assertion was perfectly encapsulated in a cartoon by Bill Mauldin in May 1966. The cartoon portrayed Kennedy taking a belt labeled "liberal support" from Humphrey, who was left holding a rock with "LBJ's foreign policy" etched on the side. The cartoon's caption read, "Sorry about that Hubert."

While the Humphrey-Kennedy rivalry would evolve in the ensuing months and have significant ramifications for the 1968 Democratic presidential nomination, buttressing public support for U.S. policy in Vietnam was the more immediate concern for the administration. Hoping to parlay the vice president's successful trip into positive coverage of the war at home, the White House carefully orchestrated Humphrey's arrival at Andrews Air Force Base and subsequent flight to the South Lawn, timing both to coincide with the evening news. Johnson met Humphrey at the helicopter, welcomed the vice president with a bear hug, and thanked him for his great service "in the mission of peace." Humphrey told the president with "a deep sense of confidence in our cause and its ultimate triumph. . . . The tide of battle in Vietnam has turned in our favor." According to Albert Eisele, "From that moment on, Humphrey was intimately and inextricably tied to the Vietnam policies that he had expressed strong doubts about only a year earlier." Humphrey, who would view and report on events in Vietnam through "politically tinted glasses" going forward, had emerged as "an enthusiastic, born-again believer in the American cause in Vietnam."[19] As the saying goes, there is no zealot like a convert.

After arriving in Washington, Humphrey presented a characteristically verbose report to LBJ on his visit to Vietnam. In it, he cautioned that the road to victory would be "long, difficult, and dangerous" and recommended several policy and personnel changes. Humphrey wrote, "In Vietnam, the tide of battle, which less than a year ago was running heavily against the Government of South Vietnam, has begun to turn for the better." While acknowledging that a "long and costly struggle" likely lay ahead, he expressed confidence that "we can prevent the success of the aggression in South Vietnam." The Vietnam conflict, Humphrey concluded, was not merely about the fight in one small country but rather part of a broader effort to "restrain the attempt by Asian Communists to expand by force—as we assisted our European allies in resisting Communist expansion in Europe after World War II."[20]

Ironically, Humphrey's enthusiasm for the war went too far even for the president. LBJ instructed Dean Rusk to tone down the vice president's report, which included a strident call for a long-term commitment to fight communism in Asia, to avoid "sniping and revitalized criticism." Rusk revised Humphrey's original fifty-page draft down to a seven-page memorandum that reflected the administration's desire to avoid controversy. Humphrey's temporizing and concerns were excised because, as Jack Valenti noted, "The President wants optimism; the President wants optimism."[21] Nevertheless, Humphrey became a major spokesman on behalf of the administration on Vietnam, "shamelessly promot[ing]" the administration's policies to the press, in speeches around the country, and to members of Congress. It was, as Robert Mann observed, "the price that a humiliated and emasculated vice president was willing to pay for Johnson's favor. Finally, he was once more included among Johnson's national security advisors. Despite what it cost him in self-respect and stature among the Senate's liberals, Humphrey loved it."[22]

Humphrey and the president went on the offensive to persuade Congress, the press, and the U.S. public that the administration's policies were solid and were working. On February 24, Johnson and Humphrey met with a bipartisan congressional delegation that included House Majority Leader Carl Albert (D-OK), House Majority Whip Hale Boggs (D-LA), House minority leader Gerald Ford (R-MI), Senate minority leader Everett Dirksen (R-IL), Senator George Smathers (D-FL), and Senator Thomas Kuchel (R-CA). Humphrey told the assembled legislators that the U.S. cause was just and that the administration's objectives in Vietnam were being achieved. Yet he also cautioned that "No one saw an easy solution. No one predicted speedy end. . . . Tide of battle has turned in Vietnam. We need to understand that this battle can be won."[23]

Johnson also invited each member of Congress to the White House to attend one of four meetings at which the vice president reported on his trip. In addition, Fulbright asked Humphrey to testify in front of the SFRC, and Humphrey agreed to do so. But LBJ immediately vetoed the idea, saying that no sitting vice president had ever testified before a congressional committee—even though he had done so himself in 1961. After a series of discussions within the administration and with members of the SFRC, however, Johnson relented and allowed the vice president to meet with the committee. But this would be a private and informal appearance; Humphrey would brief the members of the committee on his own accord and not as an official representative of the administration. That meeting would be held a week later in Mike Mansfield's office.[24]

Meanwhile, Humphrey continued his public campaign in support of the war, much to the chagrin of many of his supporters on the left. During a February 27, 1966, appearance on ABC's *Issues and Answers*, Humphrey rejected calls for a coalition government yet again, asserting that the National Liberation Front "engage[d] in assassination, murder, pillage, conquest, and I can't for the life of me see why the United States of America would want to propose that such an outfit be made part of any government." Historian and former Kennedy adviser Arthur Schlesinger Jr. later wrote (quoting his personal journal) that Humphrey's strident support of U.S. efforts in Vietnam disappointed him. "'It was a new and different Hubert,' I noted sadly as an ancient Humphrey fan—hard-faced, except for some unctuous smiles, and uncharacteristically coarse in language." Humphrey's "trouble, I fear, is that he cannot say something publicly without deeply believing it privately; and when, as now, he has no choice in his public utterances," due to his loyalty to the president, "he whips up a fervency of private belief. I fear also that someone has persuaded him that this is the issue on which he can knock out RFK."[25] Schlesinger's comments represent a preview of the battle lines for the Democratic nomination in 1968 between the antiwar left and the supporters of the administration.

The media noted the vice president's strident rhetoric as well. In the wake of Humphrey's trip to Asia, *Newsweek* reported on the implications of the vice president's turnaround on the war. "Thus began the most important—and, for better or worse, the most politically charged—assignment of his thirteen months as spear-carrier to LBJ . . . star salesman for the Administration's Vietnam line. As LBJ's VP, Humphrey could hardly be expected to oppose the war—but his field trip made him more bullish—and hawkish—than ever." The article observed that "Humphrey's hard-line advocacy was a gamble that history would prove LBJ's course right." Even with its skepticism, however, *Newsweek* could not help but be impressed with Humphrey's success in supporting the administration, as "The Veep plunged in with all his invincible faith in the power of positive talk." Humphrey "was impressive among those in Congress who remember him as the Hill's foremost liberal. Late in the week, he briefed the Democratic Study Group, a caucus of two hundred House liberals tortured by doubts about the war. 'He left a new spirit of hope and optimism' . . . one study-group leader said afterward. 'The Vice President is one hell of a salesman.'"[26]

Humphrey's change of heart on Vietnam puzzled those close to him. Thomas Hughes recalled that Humphrey returned from Vietnam "saying things that were crazy" about the "virtues of the war."[27] Many of Humphrey's liberal friends said things like, "We know you don't really believe what you've been saying about Vietnam." But as Marquis Childs noted in the *Washington Post*, "Nothing grieves and angers Vice President Hubert Humphrey more" than the implication that his support for the war was manufactured or disingenuous, because "Humphrey believes it with a passionate and—needless to say—highly articulate conviction." This was no temporary political maneuver or sycophantic conversion, Childs continued, since "Humphrey has cast his lot with no reservation whatsoever with the President and the President's policies. Whatever his political future may be, it turns on the success or failure of the Administration and particularly on Vietnam."[28] Childs's comments would prove to be prescient, as this is exactly what would undermine Humphrey's 1968 presidential campaign.

Some of Humphrey's associates believed that they understood what accounted for Humphrey's "new unrestrained support of Johnson's Vietnam policies." Ted Van Dyk noted that while Humphrey had been surprised at the level of support from U.S. allies in Asia for the U.S. presence in Vietnam, "he also wanted very badly to support the president, and I think this kind of gave him the reasons he needed. . . . That was the point at which he really began defending the administration, and you could see that he began being taken back into the inner councils a little bit." John Rielly concurred in assessing this turning point in the vice president's perspective; he believed that nothing affected Humphrey's political future more than the February 1966 tour of Asia. "That trip was the most important event of the Humphrey vice presidency. Having been cut out for a year, he was desperate to get back into Johnson's good graces, and when he got the opportunity, he oversold it. Instead of supporting the president 100 percent, he did it 200 percent." Rielly concluded, "After that trip came the period in which he did the most damage to himself politically because he was now more for Johnson's policies than Johnson."[29] Nevertheless, a sizable cohort of liberals wondered aloud whether the vice president needed to "overplay the part of cheerleader for the war in Vietnam." According to *New Republic*, "The answer is yes. Hubert Humphrey has never had it in him to be just a 'good soldier'; he is by nature a recruiting sergeant." As a result, "It is inevitable that our overcommitment in Vietnam should be matched by Humphrey's overcommitment to the overcommitment. To expect him to moderate his enthusiasm is to expect sobriety from an alcoholic."[30]

Adding to the pressure on Humphrey was the fact that those closest to him were split on the war. William Connell, the vice president's chief of staff, and Max Kampelman, a close friend and adviser, urged Humphrey to support the president unreservedly. On the other hand, Rielly and Hughes wanted to "nudge him the other way." As a result, the staff "increasingly pulled Humphrey in opposite directions on Vietnam," and while some of his aides were "determined not to let him pass a point of no return" in terms of supporting the administration, "especially in extemporaneous remarks and in interviews, he began to approach that point." Ted Van Dyk later described Humphrey as "genuinely torn" on the substance of U.S. Vietnam policy, but while the vice president may have held lingering reservations about his defense of U.S. policy, his actions and words left little room to question the depth of his allegiance to LBJ and the necessity of U.S. involvement in Vietnam.[31]

Even with this shift in the vice president's views, however, *U.S. News & World Report* considered Humphrey to be the logical choice to "try to bring the disaffected [liberals] back into the Administration fold." *New York Post* columnist James Wechsler agreed. He wrote in March that after seeing Humphrey defend the administration on television, the vice president's "righteous rhetoric was almost reminiscent of Richard Nixon."[32] But Humphrey had lost a great deal of his credibility with liberal opponents of the war. *Time* reported that many in Congress "found Humphrey unwontedly militant." One senator remarked, "He was talking 'Win.' He was much tougher than McNamara ever was before our committee, and tougher than Rusk." Mounting liberal criticism of the vice president included a reprimand by writer and literary critic Alfred Kazin, who charged that Humphry was trying to "prove his masculinity" by taking a hard line on Vietnam. Kazin, along with other liberal writers, presented Humphrey with a petition calling for a bombing halt and peace talks including the NLF, and that criticized Johnson for waging an undeclared and disastrous war. Yet their "harshest criticism was for Humphrey, whom they accused of double talk and abandoning liberalism."[33] And Wayne Morse complained that Humphrey "has lost all his persuasiveness among people who think. I never expected my Vice President to make this plea for war." The disillusionment of many liberals was summarized by George McGovern: "It really disappointed me beyond what I can tell . . . [Humphrey] was kind of an inspiration to me as a young politician," and Vietnam "was the first major separation we had on anything. It was very painful to me . . . and others."[34]

The chastisement from his liberal friends did not impede the vice president's advocacy for U.S. Vietnam policy. Humphrey recalled that he "became more and more the spokesman for the Administration. I met with reporters and with Congressional people and I supported our presence in Indochina as necessary and right."[35] Yet, as William Gibbons has observed, Humphrey's "zeal lead to increased concern in Congress about the potential commitments made at Honolulu" by Johnson. Perhaps the best example of how far out of favor with his traditional liberal base the vice president had fallen came during an unofficial meeting with members of the Senate Foreign Relations Committee on March 2 in Mike Mansfield's Senate office. The meeting degenerated into a "bitter encounter" between Humphrey and Fulbright in which the SFRC chairman questioned the vice president so sharply that Humphrey reportedly began to cry. Despite being old friends, the fault lines between Fulbright and the administration over Vietnam had become so deep that the long-standing personal and political ties he shared with Humphrey were not enough to prevent the confrontation. Despite the harsh attacks, however, at the end of the meeting, Fulbright and the others present thanked Humphrey and told him they were not trying to be critical of him personally. Fulbright even said to Humphrey, "You know we all love you," but it was clear that the vice president had become the scapegoat for the committee in their opposition to the administration.[36]

Part of the concern over Humphrey's split with the left over the war had to do with the role of Vietnam in the 1966 midterm elections. Over the next several months, electoral politics would play a key role in the vice president's defense of administration policy. On NBC's *Meet the Press* on March 13, 1966, Humphrey responded to a question about how the war would influence the midterms by saying, "this administration and any administration that is entrusted with the security of this nation cannot let the political eye govern the decisions that must be made in reference to our national interest and our national security." Humphrey pointed out that "One of the prices that you pay in public office as an elected official is the risk of making decisions at times that are rather unpopular."[37] Shortly thereafter, he framed the issue of the war in broader terms intended to resonate with the electorate that fall, telling an AFL-CIO audience in Washington, "Communism in Asia is not a subject of academic discussion. It is a matter of survival. Vietnam today is as close to the United States as London was in 1940."[38]

Humphrey went to great lengths to convince Johnson, the public, and his liberal friends that his support for the administration's policies was genuine. In an interview with *Newsweek* in April 1966, for example, he cautioned against imagining that he supported U.S. Vietnam policies because he had to; rather, "I am supporting them out of clear intellectual commitment."[39] In assessing Humphrey's place in the administration, *Time* noted that since the beginning of 1966, "Humphrey finally [found] an effectual and demanding outlet for his energies. It was then, at Lyndon Johnson's behest, that the Vice President publicly helped shoulder the increasing burdens of the war in Viet Nam. Since then, Humphrey has become the Administration's most articulate and indefatigable exponent" of U.S. policy in Southeast Asia "with all the evangelical fervor he once brought to such causes as civil rights and disarmament. Seldom have man and mission been better mated." According to the article, Humphrey's liberal credentials had "assured him a respectful hearing from foreign governments and segments of American society that had discredited the Administration's motives in Viet Nam." But along with that respect came disapprobation. Humphrey willingly, if not happily, accepted the abuse from his old friends such as members of the Americas for Democratic Action and Fulbright in order to defend the administration's policies: "I'm not quite manageable on the Viet Nam issue, and a lot of my liberal friends resent it." While *Time* suggested that "Far from reflecting political expediency, Humphrey's views on Viet Nam are a distillation of his oldest and most deeply held convictions" as an internationalist, others disagreed, as Humphrey "soon began to push his arguments beyond credible limits."[40]

On April 19, for example, Humphrey stated in an interview with Eric Sevareid of CBS that the president's summit in Honolulu represented "a pledge to ourselves and to posterity to defeat aggression, to defeat social misery, to build visible, free political institutions, and to achieve peace." With characteristic hyperbole, he asserted that the declaration that came out of the meeting was as significant to the future of Asia as the Atlantic Charter had been at the outset of World War II.[41] The next day, he told Democratic Party leaders concerned about the impact of Vietnam on the midterm elections that they should "not apologize" for the war because it was "morally right" and "aggression unchecked is aggression unleashed." If the war overshadowed the administration's domestic achievements, Humphrey asserted, it was up to the Democratic candidates to "put it in perspective."[42] Such sentiments did nothing to appease Democratic opponents of the war and foreshadowed the administration's electoral strategy that fall.

Moreover, the vice president's comments created further distance between Humphrey and the party's liberal wing, which helped to place him in an interesting political space. On April 29, the *New York Times*' Washington bureau chief James Reston depicted Humphrey as condemned by his liberal friends while being praised by conservatives for his "all out" support of the war.[43] Similarly, the conservative *National Review Bulletin* noticed Humphrey's outspoken hawkish defense of the administration's Vietnam policies. In May 1966, the editors argued that the vice president "surprised a lot of people by his hawkishness, which seemed to go further than Lyndon Johnson's." They posited that Humphrey either "intended to prepare us for more vigorous military action in Vietnam" or he "recognizes that there is no alternative than to occupy rightist territory, his rival Bobby Kennedy having dug himself in so securely on the left and Johnson being, after all, his boss." Of course, they accurately framed Humphrey's statement in political terms, suggesting that by heaping scorn on the notion of a united front government in South Vietnam with the Communists, Humphrey was "heaping scorn on Bobby Kennedy, who has great need for same," in an effort to "underscore the polarity of their Vietnam views and to try to turn it to account."[44] Of course, Humphrey would never be mistaken for a favorite of the *National Review* crowd or as a William F. Buckley conservative. Yet it is a testament to the centrifugal forces the war created that the vice president's views were more in line with those of Nixon and Goldwater than with those championed by RFK and Fulbright.

Humphrey's growing alienation from the liberal community was exemplified in July when he received a pointed and highly critical letter from Richard Hudson, editor of the *War/Peace Report*. Hudson told the vice president that he was "often the subject of discussion among liberals who used to be your most ardent supporters. One of the reasons that we campaigned for the Johnson-Humphrey ticket in 1964 was that we believed that you would have a good influence on foreign policy questions on the President. Now, to be brutally frank, we are disgusted with you." Hudson charged Humphrey with sounding like "even more of a hawk than the President himself. Is that really necessary?" While granting that Humphrey, as vice president, had to reflect Johnson's views at least to an extent, he urged Humphrey to "think afresh about the whole history of the Vietnam situation and come to your own conclusion. If that conclusion is different from the President's," he pled, "I would hope that you would seek to persuade him in another direction. If you find yourself totally out of sympathy with his course and he will not change it, I think you should break openly with the President on the Vietnam question. I believe history would justify you in this action."

Humphrey responded to Hudson three weeks later. The vice president expressed appreciation for Hudson's "candor" in discussing his status within the American liberal community. In a monumental understatement, Humphrey wrote, "I am quite aware that some of my liberal friends disagree with the position I have taken on Vietnam, and that is certainly their privilege." But Humphrey reiterated his complete confidence in his convictions about U.S. policy in Southeast Asia, although he did admit that he was "continuously examining our position in Asia and have sought to encourage some development of it."[45] The exchange with Hudson was symptomatic of the growing concern among the vice president's liberal colleagues. John Rielly informed the vice president that he would be receiving visitors—including Humphrey's former foreign policy assistant Allard Lowenstein—on August 18, 1966, to discuss the Vietnam conflict, "particularly as it relates to your status in the American liberal community. They believe they have some ideas about possible negotiations that may be worthy of consideration." But more ominously, Rielly warned, "they want to talk about your relationship to the liberal community and possible things that you might do to handle some of the problems arising from your articulate support of the President's policy in Vietnam."[46]

Clearly, Hubert Humphrey had transformed from an apostate to an apostle on Vietnam. His loyalty to the president and his understanding of politics in an election year eclipsed his long-held principles in his public appearances and statements. All of his previous concerns about the trajectory of U.S. policy were banished; in their place was a steadfast faith in the correctness of LBJ's Vietnam decisions and a full-throated defense of the conflict. But advocating for the war "was taking a personal and political toll on Humphrey." For example, journalist William Shannon, a long-time Humphrey supporter, published an article in *Commonweal* defending the vice president against charges that he changed his position on the war. The article also hinted that Humphrey's private views on the conflict differed from Johnson's but he could not express his differences publicly. Humphrey wrote to Shannon to address the issue. "There is a suggestion in your article that I may well have a different viewpoint on Vietnam from the President, but that I cannot express differences with the President because it would be highly irresponsible," Humphrey stated. The vice president agreed with the latter characterization but also dismissed the former, asserting, "I am thoroughly in agreement with the President. If somehow I should become President tomorrow, I would follow essentially the same pattern, I believe, on the basis of the evidence I now have." Humphrey copied the White House on the letter through Jack Valenti. Valenti later replied that LBJ thought the letter was "excellent," and the following week, Humphrey was invited to the Tuesday lunch meeting on Vietnam.[47]

As the November elections approached, the fissures within the Democratic Party became increasingly apparent. Nearly every important primary race in 1966 for a Senate seat or governorship became a proxy contest between those who supported the administration and those who leaned toward RFK's evolving antiwar stance. For his part, Humphrey was prepared to "lay it on the line" for his fellow Democrats and planned to campaign vigorously to help Johnson, who had effectively lost most of his congressional support. During the midterm election cycle in 1966, Humphrey campaigned across the country for Democratic candidates by championing the administration's Vietnam policies. Characterizing it as not only politically but also morally right to support the president's approach in Vietnam, Humphrey declared, "I happen to believe that the only danger at the polls for Democrats is if they weasel—or wobble—if they spread a canopy of doubt or confusion." He urged candidates to "run on Vietnam" and insist that the war there was "against hunger, poverty, illiteracy, and disease."[48]

As the campaign progressed, Humphrey's keen political instincts kicked in when Johnson decided to make a sudden trip to Manila for a summit meeting on the war in late October. Virtually alone among LBJ's senior advisers, with the notable exception of Robert McNamara, Humphrey argued that the public would see the trip as "politically diversionary and vent their anger on the Democrats at the polls." Humphrey's fears were proven correct when Republicans framed the summit as a "gimmick." Gerald Ford chastised Johnson for mixing "domestic politics and honest endeavors for peace in Vietnam," calling the meeting "some gesture aimed at taking the heat off of the Democrats on the Vietnam issue" before the election. Barry Goldwater concurred, stating, "No matter how piously the President may deny any domestic political considerations, the very fact that the meeting is scheduled so close to the congressional elections . . . makes it impossible to separate the trip from pure and simple Johnson politics." The GOP backlash notwithstanding, Humphrey's advice fell on deaf ears, and Johnson traveled to the Philippines and made a surprise visit to Vietnam.[49]

Unfortunately for the president, the trip did not achieve anything of significance. A seven-nation declaration released at the end of the summit suggested that U.S. and its allied forces would leave Vietnam within six months after Hanoi withdrew its troops to the North, ceased infiltration of the South, and the level of violence subsided. Johnson posited that the so-called "Manila formula" might lead to negotiations and allow the United States to disengage from Vietnam; those unrealistic and ultimately futile hopes failed to materialize. Moreover, the communiqué effectively committed the administration to a virtually open-ended war in Southeast Asia. The ramifications of that guarantee proved to be a political windfall for the Republicans and a political disaster for Johnson and, by extension, Humphrey. While the war played a decisive role in only a few of the midterm races, it was clear that the administration found itself in a precarious position on the war. The *New York Times* editorialized that the election indicated "widespread dissatisfaction and uneasiness about the course and the prospects of the Vietnam War."[50]

In the wake of the election, Democrats worried about the effect the war could have on the 1968 presidential election. The combination of the reaction to the Fulbright hearings, the ever-increasing casualty numbers, the escalating number and visibility of teach-ins and other protests on university campuses (and beyond), and declining support for the war in opinion polls made the conflict a potential political disaster for the administration and its supporters. Senator Stuart Symington (D-MO) told Walt Rostow, "We are getting in deeper and deeper [in Vietnam] with no end in sight."[51] Humphrey had reason to be concerned as well. Not only was the war becoming increasingly unpopular with the public, but it had also cost the vice president dearly in terms of support among liberals and especially with academics, "his most vocal constituency." As James Reston wrote, LBJ had given Humphrey the "impossible task" of persuading liberals that the war was both morally right and successful, all evidence to the contrary, and as a result, the vice president was inextricably linked to the administration's policies and decisions on the war. Indeed, the cover of *Esquire* in November 1966 portrayed Humphrey as a ventriloquist dummy on LBJ's lap.[52]

Despite the erosion of his support on the left and the stirring of some uncertainty in his own mind about the trajectory of the war, Humphrey remained characteristically optimistic about the prospects for success in the conflict as 1967 began. That perspective caused anxiety for his colleagues in the Americans for Democratic Action. The vice president, who had been a founder and motive force in the organization prior to 1964, had been invited to be the keynote speaker at their convention in 1966. According to Andrew Kopkind in the *New Republic*, "the word went out to 'be kind to Hubert.' The floor debate on Vietnam policy was moved up on the agenda to come before his appearance so that it would not appear that ADA was repudiating its favorite officeholder." According to one delegate, "Despite occasional differences, 'Hubert Humphrey and the ADA are as one.'"[53] Yet by early 1967, as the war in Vietnam bogged down and the political situation at home deteriorated due rising opposition to the conflict, many ADA members demonstrated a sharply diminishing willingness to forgive the vice president's heresy on the conflict. One news report put it bluntly: "Humphrey has lost most of the ADA's avid support. He sacrificed it by his support of the Vietnam war and the President's foreign policy."[54]

Humphrey, however, remained undaunted, and he continued his unwavering campaign of support for administration efforts in Vietnam. In March, LBJ met in Guam with the new Saigon leadership and the U.S. country team to assess the current situation on the ground. Following the meeting, the administration stressed the significance of the nonmilitary programs in South

Vietnam, but the president would simultaneously order stronger bombing of the North. Unsurprisingly, that decision did not go over well in European capitals. In an effort to address the disappointment and anger in Europe over U.S. Vietnam policy, LBJ sent Humphrey to mollify U.S. allies and attempt to repair the relationships frayed by the lack of progress toward a resolution of the conflict. The trip was a success despite widespread antiwar demonstrations and the vice president's inability to convince any European countries to provide additional support for the conflict. Humphrey met with numerous leaders, including Pope Paul V—with whom he discussed the bombing pauses and social programs in South Vietnam—and did his best to assuage concerns about the trajectory of U.S. efforts in Southeast Asia. He privately warned British prime minister Harold Wilson, with whom he was close, against "jeopardizing his relationship with the President" by backing away from U.S. Vietnam policy. Near the end of the trip, Johnson cabled Humphrey, telling him that the vice president had "done a perfectly wonderful job for the country. Your presence, your political skill, your good will and good humor have, I believe, helped us turn an important corner in our relations with Europe. I want you to know how grateful I am."[55]

Despite his success in Europe and his improved relationship with the president, Humphrey knew that many of his long-standing and most liberal friends "were deeply at odds with him" due to his support of the war.[56] That tension would be manifested clearly on April 17, 1967, when Humphrey had dinner with Joseph Rauh, John Kenneth Galbraith, Arthur Schlesinger Jr., *New Republic* editor Gilbert Harrison, and several other leading liberals in an effort to "open up a new dialogue that might tone down liberal critics of the war in Vietnam." Before Humphrey arrived, Schlesinger reminded the group that although they had strong feelings about the war, the vice president was an old friend and they owed him a polite reception. Rauh later recalled, "It was very pleasant for a while. Everyone seemed to be trying to avoid the hard issue of Vietnam."[57] Humphrey's expectation was that the off-the-record dinner might help score points both for the president's policies and for himself with the liberals with whom he had become increasingly estranged over the conflict in Southeast Asia. Those hopes would be dashed before the evening concluded.

According to journalists Rowland Evans and Robert Novak, the "mere fact the Vice President felt it necessary to seek the meeting tells much about the escalating political war between the Administration and the liberal establishment. As a well-disciplined soldier in the highest Johnson ranks, Humphrey has carried his full share of the burden of Vietnam." The dinner did not change any minds, but one participant told Evans and Novak, "Humphrey made 'the most convincing, persuasive argument for Mr. Johnson's handling of the war that could possibly be made.'"[58] Schlesinger "gratuitously suggested that the group understood Humphrey could not speak freely because of his loyalty to Johnson. Humphrey assured everyone present that he would speak candidly and wanted them to, an assurance that touched off forty-five minutes of continuous and acrimonious exchange on the subject of Vietnam, most between Humphrey and Schlesinger, with Rauh trying unsuccessfully to act as moderator."[59]

There were signs during the night that Humphrey's discomfort with the war had not been completely repressed. In a memorandum of the meeting prepared by one of the participants, the "bitterest debate centered on Arthur's charge that the administration stupidly failed to understand that there had been tremendous changes in the Communist world and was still basically clinging to the view that Communism was a monolithic structure. Humphrey took sharp issue with this." According to the memo, "They went back and forth on this point somewhat in the fashion of two bar room brawlers who keep repeating themselves for many moments." In the ensuing discussion, Humphrey stated, "Now suppose I were president and you were my advisers, what would you tell me to do to get us out of this morass?" The author of the memo opined, "I thought it [the use of the word *morass* several times] reflected his own deepening despair about the entrapment." When the subject of a bombing halt was broached, Humphrey polled the group, which was unanimous in their support of such a move. According to the memo, Humphrey said "very quietly: 'On balance, I think you are right that the risks of stopping the bombing are less significant than the other factors. But the president's advisers obviously don't agree.' He then went on to emphasize that he had only periodic, fragmentary participation in the foreign policy discussions." The author characterized Humphrey's own view on the war as "far less optimistic and self-righteous than he has on other occasions," and Humphrey "listened very intently as they spoke."

When the meeting finally broke up after lasting nearly five hours, Humphrey went "out of his way to put his arm around Schlesinger and Schlesinger apologizing for the vigor of his arguments." The effort at reconciliation notwithstanding, "it was the last serious attempt by Humphrey's old liberal friends to change his mind on the war. He had convinced them that if he had to choose between his old liberal constituency and supporting the president, he would do the latter." As one of the participants later observed, "Most of us were struck by the sense that he was increasingly conscious of the dead end into which his own political life might be headed as a result of the war."[60] Schlesinger recalled, "An impassioned Humphrey gave us a defense of the war, at once voluble and pathetic. He talked as if the whole thing were a Chinese Communist plot." He later wrote, "I was most depressed of all . . . by the lack of the sense of the concrete human dimension of problems which had characterized the old Hubert. Not once in his long discourse did he express any dismay over the human wreckage wrought by American policy."[61] The gathered liberals left the dinner convinced that if forced to choose,

Humphrey would side with the president rather than go with his natural political instincts on Vietnam.

The confrontation at dinner likely forced Humphrey to at least consider reevaluating his strident defense of U.S. Vietnam policy, if for no other reason than the voices arguing against the war continued to grow louder both within and beyond the administration. Humphrey later wrote that by mid-1967, dissenters within the government began to have more influence in internal discussions. He noted that Assistant Secretary of Defense for International Security Affairs John McNaughton and General Counsel to the Secretary of Defense Paul Warnke—who would succeed MacNaughton following the latter's death in a plane crash in July—had started to work on convincing Robert McNamara that the bombing strategy was not working. Shortly thereafter, rumors began to circulate that the secretary of defense was beginning to have second thoughts about the U.S. involvement and strategy, but Humphrey made it clear that he "never heard McNamara dissent from the President's views in those private discussions [with the president, Rusk, McNamara, Walt Rostow, Richard Helms, and Humphrey], including the very private Tuesday luncheons." Had McNamara come out against the war, Humphrey implies in his memoirs, then perhaps the vice president's own reemerging concerns about the war might have been expressed earlier.[62]

As the polarization of the country increased and the reluctance of those in the administration who supported alternative policies to express their views faded, Johnson faced an uncertain future. As he looked forward to the 1968 election, the president realized that Vietnam would override virtually every other campaign issue. While the White House's response to dissenters had been somewhat contained in previous years, it became increasingly clear that the administration's strategy entering 1968 would subject critics "to unremitting pressure from every quarter where Lyndon B. Johnson commands or can muster support." According to *Newsweek*, "This is a formidable task, but . . . he has at his disposal the all but inexhaustible resources of his incumbency. These include the power to put the Vietnam critics' chief talking point to a clear-cut test and proclaim a halt in the bombing of North Vietnam." Johnson could rely on "the scrappiest warrior in the White House phalanx," Humphrey, who "has hammered lustily away at Vietnam dissenters . . . for 'bad-mouthing our cause there.'" As the magazine concluded, "It promises to be a long and bitter year, for, barring a major turn in the course of the war, the debate on Vietnam looms as the most divisive political issue the U.S. has known in decades."[63]

Just how contentious became obvious when, in the spring of 1967, the Reverend Martin Luther King Jr. joined the national conversation on the war. Because of his stature, he quickly established himself as a key figure within the antiwar movement. While he had evinced private doubts about the conflict for years, King remained conspicuously silent on the war in public statements. He did participate in an antiwar forum in Los Angeles in late February with, among others, notable GOP dove Senator Mark Hatfield (R-OR), and he marched in an antiwar demonstration in Chicago a few weeks later. Finally, though, he had enough; as he told a close adviser, "I can no longer be cautious about this matter. I feel so deep in my heart that we are so wrong in this country and the time has come for a real prophecy and I'm willing to go that road."[64] On April 4, 1967, King delivered a politically explosive speech at Riverside Church in Manhattan. It was a blistering attack on the administration's conduct of the Vietnam War that caused many of King's allies to distance themselves from the civil rights leader. King's condemnation of U.S. Vietnam policy "elicited a sharp backlash of criticism" from notable figures like Ralph Bunche and Roy Wilkens, as well as from members of the administration, including Humphrey. The vice president suggested that the civil rights leader had "made a serious misjudgement," and the following week, he told students at the University of Georgia that King "had erred by aligning the civil rights movement with the growing peace movement." According to Charles DeBenedetti, King was "badly shaken—even stunned—by the ferocity of the prowar attack."[65]

Despite his shock, King would become more vocal about his opposition to U.S. involvement in Vietnam, focusing on both racial and socioeconomic problems in the United States that the war exacerbated. To be sure, King's public denouncement of the war caused his popularity to wane, but, more significantly, it symbolized the growing discontent with the Vietnam conflict that steadily escalated in mid- to late 1967. Public opinion swung against the administration as frustration with the lack of progress despite the repeated assurances from LBJ, General William Westmoreland (commander of U.S. forces in Vietnam), and others that success lay just around the corner. As attitudes toward the war soured and his own popularity dropped precipitously, Johnson became increasingly obsessed with the problem of how to demonstrate to the country that the administration's policies were working. At the same time, as opposition to the war grew and protests became more widespread—both on university campuses and with the general public—Humphrey's defense of the administration's policies grew correspondingly strident.

Yet some who knew the vice president well wondered if his commitment to the administration's policies was wavering. In a column on August 24, 1967, for example, *New York Times* columnist Tom Wicker wrote that Humphrey's recent speeches did "not suggest a serenely convinced mind" despite claims to the contrary. He argued that Humphrey was undergoing an "emotional struggle" due to the lack of progress with the war and the negative ramifications that had for the Great Society. Wicker concluded that the conflict challenged "Humphrey's sense of decency" and "raised the issue that even if the war was right in principle, can these costs be decently borne?"[66] It would be a question with which Humphrey would grapple, largely unsuccessfully, over the course of the next year.

For the time being, however, the vice president remained committed to defending Johnson's decisions on the war. In October 1967, for example, Humphrey affirmed his position and his personal dedication to the official administration position in two sentences: "I support the President and I support the course he is following because I, too, believe it is right. And no amount of popularity gained is worth the abandonment of conscience."[67] Two weeks later, Humphrey spoke to the National Defense Executive Reserve in Washington, D.C. He dismissed those who marched on the Pentagon to protest the war as "incredibly ridiculous," saying that they gave aid and comfort to the enemy. "I think it is time that all Americans realized that we are in the midst of a protracted, costly struggle" that "will probably not end until Hanoi comes to believe that we have the will, the determination, the perseverance, patience and strength to see it through." He explained that the United States was engaged in Vietnam for two "clear and interrelated reasons: We are there, first of all, in the interest of our own national security. We are there also to increase the possibilities of a stable and peaceful world." The United States was "meeting aggression at a limited level so that it will not have to be met later at a far wider and more dangerous levels. We are resisting once again a militant, aggressive communism."

But even if "were we to reduce our assistance to the nations on the Asian rim, were we to withdraw from Vietnam, as I see it, short of a just and peaceful settlement, I believe the ultimate goal of reconciliation and peaceful settlement would not be served. I believe it would be threatened." Citing his long experience in the Senate, including twelve years as a member of the SFRC, Humphrey forcefully asserted that "I supported then and I support now, our policy in Southeast Asia. . . . I have not forgotten the lesson of the thirties, when men who cried out 'PEACE' and sought to adjust themselves to the dictators and the aggressors, failed their time and their generation." That said, the vice president left the door open for a resolution to the conflict. "We have been, and we're ready to accept an immediate cease-fire by all combatants now, this afternoon, tomorrow; we're ready to attend a reconvening of the Geneva Conference now, to cease all aerial and naval bombardment of the North when this will lead to productive discussions. The road block to peace, my fellow Americans, is not in Washington, the road block to peace is in Hanoi." He ended the speech with a ringing endorsement of LBJ: "Today President Johnson feels that he is following the course that he believes to be right in Vietnam and in Southeast Asia. . . . And I believe that, as other strong Presidents in the past that, he will be proved to be right by history." It was fortunate, the vice president argued, that the country had LBJ, "a man who put principle above popularity" and was "as resolute as Washington, Lincoln, Roosevelt, Truman, and Kennedy."[68] The depth and ferocity of Humphrey's defense of both the president and U.S. policy, even at this late date, reflects just how strongly he felt about the importance of loyalty to Johnson.

The following week, Humphrey traveled to Vietnam again, this time as the U.S. representative at the inauguration of Thieu and Ky in late October 1967. On the trip, he spoke out strongly in support of reform and a stronger commitment to the war by the new South Vietnamese government. But as important as it was to demonstrate U.S. support for the struggling Saigon leadership, this trip needed to be viewed through the lens of domestic political considerations. According to Arnold Offner, Humphrey's trip and reports "seem to have been directed less to the Vietnamese people than to the American public" due to Eugene McCarthy's imminent challenge to Lyndon Johnson for the 1968 Democratic presidential nomination.[69] Being able to present a compelling narrative of progress and success in Vietnam became an absolute priority for Humphrey and other administration proxies as the 1968 presidential campaign inexorably approached.

The day before the inauguration took place, the vice president sent LBJ a telegram with an overview of the situation on the ground as he perceived it. Humphrey informed Johnson, "I am encouraged not only by the evident progress I have seen over February 1966, when I was last here, but by the expressed determination of both Thieu and Ky. . . . There is solid reason for satisfaction and optimism if the true picture can be shown and the public can be made to understand it." He concluded his interim report by saying, "We are winning—steady progress is everywhere evident. . . . More than ever, I am convinced that what we are doing here is right and that we have no choice but to persevere and see it through to success."[70] While Humphrey's comments to LBJ seemed typically optimistic and positive, the vice president's trip to Vietnam had "brought back many uncertainties." While he still believed that communist aggression should be stopped, he harbored serious doubts as to whether success in Vietnam—however that could be defined—was still possible. According to Humphrey, "I knew that the American people would not stand for this kind of involvement much longer."[71]

Indeed, the documentary record is clear that the administration's view was much more somber and realistic in confidential discussions of the war than in statements for public consumption. Humphrey was equally pessimistic. He told his close friend Edgar Berman, who had accompanied him on the October trip, "From what I know and see here now, I think we're in real trouble. America is throwing lives and money down a corrupt rat hole." On the trip back to the United States, Berman asked Humphrey what he would report to the president. Humphrey responded "obliquely," according to Berman: "I hope they know what they're doing. As of right now I'm damn sure we're not doing the Vietnamese or ourselves any good." The vice president continued, "We're murdering civilians by the thousands and our boys are dying in rotten jungles—for what? A corrupt, selfish government that has no feeling—no morality. I'm going to tell Johnson exactly what I think, and I just hope and pray he'll take it like I give it."[72]

When Humphrey reported to the NSC on November 8, however, he did not go quite that far. Before he started speaking, Johnson handed him a note ordering the vice president to "make it short, make it sweet, and then shut up and sit down." Humphrey complied, giving an upbeat assessment of the war's progress and Saigon's evolution toward political democracy. The vice president stressed that pacification was "beginning to move," action was being taken to eliminate corruption, and that the election had produced a "very good affect." He also noted that the spirit and morale of U.S. troops were high and concluded, "On my last trip to Vietnam, I came back 'impressed.' Today, I return 'encouraged.'"[73] Humphrey's superficial optimism clashed with the prevailing pessimism in the White House. That became more apparent when the vice president's staff informed the press that unless the administration could persuade voters of significant progress in Vietnam over the next six months, both Humphrey and Johnson would suffer "sure political death" as the 1968 presidential election approached.[74]

In *The Education of a Public Man*, Humphrey engages in an interesting counterfactual exercise: "Would I have behaved differently had I remained in the Senate instead of becoming Vice President?" His answer was yes, and his explanation was simple: "Where you stand often depends on where you sit." Humphrey wrote, "Once a wartime decision has been made and men's lives have been lost, once resources are committed—and most dangerously, once a nation's honor has been committed—what you are doing becomes almost Holy Writ. Any division, dissension, or diversion is suspect." As a result, "Your future judgments become tied to what has been done. In my own case, I came to feel, strongly and not indifferently, that what we were doing had to be done."[75] That attitude was reflected when Humphrey spoke in Hollywood, Florida, on November 18, 1967, to the Young Democrats' National Convention. He put the issue of the war on center stage. The "American people must decide what they want to do about the immediate issue of Vietnam. Are we going to last it out until there is a just and peaceful settlement? Or are we going to withdraw, short of such a settlement [and] abandon the people of South Vietnam?" Or, he continued, "at the other extreme—are we going to impetuously reach for the weapons that would settle the issue in Vietnam by burying it in World War III?"[76] One can be forgiven for reading too much into this speech, but the level of uncertainty and introspection about the current state of the conflict is striking.

As 1967 drew to a close, Hubert Humphrey had completely changed his position on Vietnam from his skeptical outlook in 1964 and 1965. Prior to his exile, he had urged Johnson to disengage from the conflict and had strongly opposed an expanded bombing campaign. By early 1966, however, he had become a hawk on the war and would, over the next two years, be perhaps the most vocal supporter of the administration's policies in the country. Had he remained in the Senate, it is entirely possible—if not likely—that his views would not have changed so drastically. Yet because of his commitment to be completely loyal to the president, and due to his embrace of political expediency driven by his own ambitions, he "tied his political fortune to staying the course" with LBJ and his Vietnam policy "in the hope that the outcome in Southeast Asia would justify his decision."[77] Those choices would have serious consequences, however, especially for the looming presidential election. The left had abandoned the president, the Republican Party was resurgent in the wake of the 1964 Goldwater debacle and its significant gains in the 1966 midterm elections, and there was no end in sight for the war despite the commitment of half a million U.S. troops and the expenditure of billions of dollars. For his part, Humphrey realized that he was irrevocably linked to LBJ and his policies, especially in Vietnam. While in Asia for Thieu's inauguration, he had commented to reporters, "If the war in Vietnam is a colossal failure, I know what happens to me."[78] Humphrey's words would prove to be prophetic during the 1968 presidential campaign.

Chapter Four

"When the Gods Wish to Punish Us . . ."

A politician never forgets the precarious nature of elective life.
—Hubert Humphrey

Never was anything great achieved without danger.
—Niccolò Machiavelli

Hubert Humphrey's presidential ambitions had long been obvious to his friends and admirers. But as the pivotal election year of 1968 opened, it was patently obvious that the vice president's political fortunes were inextricably connected to Lyndon Johnson and the outcome of the Vietnam conflict. Would the president be able to navigate the war issue successfully and earn another term in the White House? If he did, would Humphrey still be his running mate in 1968? Or would the conflict drag on through the fall campaign without a resolution, leading to LBJ's electoral downfall? And what would each of these scenarios portend for Humphrey's political future? Soon, however, those questions would be moot. The entire political landscape was irrevocably altered for both the vice president and the country in the wake of the Tet Offensive in late January, the stunning results of the New Hampshire primary six weeks later, and LBJ's unexpected decision to withdraw from the presidential race at the end of March. Those events changed everything.

Despite all of the upheaval, however, one thing remained the same: the decisive influence of the Vietnam conflict on Humphrey's future. Indeed, the most crucial questions for the vice president by the spring of 1968 would be whether he would be the Democratic nominee and, if so, where and how he would position himself on the Vietnam War. This chapter explores how Humphrey grappled with the political implications of the conflict in Southeast Asia in the months leading to the Democratic convention in August 1968, the strife in Chicago caused by the war, and what the Minnesotan's struggle to stake out a broadly acceptable position on the conflict distinct from the administration meant for his candidacy and the country. What will become tragically apparent is the vice president's inability or unwillingness to break with LBJ on the war due to his allegiance to the president. Moreover, Humphrey's uncertainty about the conflict would have devastating consequences for his presidential campaign, the cohesion of the Democratic Party, and the future of liberalism in the United States.

One of the traditional duties for a vice president is travel—to funerals, to inaugurations, or just to represent the administration's interests to foreign leaders. From December 1967 to January 1968, Humphrey embarked on yet another long trip on Johnson's behalf, this time a 22,000-mile journey to nine African nations as part of a goodwill tour with newly confirmed Supreme Court justice Thurgood Marshall, the first African American to sit on the Court. It would prove to be an enjoyable and successful tour for Humphrey, particularly given the fact that it allowed the vice president to avoid most of the incessant questioning about Vietnam that he had to endure from the media and frequently hostile audiences at home. At one point on the trip, Humphrey told reporters that he was "delighted" not to have spent "even 30 minutes discussing Vietnam with his hosts" in Africa.[1]

Humphrey's respite from dealing with the war would be short-lived. Shortly after returning from Africa, Humphrey spoke to a group of Democratic supporters in Fresno, California. Humphrey explicitly tied himself to the president, saying, "this is the Administration of President Johnson and I take my share of the responsibility." That included responsibility for the administration's Vietnam policy, and the vice president asserted that his views on the war "haven't changed" since 1954: "we have a responsibility as a member of the United Nations, as a leader of the free nations, to try to preserve world order." Humphrey defended the war as "moral" since "we're in Vietnam. . . . Not to conquer, but to save." He told the audience that it would be "immoral" and "hazardous, foolhardy and indecent to turn our backs on 10 free countries and 250 million free people in Southeast Asia." What was honorable, he concluded, was "keeping our commitments."[2]

Honor and morality notwithstanding, the situation in Vietnam continued to deteriorate and loomed as a significant political issue in the presidential election. Yet the vice president remained utterly convinced that Johnson would be renominated and reelected that fall. Indeed, Humphrey made it clear that he supported the president "without equivocation," indicated that he felt closer than ever to LBJ, and asserted that he would campaign for

Johnson regardless of whether he stayed on the Democratic ticket.[3] That loyalty, still unwavering despite the uneven relationship between the two men and the complete lack of improvement in the situation in Southeast Asia, would be tested in the weeks that followed. The surprise attacks of the Tet Offensive at the end of January 1968 shocked the administration and had a devastating influence on U.S. public perceptions of the conflict—especially given recent comments from Johnson and other administration officials that meaningful progress was being made in the war. Although from a strictly strategic perspective the attacks had little in the way of long-term consequences, the negative effect on public perceptions of the conflict was palpable. Perhaps the lowest point for the president came when venerable CBS journalist Walter Cronkite exclaimed on a live broadcast, "What the hell is going on? I thought we were winning the war," and told his audience that the war was "mired in stalemate." Johnson noted sullenly, "If I've lost Cronkite, I've lost the country."[4]

The administration scrambled to respond. Initially, the Joint Chiefs of Staff (JCS) requested 45,000 additional troops; by the end of February, however, the JCS and Westmoreland revised their estimate upward nearly five-fold to 206,000. Almost overnight, opinion surveys demonstrated the debilitating effects of the Viet Cong attacks on public support for the war. A Gallup poll revealed that approval ratings for Johnson's Vietnam policies fell to 35 percent by early February 1968.[5] In an effort to shore up support, Humphrey immediately went on the offensive to defend the administration. In an article in *Pageant Magazine* in February, for example, the vice president addressed the question of why the United States was involved in Vietnam. Among the reasons he cited were the argument that "Aggression is best stopped in its earliest stages," national self-determination, and the U.S. "obligation to back up the self-help efforts of the less fortunate majority of mankind." Humphrey claimed that "our long-range objective remains unchanged—securing peace and stability in Southeast Asia. So does our assessment that South Vietnam is critical to that stable peace, and ultimately to the security of America." He concluded by asserting, "I believe that to withdraw from Vietnam would be a serious mistake, and that the security of Southeast Asia—call it the 'domino theory' if you like—depends upon preserving the independence of South Vietnam."[6]

While Humphrey tried to rally public support, he also worked behind-the-scenes to provide a potential solution to the administration's cascading problems in Vietnam. In late February, Humphrey drafted a memorandum for Johnson titled, "Regaining the Initiative." The vice president proposed to fund the troop increase with a special 1 percent war tax, step up the Army of the Republic of Vietnam's arms modernization program, and demand better battlefield performance from the Saigon regime. As with his memorandum in February 1965, however, Humphrey's suggestions were flatly rejected by the president, this time because of domestic political considerations rather than in spite of them. LBJ was already concerned about his political credibility and electoral prospects that fall—which made the imposition of new taxes or the mobilization of the reserves inconceivable—but he also worried about the fragile U.S. economy. An imbalance of payments had caused a devaluation of the dollar and a run on gold, and the mounting costs of the Vietnam conflict had begun to cause weakness in a number of key economic indicators. Rather than relying on Humphrey's advice, Johnson turned the question of how to proceed with the war over to his new secretary of defense, Clark Clifford, who succeeded Robert McNamara on March 1. By the beginning of March, Clifford and his task force had become "convinced of the need to start peace talks" due to the glaring deficiencies in U.S. policy and the lack of progress in the fighting.[7]

Meanwhile, Johnson faced a political threat closer to home. Winning a presidential election against a sitting president in a time of war is difficult, to say the least—just ask George McClellan, Wendell Willkie, or John Kerry. Challenging a sitting president in one's own party for the nomination under the same conditions is virtually impossible.[8] Yet that is exactly what Eugene McCarthy decided to do in 1968 as a result of his opposition to the war. McCarthy was a traditional Cold War liberal who had supported the U.S. involvement in Vietnam until late 1965. As tens of thousands of U.S. combat troops poured into South Vietnam, the Minnesota senator expressed concern about the militarization of U.S. foreign policy, concluded that LBJ had lied about the events in the Tonkin Gulf in early August 1964, and believed that the administration had "grossly misused" the ensuing congressional resolution to expand the war. McCarthy came to view the conflict as a Vietnamese civil war rather than externally inspired aggression and began speaking out against Johnson's policies from his seat on the Senate Foreign Relations Committee. By late 1967, McCarthy's disillusionment found an outlet as he agreed to be the candidate of the "Dump Johnson" movement led by former Humphrey foreign policy assistant Allard Lowenstein. McCarthy would compare his Vietnam-centric campaign to Humphrey's audacious effort to force the Democratic Party and Harry Truman to confront the issue of civil rights at the 1948 convention.

McCarthy announced that he would enter four primaries in 1968. His justification for doing so was that he sought "an honorable, rational, and political solution to the war," which he characterized as too costly in terms of lives lost on both sides and the destruction of Vietnam and that could not be justified morally or before "the decent opinion of mankind." Humphrey downplayed McCarthy's candidacy. The vice president told Johnson that while he was "very much upset" with his fellow Minnesotan and had tried to dissuade him from running, the president should not be concerned about the challenge. Humphrey called it a "lark" and noted McCarthy's "casual manner toward major undertakings." The vice president also acknowledged to LBJ, "I guess I have no influence on these friends of mine," an admission that probably bruised Humphrey's ego but accurately reflected his fractured relationship with the left as a result of his vocal support of the war.[9] Unfortunately for Humphrey and Johnson, however, McCarthy's insurgent campaign would be far more problematic for the president than either of the two men anticipated.

The results of the New Hampshire primary on March 12 stunned the country and emphasized just how important Vietnam could be in the race for the White House in 1968. McCarthy's "tremendous showing," as Humphrey called it, completely shook up the Democratic race. Not only did the Minnesota senator get over 42 percent of the vote and become the overwhelming favorite to win the Wisconsin primary, but the results prompted LBJ's political nemesis Robert Kennedy to announce his candidacy the following week, further muddying the political waters. Humphrey was "torn." He worried about losing support from key Democratic constituencies like African Americans, especially given Martin Luther King Jr.'s opposition to the war, which the vice president knew could jeopardize the black vote for the party in November. But he still believed that when it came down to it, the American people would stick with the "hard task" of the Vietnam War. The vice president was so sure that was the case that he told a regional conference of Democratic activists in Rhode Island that McCarthy's presidential campaign was just the party's way of debating the issues. Lyndon Johnson, he asserted confidently, would be elected to a second term that fall and bring peace to Vietnam "without appeasement."[10] It was a bracing statement, but one that would prove to be overly optimistic.

In private, however, the vice president's enthusiasm for the war had waned. The accumulated problems of early 1968—combined with his lingering uncertainty about U.S. involvement in Vietnam that he had cautiously expressed on rare occasions over the past three years—forced Humphrey to reconsider his position on the war. As a result, he urged Johnson to use the impact of the Tet Offensive and public opposition to the war to press South Vietnamese president Nguyen Van Thieu to propose U.N. supervision of a cease-fire, withdrawal of all foreign troops from South Vietnam, and general elections that included all parties. Meanwhile, the United States would halt bombing above the 20th parallel—sparing the densely populated cities of Hanoi and Haiphong from aerial attack—in the hope of inducing the North Vietnamese to come to the negotiating table.

But Humphrey wanted to go further than that. Late one night in the president's White House bedroom, Humphrey talked to LBJ about the situation in Vietnam. He told Johnson, "From a political view here at home, that [pullback to the 20th parallel] is not going to do much good. What you should do is stop it all. You should cease bombing north of the 17th parallel."

As Humphrey's biographer Carl Solberg noted, this was "Humphrey's first recorded statement at variance with the president's policy" since his efforts in early 1965 to convince LBJ to abandon the war. The vice president believed that Johnson would reap political and electoral benefits if he took these actions, but, yet again, Johnson rejected Humphrey's advice. For Humphrey, "it was the worst time of the war," as he realized just how entangled his political future was with Johnson's Vietnam policy. As Humphrey's protégé Walter Mondale would later observe, at that moment, "I think Humphrey thought his political career was destroyed."[11] That statement would be both accurate and prophetic.

For his part, Johnson struggled to find a solution that did not involve military defeat, diplomatic capitulation, or political disaster. By early 1968, LBJ had retreated into a bunker mentality as the war deteriorated and politics consumed him. After rejecting the request by the JCS and Westmoreland for a massive infusion of troops, the president convened a gathering of distinguished elder statesmen known as the "Wise Men" on March 22 to consider the administration's options.[12] Former secretary of state Dean Acheson admitted that he had changed his mind on the war and urged LBJ to initiate a bombing halt to stimulate peace talks. Nearly everyone in the meeting agreed with Acheson's judgment. The president was shocked, later asking Clifford and Dean Rusk, "Who poisoned the well with these guys?" and remarking to an aide, "The establishment bastards have bailed out." Hoping to find support elsewhere, Johnson met separately with Humphrey and several civilian and military advisers. The assessment in that meeting from George Carver, special assistant for Vietnamese affairs to CIA director Richard Helms, paralleled that of the Wise Men and would later be described by Humphrey as having a "profound effect" on U.S. policy in Vietnam. Indeed, as Arnold Offner has written, these briefings in late March, combined with a series of increasingly pessimistic military and intelligence reports that had changed the thinking of many administration officials even prior to Tet, "compelled Johnson to change course. . . . He ordered his speechwriters to craft a 'peace with honor' address."[13] What happened next would send a seismic shock through the country and create an unexpected opportunity for Humphrey.

Given the trajectory of events and the pessimistic conclusions being reached by his advisers, LBJ privately began contemplating a more drastic step than just altering course to seek a peaceful resolution to the conflict. The combination of the McCarthy challenge in New Hampshire, the increasing discontent with and unpopularity of the war, and the devastating visuals of the Tet attacks that played out live on television sets across the country forced the president to reevaluate his political future and whether he would indeed seek another term in the White House. Although he would not make an irrevocable decision until just before his nationally televised speech on March 31, Johnson indicated to those close to him his uncertainty about running for another term. He made it clear that his efforts to bring the war to an end would likely be seen as a callous political move if he was the Democratic nominee in the fall—hence the deliberation about withdrawing from the race.

Once Johnson made his preliminary decision during the last week of March, he visited Humphrey at the vice president's apartment. The president knew that Humphrey would be leaving for a conference on nuclear nonproliferation in Mexico City the next day, so he wanted to keep the vice president informed about both the announcement regarding peace talks and the possibility of LBJ's withdrawal from the presidential campaign. Johnson showed Humphrey a draft of the speech, which included the limited bombing pause they had already discussed. Humphrey, with palpable relief and undisguised delight, called the president's decision "just great, the best thing I ever heard you say," and suggested a few changes that LBJ included in the speech.

Then the president showed Humphrey an alternate ending to his remarks in which LBJ would announce that he would neither seek nor accept the Democratic presidential nomination in 1968. The vice president was shocked and bewildered. He teared up and "expressed his dismay and surprise," telling Johnson, "You can't do this, you can't just resign from office. You're going to be reelected." LBJ told Humphrey that he was not sure which ending he would use but made it clear to his vice president that ending the war, not reelection, was the priority: "Hubert, nobody will believe that I'm trying to end this war unless I do that. I just can't get them to believe I want peace." As Johnson got up to leave, the two men shook hands, and Humphrey simply said that "he hoped to God [LBJ] wouldn't go through with it." The president replied, "If you're going to run, you'd better get ready damn quick."[14] On that ominous note, Humphrey left for Mexico City, which is where he watched on television as Lyndon Johnson made his fateful and historic announcement.

In the immediate aftermath of LBJ's speech, Hubert Humphrey faced the biggest and most complicated decision of his political career. Would he enter the campaign to replace Johnson in the Oval Office and fulfill his long-held dream of being elected president, or would he allow Eugene McCarthy and Robert Kennedy grapple for the Democratic nomination and stay out of the fray? Humphrey was unsure whether he could actually capture his party's imagination and be selected as its presidential candidate. When Johnson had mentioned his potential withdrawal from the race, Humphrey had commented that "There's no way I can beat the Kennedy machine." Now, he expressed additional doubts about running: "Would I just be a punching bag for Kennedy, only to be humiliated in the Convention? Quite frankly, I am not sure that I have the stomach for it, knowing the ruthless methods that are employed by both Kennedy and Nixon."[15]

What Humphrey may not have fully appreciated at the time—but what is certainly obvious in retrospect—is the fact that he had the inside track on the Democratic nomination that spring despite McCarthy's domination of voting in the early primary states and the rising popularity and momentum of RFK's campaign. Even without entering the Democratic primaries, Humphrey had an unambiguous path to the nomination based on his widespread support with the party establishment. He had accumulated countless political IOUs over the past four years, traveling more than 250,000 miles to all fifty states and campaigning vigorously for Democratic candidates at every level of politics. Moreover, Humphrey's chief of staff William Connell told Humphrey when the vice president returned from Mexico that all the key Democratic Party officials Connell had contacted since the president's speech had agreed to delay any decision on who to support for the nomination until the vice president announced whether he would be a candidate.

Yet Humphrey understood that even with these structural advantages, he would have to overcome his connection to the administration's Vietnam policies if he hoped to convince the antiwar faction of the party to rally behind him both in Chicago and during the fall campaign. As the vice president told his confidant Edgar Berman, "the only way I can unite the nation is to do something about Vietnam now." The *New York Times* suggested that thanks to the Vietnam conflict, Humphrey "seems to be shaping up as the favorite of the middle-of-the-road forces." Despite that perspective, however, it was clear that Humphrey "became noticeably reticent about the Vietnam War," perhaps because one of his biggest political obstacles within the Democratic party was "how to regain liberal support that he lost through association with that war policy." Regardless of his decision on whether to challenge McCarthy and Kennedy, Humphrey's campaign would inevitably be negatively influenced by his ties to the administration. As one observer put it, the "Johnson mantle, it has been assumed, could give its wearer nothing but an itch."[16] In the end, however, it would be an easy decision for Humphrey: he would run, Vietnam notwithstanding. His presidential ambitions trumped any reservations he may have had.

On April 27, 1968, Humphrey officially announced his candidacy for the presidency, "an office that demands perhaps more judgment, wisdom and maturity than any single man possesses." In his speech, he talked about the "practical possibilities of peace" and called for an end to the war without "humiliation or defeat," asserting that "I shall, as the President has, observe the absolute priority of peace over politics."[17] The vice president now had four months to convince his Democratic colleagues and constituents, especially his former allies on the left, that he could be trusted to bring the war to an end. This would pose a challenge; a few days later, RFK won the Indiana primary and McCarthy won in Oregon, demonstrating the potent influence of antiwar sentiment within the party. As Chester Cooper cogently observed,

"Humphrey found himself in a very uncomfortable spot. It was difficult to carve out a position on Vietnam that would maintain whatever lukewarm support he still had from President Johnson on one hand, and compete with McCarthy and Kennedy on the other." In *Newsweek*, journalist Kenneth Crawford similarly concluded that Humphrey, "coming late to the campaign, poor both in finances and organization, and bearing the scars of loyal service in the Johnsonian wars . . . faced an upstream swim."[18]

Even more problematic was the fact that the vice president's loyalty was rarely reciprocated by LBJ, which limited Humphrey's options in terms of how far he could stray from the administration's official policy. Frequently, the president came down on Humphrey "like an avenging general" when he diverged from the party line—such as Humphrey's proposal for negotiations with noncommunist elements of the National Liberation Front. If that were not enough, Humphrey also had to deal with another major obstacle to his presidential aspirations. "For many, if not most, of his liberal friends, the old firebrand transformed himself all too swiftly into the new fire-eater for the Administration. Particularly as the debate over Vietnam grew in intensity, HHH seemed to carry loyalty to the point of lackey-hood to Lyndon Johnson."[19] Indeed, Humphrey's hawkishness on Vietnam remained "a stumbling block even for steadfast admirers." Humphrey had "repeatedly braved pickets and hecklers to proclaim his unstinting public support of the full Johnson record—not excepting the war in Vietnam."[20] The distance between Humphrey and the liberals would plague his campaign throughout the rest of the year despite his best efforts to make amends and unite the party.

The vice president appeared on NBC's *Meet the Press* the day after he announced his candidacy. Humphrey made it clear that he had not "asked the president to take any part" in his campaign because the vice president was "going to put the priority of peace above partisan politics." During the interview, Humphrey framed his contributions to the administration, stating that he "had the opportunity to participate in the discussions that have taken place that led to decision-making," although he did not want to "exaggerate the importance" of his contribution. When asked by James J. Kilpatrick about the peace process, Humphrey said, "I think you have to be willing to take some chances in seeking peace." Straddling the divide in Nixonian fashion, Humphrey said that "intervention in Vietnam was required" but also opined that the United States "ought to pursue as effectively as we can an honorable peace." James Reston pushed Humphrey to be more specific, asking him if he would "be able to be absolutely free to speak out for Humphrey and not merely just defend the Administration during the campaign." Humphrey responded forcefully, stating that he would "run on the record of the Kennedy-Johnson, and the Johnson-Humphrey Administrations, but I will not rest on it. . . . I am my own man and I will be my own man." But, he noted, "I see no reason to repudiate what we have done."[21] The vice president's comment perfectly encapsulated Humphrey's dilemma on Vietnam. He remained trapped between the Scylla of his loyalty to LBJ and the administration's policies and the Charybdis of the antiwar forces in the country that may have more accurately reflected his own principles.

In a conversation with John Osborne of *New Republic* in May, Humphrey repeated similar themes. At one point, he stated, "No Vice President can be a free spirit. If you want to be a free spirit, be a poet. But a man can be the Vice President and never lose his soul and his spirit, and I feel that that is what has happened to me. If I had it to do all over again, I'd make the same decision I made in 1964." One could be forgiven for being skeptical of Humphrey's claim, but realistically he could not have said anything else. Osborne opined that "In order to be a convincing candidate, Hubert Humphrey will have to manage what amounts to a resurrection after his years in the shrouding shadow of Lyndon Johnson. . . . He will have to erase the image of the lackey, the willing slave, which he has fashioned for himself . . . [that] haunts Humphrey still." Ultimately, Osborne concluded, "Humphrey's record of support for the war is too complete and too familiar to be evaded, and he is no man to evade either it or his conviction that the United States has an inescapable responsibility to 'protect world security with its power.'"[22]

The political calculus for Humphrey changed dramatically with Robert Kennedy's tragic death in early June. Over the previous weeks, McCarthy's candidacy had faded as mainstream Democrats refused to support his antiwar message. It appeared likely that the more popular and dynamic RFK would take up the mantle as the peace candidate for the party while still appealing to moderates. Kennedy's strong performance in the primaries vaulted him to second place in the delegate count with tangible momentum only three months after entering the race on March 16. When Sirhan Sirhan assassinated RFK in the immediate aftermath of Kennedy's victory in the California primary, however, the Democrats were left with no realistic alternative for their presidential candidate but the vice president. Ironically, while Kennedy's death effectively clinched the nomination for Humphrey, it likely cost him in the general election against Richard Nixon. Had RFK lived and the nomination come down to a floor fight at the convention in August, it is entirely plausible that Johnson would have allowed Humphrey to distance himself from the administration on the war in order to prevent a Kennedy coronation in Chicago. Such was LBJ's insecurity about and animus toward Bobby Kennedy.

The day after RFK's death, Humphrey met with McCarthy at the vice president's office. Reporters described McCarthy as looking "weary beyond belief": the campaign and Kennedy's death had taken a toll on the Minnesota senator. McCarthy told Humphrey that he viewed the vice president's nomination as "inevitable" and that he wanted to make a graceful exit from the presidential race. But, the senator cautioned, his supporters would denounce him if he left the campaign without at least "symbolic" concessions on Vietnam. McCarthy pleaded with Humphrey to make some gesture toward the antiwar left. Humphrey refused to make any promises, as he was still beholden to the administration and uncertain how LBJ might react. McCarthy left, dejected and disappointed. Immediate after the meeting, Humphrey summoned his aide Ted Van Dyk and informed him about the conversation. As Van Dyk recalls, "They had come to no agreement, Humphrey said, and he found it difficult to see how they could." But Van Dyk pushed back, arguing that McCarthy's proposed *quid pro quo* "was an offer [the vice president] should not lightly refuse. If McCarthy were to formally withdraw from the nominating race and endorse Humphrey, it would be worth some concessions on Humphrey's part," given how valuable the senator's endorsement could be to the vice president going into the convention.[23] Yet Humphrey's reluctance to abrogate his allegiance to the president still trumped all other considerations.

McCarthy was not alone in his efforts to convince Humphrey to change his public position on the war. The following week, former Johnson administration official Bill Moyers told a New York radio station, "The problem is whether or not Humphrey can free himself from the incrustations of the last four years and emerge as the Humphrey who really wrote the script for most of what Eugene McCarthy and Robert Kennedy have been saying this year." He went on to urge Humphrey—to whom he had spoken frequently in recent weeks and on whose campaign Moyers was expected to advise—to publicly say what Moyers asserted that the vice president believed privately: "that present policies are inadequate, present personalities are inadequate, that we must move away from where we have been, we must liquidate the war in Vietnam in one way or another." The next day, Moyers suggested that Humphrey "has always questioned the efficacy of American military power in a situation like Vietnam" and predicted that the vice president would "emerge on his own within the next week or so."

Contrary to Moyers's hopeful prognostication, however, Humphrey continued his unambiguous public defense of the administration. "No man agrees with the President on every detail," he averred in an article in *New Republic* two weeks later, but "I have supported this policy enthusiastically." Humphrey also responded defiantly when asked about Moyers's comments. "I may be wrong or stupid," the vice president said, "but I'm not a hypocrite." While Moyers did not have any specific information about Humphrey's plans and later apologized for implying that he did, the former administration official claimed his motives were pristine and that he was trying to push the vice president in the direction that was best for the country and the candidate: away from his loyalty to LBJ and back toward his liberal principles.[24] There is evidence to suggest that Moyers was not speaking completely out of turn. In a speech to the National Press Club on June 20, for example, Humphrey said that he had always favored a negotiated rather than a military solution to the conflict and reiterated his position that as vice president, he had simply been "a member of the team." He also emphasized that as president, he would be the "captain of the team. There's a lot of difference."[25] The balancing act between loyalty to the administration, domestic political and electoral considerations, and personal principles that the vice president attempted in the speech foreshadowed his vacillations and repeated course reversals on Vietnam over the next several months.

Humphrey's dilemma as the convention approached was summarized succinctly by Tom Wicker in the *New York Times* on June 23. Humphrey, as "a part of the Johnson Administration, has roundly praised its works and its master at every opportunity, and now has to take the political responsibility for four years of enthusiastic association with those words and that master. . . . One thing is plain. . . . Whatever the nation wants, it does not want more of the same."[26] As political scientist Marie Natoli has written, few vice presidents have been in "as awkward a position" as Humphrey was in 1968. He had spent four years "under the tutelage and subordination of Lyndon Johnson—and he had kept his promise of loyalty . . . despite his disagreement privately. Time after time, in arena after arena, he had publicly defended the Administration policy on Vietnam." What Humphrey needed to do was to "somehow strike a balance between the loyalty he had promised and the independence he so desperately needed." Some of Humphrey's advisers suggested that might prove to be an impossible needle to thread; indeed, a few argued that he should consider resigning as vice president to allow for more flexibility on Vietnam and to establish his independence from the administration. But Humphrey predictably refused, arguing that "He had a contract with the American people; to resign would be to break that contract."[27]

Moyers may not have had direct knowledge about Humphrey's true intentions, but his political instincts were correct, at least insofar as Humphrey's campaign team was concerned. Humphrey's foreign policy advisers—including George Ball, now U.S. ambassador to the United Nations—were convinced that the vice president needed to come out for an unconditional bombing halt. A major influence on the vice president's thinking was John Rielly, Humphrey's long-time aide whose advice had been so prescient early in the Johnson presidency. Rielly urged the vice president at every opportunity to state explicitly his opposition to the war and break with LBJ. Rielly was part of the campaign's Vietnam policy task force that Humphrey had authorized to experiment with language providing the vice president with a workable policy on the war that would be distinct from that of the administration.

The Rielly-led working group completed a final draft at the end of June that it considered to be a worthy independent statement for Humphrey. It called for a reduction in American forces and overall presence in Vietnam, suggested reciprocal steps by both sides that could reduce the level of conflict, and proposed that, if North Vietnam showed good faith, bombing of North Vietnam might be suspended. While the draft did not propose a unilateral U.S. withdrawal from the country or the imposition of a new regime on Saigon, it was "an unmistakably more accommodating posture on the war than that of Johnson." Humphrey agreed that he would present the document to Johnson and inform the president of his intention to issue it promptly. He would explain that he continued to support Johnson's efforts toward peace, but that, as a presidential candidate in his own right, "he had an obligation to tell the party and the country what he would do about Vietnam if elected."[28]

As the task force worked to craft Humphrey's potential statement, Chester Cooper consulted with Humphrey's campaign aides about the vice president's position on Vietnam. The staff informed Cooper somewhat prematurely that Humphrey had prepared a major speech on Vietnam that he hoped to deliver prior to the meeting of the Democratic platform committee. According to Cooper, who had consistently urged a political solution over a military one during the Johnson administration, "Humphrey was caught between a desire not to prejudice the talks in Paris and a need to establish himself as a candidate with views on Vietnam distinguishable from those of President Johnson." Humphrey's aides wanted assurances that if the vice president went ahead with the speech, the negotiators in Paris "would not cut the ground from under him." Cooper traveled to Paris for consultations with Cyrus Vance—who, like Cooper, served as a deputy to Averell Harriman in the Paris negotiations—and upon his return he made it clear that "Humphrey's public advocacy of a bombing cessation would be the kiss of death." Humphrey agreed that the points he would score with liberal Democrats would not be worth undermining negotiations. In what Cooper described as "an impressive act of statesmanship," Humphrey decided not to give the speech.[29]

Yet as the summer wore on, the Paris peace talks failed to gain any traction. As Johnson continued to push the "San Antonio Formula" and pressure the Saigon regime to make concessions on several issues—most notably the inclusion of the Viet Cong in negotiations and a coalition government—domestic opponents of the war pushed for an unconditional bombing halt, a phased withdrawal of U.S. troops, and expedited negotiations. Concurrently, the vice president hoped to fashion a compromise and prevent a major clash at the convention over the Vietnam plank that could derail his campaign before it launched. But the efforts to find common ground with the doves placed Humphrey squarely in the firing line of the president, who grew increasingly agitated and bitter over his lack of success in brokering a peace in Vietnam. The president's frustration with the negotiations reinforced his overall lack of respect for his vice president, whom LBJ thought sided with the antiwar forces far too often. While Humphrey remained a loyal and dedicated member of the administration, Johnson failed to repay that allegiance. As Kyle Longley notes, he frequently "chastised Humphrey for lacking the backbone to confront his enemies and accused him of vacillating, especially on Vietnam. It created tension between the two, especially as the vice president tried to establish his own place in the political arena."[30]

By the middle of the year, Hubert Humphrey found himself in an unenviable position despite being the presumptive Democratic nominee. He faced countervailing pressures from all sides—LBJ, the vice president's advisers, domestic political considerations, the deteriorating situation on the ground in Vietnam, the antiwar movement, and his own principles and conscience—that made it virtually impossible to avoid conflict on the war. More generally, the summer of 1968 saw little progress on the military front in South Vietnam. Since his withdrawal announcement at the end of March, Johnson had insisted that the South Vietnamese take more responsibility for the fighting, and the Army of the Republic of Vietnam was increased to 850,000 troops and began to conduct expanded joint military operations with U.S. forces. In addition, while more emphasis was placed on the pacification programs, including the notorious Phoenix Program, few of these initiatives made a tangible difference to either the political or military situation on the ground.[31] Meanwhile, U.S. soldiers continued to come home in body bags, and antiwar sentiment across the country continued to grow.

Indeed, nothing the Johnson administration or the Saigon regime attempted could change the underlying reality of the conflict: despite the vicious losses inflicted upon them during the Tet Offensive, the NLF and North Vietnamese refused to buckle to American pressure, either on the battlefield or at the negotiating table. And so the stalemate continued. At home, John Wayne's *The Green Berets* was released to a skeptical American audience that no longer believed in the patriotic and heroic conflict championed by the film. Antiwar protests increased exponentially, with serious clashes between students and law enforcement on university campuses and growing discontent within the general public. With over thirty thousand American soldiers dead, over half a million still deployed in South Vietnam, and no end to the fighting in sight, a country weary of war desperately hoped that a new administration would be able to bring the conflict to a conclusion.

An increasingly frustrated Humphrey appeared on ABC's *Issues and Answers* on July 7. Humphrey said, "I have watched the leader of this country, the President, face this horrendous problem of Vietnam. I have watched the agony of it. I have watched the seriousness of the decision-making process." Given that, he believed that Johnson would "try to find an honorable peace." He then told Sam Donaldson that he wanted "to see this struggle deescalated. I have called for a cease-fire on the part of all parties. . . . I want a political settlement in this struggle." When asked what he would do if elected, the vice president responded, "I will try to use the powers of the office of the

Presidency to . . . seek every honorable way to bring this struggle to a prompt conclusion and to deescalate the struggle as quickly as possible." When asked by Frank Reynolds about a coalition government, Humphrey said, "I really believe that for a candidate for public office at this stage to start to spell out what would be the ingredients of an acceptable political settlement would be a great disservice to the men who are conducting our negotiations in Paris. . . . So I have had to make some sacrifice . . . in terms of some of the things that I might want to say." Humphrey's answer could have been taken word-for-word from the campaign statements of Richard Nixon, who attempted to be the Delphic Oracle on Vietnam throughout 1968 to avoid committing to any politically dangerous policy. Sam Donaldson then suggested that "many people in this country view you as someone dedicated to the escalation of the Vietnam War" and say that "Hubert Humphrey is a warmonger." Humphrey fired back defensively, "Of course it isn't true. Some people still believe the world is flat."[32]

But, of course, the perception of Humphrey as a staunch advocate of the war continued to define the vice president in the eyes of many on the left. On July 9, Arthur Schlesinger wrote to David Ginsburg, New York attorney and steadfast Humphrey supporter, regarding the vice president's recent public statements on the war. Schlesinger sadly noted that the vice president's comments led one to conclude that "Hubert really believes in this ghastly war." Ginsburg passed the letter on to Humphrey, who "responded passionately and at length" to Schlesinger on July 13 to deny the allegations. Schlesinger, in turn, wrote back on July 24 and explicitly told Humphrey that his failure to recognize that his long-time liberal friends opposed his candidacy on principle because of his position on the Vietnam War meant that "you had lost your own sense of reality and are in deep trouble."[33] The constant pressure and criticism emanating from the left stirred Humphrey's traditional liberal principles, and it demonstrably contributed to both his internal and public struggles with the Vietnam issue.

That uncertainly percolated to the surface more often as the campaign evolved. Humphrey intended to speak to the Commonwealth Club in San Francisco on July 12, 1968, but illness prevented his appearance. In his prepared remarks, however, he suggested that the United States had reached "a turning point" and that "Communist countries no longer pose a monolithic threat," arguing that U.S. foreign policy had to craft "new priorities, new policies and a new sense of purpose in our engagement in the world. They demand a shift from policies of confrontation and containment to policies of reconciliation and peaceful engagement." The task of reconciliation "can obviously proceed much more quickly once peace is achieved in Vietnam. It must be a lasting and stable peace." He made it clear that he wanted to end the war but that he wanted "to end it the only way it can be ended—by a political settlement . . . which will permit the people of South Vietnam . . . to shape their own future. And I want to see a cease-fire at the earliest possible moment." The speech concluded by emphasizing that "Right now, however, the most effective peace effort we can make is to back our negotiating team in Paris. We must not make their job more difficult by misleading Hanoi into the belief that our negotiators may not be speaking for America."[34] This brief glimpse into Humphrey's thinking is intriguing; the fact that he did not give the speech is an indication of his reluctance to challenge the administration on any level on the war.

One of the major problems Humphrey faced over the summer was a lack of information on the progress of the war and the negotiations in Paris. Johnson, always paranoid about potential leaks, kept his circle of trust tight, which meant that Humphrey frequently found himself out of the loop regarding key military and diplomatic decisions.[35] For example, LBJ met with the South Vietnamese leadership on July 19 and 20 and declared his support of their government, with no mention of either a bombing halt or negotiations that might include the NLF, which the Saigon regime refused to even consider. Humphrey told syndicated columnist Drew Pearson that he was "crushed" by Johnson's speech, saying, "He pulled the rug right out from under me. It gave me an awful wallop." As Tom Wicker opined in the *New York Times*, this episode added to Humphrey's "politically painful" identification with the war and administration policy.[36]

That link prevented the vice president from making any drastic change to his position on the war. Journalist Roscoe Drummond interviewed Humphrey in mid-July and reported that despite rumors to the contrary, the vice president would not "go dovish" in an effort to win the White House. Instead, "he will stand by his convictions even if it hurts politically." Humphrey believed that his prospects for electoral success would be undermined if the hard-core antiwar left was "determined to punish him for disagreeing with them," or if he tried "to wiggle out of his strong support of our defense of Vietnam in the hope he can pacify one side without alienating the other." Drummond argued that Humphrey would not "repudiate his convictions, nor try to find some set of words which will appear to dilute them in an effort to persuade the anti-Vietnam voters that he has changed and the pro-Vietnam voters that he hasn't." This would "come as a surprise only to those liberal intellectuals and cynics who used to wring their hands over Humphrey's support of the President on Vietnam hoping and often suggesting that Humphrey was only 'going along loyally' with President Johnson, and didn't really believe what he was saying." This, Drummond concluded, was consistent with Humphrey's long-standing support of U.S. support for South Vietnam, even if the vice president did believe that the war "must and should end in a negotiated political settlement."[37]

But the idea that Humphrey secretly harbored doubts about the war would not go away. According to *Time*, "Friends and commentators kept hinting that Humphrey was about to break loose from Johnson on Viet Nam or was preparing to fight Johnson over the Democratic platform." Humphrey remained steadfast, declaring, "We don't need an Aaron Burr in this Republic." Yet it was clear that "Humphrey cannot realistically hope to placate the hardcore opposition on his left. He can merely chip away at it by edging further away from the Johnson Administration."[38] Those efforts proceeded as Humphrey's campaign staff tried to draft a Democratic platform plank on Vietnam behind which the party could unify. Meanwhile, Humphrey's political allies and friends continued to urge him to distance himself from LBJ on the war. Averell Harriman urged Humphrey to "get out from under" current policy or to just "get out" by resigning the vice presidency. Similarly, David Ginsburg, who would lead the Humphrey team's efforts to shape the platform at the convention, pressed Humphrey to "make the break now" before arriving in Chicago.[39] Humphrey found himself between the proverbial rock and a hard place. He had to deal with antipathy from the antiwar left due to his loyalty to LBJ while simultaneously being hamstrung from moving away from the administration's policy on the war because the president feared it would undercut his negotiating position.

After weeks of preparation with his campaign task force on Vietnam and extended consultations with his advisers, Humphrey met with the president on July 25 to seek permission to break with the administration and call for a total halt to the bombing of North Vietnam. LBJ summarily rejected the request. Johnson was so disturbed by the vice president's proposal that he later told an adviser that the "GOP may be more of a help to us than the Democrats in the next few months."[40] The president's annoyance with Humphrey should be understood in context. Throughout the summer, rumors had swirled from Moyers and others that the vice president might abandon the administration's position on Vietnam, so when Humphrey finally approached LBJ with his proposed statement, it riled up the president to an even higher degree. Clark Clifford noted that in some of his meetings with LBJ that summer, "he branded Humphrey weak and 'disloyal.'" Clifford also reported that former Truman administration official George Elsey told him of a conversation in which Johnson said that if Humphrey did not stand firm on Vietnam, a Nixon victory "would be better for the country" because he "may prove more responsible" than the vice president on Vietnam.[41] The widening breach between Johnson and Humphrey would only intensify over the next several weeks, and the question of who LBJ actually preferred as his successor remains open for debate.

His effort to carve out a workable position on Vietnam now proscribed by the president, Humphrey returned to his office from the White House, unhappy but resigned to the situation. He told Ted Van Dyke about the meeting and tried to put the best spin possible on the conversation. The vice president explained, "Johnson said he was doing his best to negotiate a peace. He thought my paper would complicate and confuse the negotiations." But Humphrey also relayed LBJ's explicit threats, noting that "he told me that it would endanger American troops like his son-in-law and cost lives. I would have blood on my hands. He would denounce me publicly for playing politics with peace." Then Humphrey—who by this point was clearly near the end of his rope and weary of the toxic relationship he shared with the president—declared dejectedly, "I've eaten so much of Johnson's shit in this job that I've grown to like the taste of it."[42] Humphrey was beginning to realize the price of his loyalty.

As the comments by Clifford and others indicated, LBJ complicated Humphrey's candidacy—and not just because the vice president would be linked to the administration's policies. Johnson "showed a surprising lack of enthusiasm" for Humphrey's candidacy. Many pundits believed that LBJ would support his old friend, but their relationship had deteriorated. Johnson had, over the previous months, "made a series of disparaging and contemptuous comments about his vice president" and was "ambivalent" about Humphrey's candidacy.[43] Humphrey did not help in this regard. He increasingly referred to the "Johnson-Humphrey administration" in his speeches, which allowed him to take at least partial credit for the administration's successes, even though it also implicitly made him culpable for its failures—most especially in Southeast Asia. Unfortunately for the vice president, that approach also had the negative effect of undermining LBJ's fragile ego and reinforcing the president's insecurity, both of which the president took out on Humphrey directly and indirectly throughout the campaign. Moreover, Johnson was convinced that he would be able to negotiate better terms with Hanoi if the Democratic candidates did not offer better terms than he did. LBJ wanted the credit for resolving the war, especially if it meant the possibility of an adoring party offering him the nomination at the eleventh hour.

Humphrey's advisers persevered, insisting that he would help himself the most by issuing a statement prior to the convention. But the vice president continued to hold back. Humphrey went so far as to avoid giving direct answers to questions about a bombing halt during an appearance on ABC's *Issues and Answers* on August 11.[44] In addition, he told his staff that after talking to LBJ about the progress of negotiations in Paris, "events may be on our side," and he did not "want to say something that will screw things up and have the President come down on me hard." Clearly, the prospect of Johnson's wrath represented a major obstacle to Humphrey finally taking the leap and staking out his own position on the war. That task became even more daunting when LBJ constricted Humphrey's room to maneuver on the war even further in a speech to the Veterans of Foreign Wars on August 19. LBJ asserted that he alone was responsible for U.S. policy in Vietnam and that the United States would take no further deescalation steps or halt the bombing "until it has reason to believe that the other side intends seriously to join with us in de-escalating the war and moving seriously toward peace." Humphrey had to back off his compromising rhetoric in the face of what he considered one of the president's "hardest-line speeches" on the war.

The following day, LBJ "launched into almost a tirade about Humphrey and Vietnam," insisting that the vice president was "all over the place" on the war and should not be seeking to get McCarthy's delegates. Even though that was unlikely—as one observer noted, "Nothing would bring the real peace-niks back to our side unless Hubert urinated on a portrait of Lyndon Johnson in Times Square before television and then they'd say to him, why didn't you do it before?"—the president saw such overtures as nearly treasonous.[45] If that were not enough, whatever slim chance existed that Humphrey might be able to support a peace plank on Vietnam at the convention, no matter how carefully crafted to avoid angering LBJ, evaporated when Soviet tanks rolled into Prague on August 20, 1968. The invasion provided Johnson's allies on the platform committee with a perfect Cold War rationale for approving a hard-line plank on the war in Southeast Asia.

Given the fractures extant in the Democratic Party over Vietnam, a convention fight on the platform was virtually inevitable, with the president and Humphrey potentially on opposite sides. According to columnists Rowland Evans and Robert Novak, such a scenario was actually preferred by some of Humphrey's lieutenants—particularly if it took place in public—since Humphrey and LBJ "have diametrically opposed interests in what the platform ought to say about the Vietnam War. The President, retiring from politics, naturally wants the platform explicitly to validate every action he has taken on the war. Not so Humphrey." The vice president, they argued, would rather gloss over or avoid the administration's record in Vietnam since 1963 and use the platform as "a departure point for a Humphrey-made, Humphrey-led policy in Asia which promises an early, negotiated end of the war."

But, they continued, Humphrey would be hamstrung in that effort by the appointment of Hale Boggs as the platform committee chair. Boggs, the House majority whip and a vocal hawk on the war, had agreed that LBJ would be the final arbiter of the platform language. It was clear to Evans and Novak, as well as most contemporary observers, that Humphrey could establish his independence from LBJ only by "splitting publicly over Vietnam." Yet some of Humphrey's advisers disagreed, arguing that since Humphrey was tied to every decision on the war, "any attempt by Humphrey to fudge up that record might expose him to charges of hypocrisy." In the end, Evans and Novak pointed out that Humphrey and LBJ "now seem headed for a collision course on Vietnam" and that unless Johnson "relaxes his determination to hold the Party's policy reins in his own hands until forcibly removed or Humphrey relaxes his determination to declare his independence, an explosion is unavoidable."[46] Humphrey needed to "tread carefully on Vietnam. If he strayed from Johnson's policy of keeping the United States actively involved, he would incur Johnson's wrath and the possibility of losing the president's support." As E. W. Kenworthy wrote in the *New York Times* on the eve of the convention, "so long as party divisions over Vietnam remained unhealed, the Vice President faces the possibility of a stay-home vote large enough to cause his defeat." What Humphrey needed to do, therefore, was to "have the Resolutions Committee adopt a Vietnam plank that would liberate him from Lyndon Johnson and his own past position and that might go far enough to give McCarthy a basis for accepting second place on the ticket."[47]

Kenworthy had described a Herculean task for the vice president, the challenge of which would be exemplified at a cabinet meeting on August 22. At the meeting, Johnson upbraided Humphrey over his comments on Vietnam, lecturing him at length about the realities of dealing with the Communists. The only way they would be persuaded to talk, LBJ insisted, was if they were faced with a tough, unrelenting position. Obviously, Johnson saw the vice president's heresies as violating that principle. For Humphrey, this reprimand would set the stage for the difficulties that he would face as he prepared for the Democratic convention in Chicago. As John Morton Blum has written, Humphrey "had no influence on Johnson, who had been mocking him in private for weeks. Sullen and mean in his exile, the president appeared determined to display his power over the party and his disdain for his chosen successor. Outmaneuvered by the president and emasculated by his own ambition, Humphrey glumly accepted his humiliation."[48]

Two days after the *auto-da-fé* before the cabinet, Humphrey and his staff met with other members of the Democratic platform committee to work on the Vietnam plank that would define Humphrey's campaign and help determine the level of support he would have within the party during the fall campaign against Richard Nixon. As negotiations progressed, Humphrey genuinely thought that they had been able to craft a widely acceptable statement on Vietnam. Working with former JFK speechwriter and special counsel Ted Sorensen, the vice president's proposed plank did not call for an unconditional bombing halt, nor did it insist on North Vietnamese guarantees not to exploit the halt. Instead, it called for an end to the bombing that "took into account . . . the risk to American troops as well as the response from Hanoi." After extended discussions with representatives of the various party factions, the vice president's team believed that they had drafted language that could bring the party together behind its candidate.

Indeed, David Ginsburg, who prepared the Humphrey draft statement on the war, said that there was "not ten cents worth of difference between this and the vice president's policy." At the same time, the proposed plank did not represent much of a deviation from the administration's position, but it did placate the party's antiwar forces sufficiently to gain wide acceptance. Now the language had to clear the final hurdle: Johnson's imprimatur. Prior to Humphrey's departure for Chicago, LBJ had instructed him to clear any compromise language to be included in the Vietnam plank with Dean Rusk. The secretary of state approved the wording and told Humphrey, "We can live with this, Hubert." Hoping to cover all of his bases, Humphrey then called the hawkish national security adviser Walt Rostow, who also signed off on the framework. Thus, Humphrey had a plank that simultaneously met the vast majority of the McCarthyites' demands and had been given an endorsement by the highest levels of the administration; he was on the verge of uniting the party.

Unfortunately for Humphrey and the Democratic Party, however, Johnson refused to give his blessing to the compromise language. On the president's orders, Marvin Watson—who had been appointed as postmaster general in April but had been LBJ's *de facto* chief of staff since 1965—summoned Humphrey to his hotel suite and berated the vice president for betraying Johnson. Humphrey responded bluntly, "Well, Marvin. I cleared it with the secretary of state, and I've cleared it with Walt Rostow." Watson fired back, "That doesn't make any difference. It's been looked over again and it just doesn't meet the president's approval." The heated exchange between the vice president and postmaster general continued for a while with both men refusing to give any ground, but as the meeting finally concluded, Watson emphasized the fundamental, unequivocal point to Humphrey: "You must stay the course on Vietnam if you expect to be nominated."[49]

Not satisfied with Watson's intervention in the process as the president's proxy, the vice president went directly to Johnson and asked him to accept the draft statement. LBJ refused. When Humphrey protested, pointing out that both Rusk and Rostow had approved it—just as they had agreed only days earlier—the president retorted angrily, "this plank just undercuts our whole policy and, by God, the Democratic party ought not to be doing that to me, and you ought not to be doing it. You've been part of this policy." Humphrey, completely at a loss, brusquely told Johnson, "We'll have to do the best we can. Possibly we can get something that is acceptable, but I'm afraid we're going to have serious troubles here." As Kyle Longley observed, "it remained unclear what the president wanted other than to have his plank as written. He seemed almost irrational, as often the case on Vietnam, as nothing seemed to please him." Humphrey had "shown real statesmanship in crafting a compromise, but Johnson clearly sabotaged the process by rationalizing that it might send a confusing message to the North Vietnamese or South Vietnamese."[50] More likely, LBJ simply did not want his legacy and image tainted by a Vietnam plank in his party's platform that did not completely support his administration's policy.

Humphrey briefly considered defying Johnson and taking a stand on the Vietnam issue once and for all. Frankly, had he called LBJ's bluff, he might have gotten away with it. After all, Johnson certainly would not have backed McCarthy (or Pigasus) for the nomination, and it is unlikely that LBJ would have come out explicitly for Nixon in the event of Humphrey's complete renunciation of the administration's policy. But the politically shrewd president remained one step ahead of his vice president. In an effort to exert additional pressure on Humphrey, LBJ asked Boggs and Senator Jennings Randolph (D-WV) to return to Washington. There, Westmoreland briefed them on the dangers of suspending the bombing. After returning to Chicago, Boggs visited Humphrey's suite, where he made it clear no compromise on Vietnam would make it to the floor without Johnson's approval. Boggs further threatened that he would resign as chair of the platform committee if Humphrey tried to circumvent the president with different language than that which had been sanctioned by the White House. Faced with no other realistic option than an outright break with LBJ, and realizing that discretion was the better part of valor, the vice president backed down completely and reluctantly supported the president's plank.

With Humphrey's surrender, Johnson prevailed in the dispute over the language of the Vietnam plank. The problem for the candidate and the party, however, was that the president's fixation with the perception of his Vietnam policy and unwillingness to defer to Humphrey as the nominee damaged the Democrats almost irrevocably and militated against any chance of the party emerging from the Chicago convention even partially unified. For his part, Humphrey confided to Edgar Berman that fighting Johnson on the Vietnam plank would be "suicidal" and the president "would cut me up and out of the nomination." The vice president did what he believed was required at the time given the circumstances. Consequently, as Tom Wicker wrote, this meant that if Humphrey went into the fall campaign against Nixon with the president's Vietnam plank rather than his own, the vice president would be viewed as presenting "his master's voice." Looking back, however, Humphrey wrote with regret, "I should not have yielded," an assessment that might just have been the understatement of his career.[51]

As the platform committee fight on the Vietnam plank neared a resolution, Humphrey appeared on NBC's *Meet the Press* on August 25. The vice president's comments during the interview reflected his conflict on Vietnam. Vermont Royster of the *Wall Street Journal* pointed out that while the Johnson administration had consistently taken the position that it would not stop bombing North Vietnam unilaterally, the McGovern-McCarthy forces supported a peace plank that would immediately institute an unconditional bombing halt, withdraw all U.S. combat troops, and support a coalition government in South Vietnam that included the Viet Cong. Would Humphrey run on such a platform? Humphrey responded unequivocally: "That will not be the platform. That is a minority position." Instead, he stated, "I believe that we could and should stop the remaining bombing of the North if we receive an indication that there is restraint and reasonable response from Hanoi. I think that is a common sense provision." He also confirmed his support of free elections in South Vietnam including "all people who are willing to accept the results of an election and engage in the peaceful political processes of an election." Erwin Canham of the *Christian Science Monitor* then asked Humphrey whom a person could vote for if they wanted to express dissent with U.S. policy in Vietnam. Naturally, Humphrey said to vote for him, making it clear that "I do not believe the American people want the next President of the United States to either unilaterally withdraw or to leave our forces subject to unlimited punishment from the North, or in any way to make adjustments or political concessions that would make the sacrifice that we have made in the past seem meaningless."[52]

As the televised interview concluded, Thomas Vail of the *Cleveland Plain Dealer* asked the vice president to summarize where he specifically disagreed with Johnson's Vietnam policies. Humphrey responded in typical fashion: "I think that the policies that the President has pursued are basically sound. . . . There may have been some nuances of differences if I were the President of the United States," he admitted,

> but the Vice President of the United States has a special responsibility because he is the partner of the President. One thing I have tried to do is to respect the limitations of that office. It has great responsibility with little or no authority, and I believe that I would have served to injure the cause of the United States and to injure this republic if I were to have injected myself with any little differences that I might have had into the public arena. I have to present those points of view privately in the councils of this government, and I think you men know that I am not exactly the silent type, that I have been willing to present them on the occasion when I thought they were needed.[53]

Clearly, loyalty—or at least Humphrey's anxiety over LBJ's potential reaction to any perceived disloyalty—trumped policy differences for the vice president.

Later that day, Humphrey explicitly and publicly endorsed "without qualification" the administration's Vietnam policies, promising Hanoi that they were "not going to get a better deal out of me." These remarks seemed odd in light of the imminent Democratic convention, particularly since they "represented a change from the conciliatory tone" he had taken toward war critics in recent weeks. In the same speech, he implicitly rejected the McCarthy-McGovern plank on Vietnam." Humphrey's comments clearly reflected Johnson's influence and intimidation over the preceding days, weeks, and months.

On the eve of Humphrey's nomination by the convention, the *New York Times* editorialized that the "incubus of the Johnson administration policy on Vietnam has never weighed so heavily on Vice President Humphrey as in these last few crucial days." The editorial noted that Humphrey "has long publicly, and enthusiastically, supported the President on virtually all aspects of the war; but somehow he had managed to give the impression that he really wasn't fully sympathetic to the course that has been so unsuccessfully pursued in Southeast Asia in recent years." The editors noted that while Humphrey had begun to "sound a little more dovelike than he used to," over the past few weeks "and especially in recent days he has reverted strongly and emphatically to his original position." In the wake of the platform fight, the editor wrote, Humphrey "once again fully aligns himself with Mr. Johnson's Vietnam policy and cannot pretend otherwise . . . we think the Vice President would have done better to have shaken off the incubus once and for all" in order to reaffirm his own independence as well as differentiating himself from Nixon's stance. [54]

After nominating Humphrey with barely disguised apathy, the fractured convention turned its attention to the Vietnam plank, which had been formulated by the platform committee and authorized by Johnson. As columnist Drew Pearson wrote, "The most disruptive debate was that over peace in Vietnam. It left wounds that probably would not heal, either before or after November. The tragedy is that it didn't have to happen." If LBJ had taken his hands off the reins of the convention, Pearson suggested, the internecine brawl over the plank might not have happened at all. But he did not, preferring to stay out of sight at his ranch in Texas while the convention devolved into chaos. LBJ, Pearson concluded, "seemed more interested in vindication for his own Vietnam policy than in the election of Hubert Humphrey.'"

Insurgents who opposed the language in the Vietnam plank argued in vain that Humphrey could not win the election if he were forced to run on the administration's discredited policy. Their effort to replace the platform committee's language with a plank that called for de-escalation and a negotiated settlement, however, was defeated handily. The balloting on the proadministration Vietnam plank on August 28 resulted in 1,567 votes in favor, 1,041 opposed. In the wake of the voting, protests broke out throughout the International Amphitheater. Several hundred antiwar delegates donned black armbands and sang "We Shall Overcome" while peace advocates prayed and protesters chanted "Stop the war!" If that were not enough, a Kennedy loyalist named William vanden Heuvel threatened to place Johnson's name in nomination against Humphrey to protest the Vietnam plank. His rationale? Johnson was "the only one who can run on the Vietnam plank they have given us." [55] Chaos reigned.

That afternoon, Humphrey and the president spoke on the phone, and the president—without any hint of irony—said that Humphrey did "a good job" with the Vietnam plank. He also suggested that the vice president allow word of LBJ's support for him leak out. [56] But that modicum of support from Johnson could not counterbalance the weight of Johnson's petulant actions against the vice president at the convention. The president's distrust of Humphrey was palpable. For example, to ensure that Humphrey was not planning to break with the administration on Vietnam, LBJ ordered the FBI to tap his phones. Even more emasculating for the Democratic candidate, Humphrey's own son-in-law was forced to get in line every morning to obtain tickets for the vice president's family for seats at the convention.[57]

But the most problematic result from the week of upheaval in Chicago was the platform statement on the war. While the Democratic plank differed little in substance from the one adopted by the GOP, it did save the vice president from having to break with the administration. That was a small consolation for Humphrey. After the vicious debates at the convention, he would have been ecstatic not to discuss Vietnam at all during the campaign, but now he was encumbered with a plank that did not reflect either his principles or the position of a sizable proportion of the party. Clark Clifford acknowledged that Johnson's victory on the Vietnam plank "was a disaster for Humphrey. At the moment when he should have been pulling the party back together to prepare for the battle against Nixon, Humphrey had been bludgeoned into a position that had further split the party and given more evidence of his own weakness."[58]

With the most contentious issue finally resolved, the jaded and fatigued convention turned its attention to the selection of Humphrey's running mate. Fortunately, this process faced far fewer hurdles than had the Vietnam plank. Senator Edmund Muskie (D-ME), who had led the debate to ratify the administration's plank on Vietnam, accepted Humphrey's offer to be the vice-presidential nominee and was easily confirmed despite lingering outrage from the antiwar forces. Marvin Watson later admitted the president "did not insist" on anyone but wanted "a Humphrey running mate who would shore up Humphrey and prevent him from wandering from his commitment to support the programs of the President, including especially Vietnam."[59] This would be one moment when LBJ's and Humphrey's interests coincided, as Humphrey saw Muskie as the perfect political partner in the election, someone who could balance the ticket in terms of their respective personalities and backgrounds. Now, only one task remained: for Humphrey to accept the party's nomination.

Looking back at Humphrey acceptance speech on August 29, one could be forgiven for seeing it as anticlimactic in the narrative of the convention. The riots in Grant Park, the violence on the convention floor, the actions of Mayor Richard Daley and the Chicago police, the protests by the National Mobilization Committee to End the War in Vietnam and other groups, and the nomination of an actual pig for the presidency by Jerry Rubin and the Yippies represent only the tip of the iceberg of what was an absolutely chaotic week in Chicago. For the new nominee, this would be the last chance to transcend the bedlam of the previous week and attempt to bring the various factions of the party together. To begin his remarks, Humphrey praised Johnson's leadership over the previous five years. Then, rather than avoiding the discordant issue of the war, the vice president immediately addressed Vietnam directly. "The first reality is the necessity for peace in Vietnam and in the world," he asserted, reaching out to the antiwar forces he so desperately needed in the fall. While admitting that "There are differences, of course—serious differences—within our party on this vexing and painful issue of Vietnam," he expressed hope that the delegates would "recognize the much larger areas of agreement."

Humphrey also tried to make the party feel better about the melee over the Vietnam plank. "Had we just papered over the differences between us with empty platitudes instead of frank, hard debate," he explained, "we would deserve the contempt of our fellow citizens and the condemnation of history." Surprisingly, the vice president made the closest thing to a break with Johnson that would have been possible under the circumstances. The newly crowned nominee stated, "If there is any one lesson that we should have learned, it is that the policies of tomorrow need not be limited by the policies of yesterday." He promised that, if elected, "I shall apply that lesson to search for peace in Vietnam as well as all other areas of national policy. . . . I shall do everything within my power, within the limits of my capacity and ability, to aid the negotiations and bring a prompt end to this war."[60]

With that, the 1968 Democratic convention came to an ignominious end. The week in Chicago had been a disaster of epic proportions for everyone involved. But now Humphrey and the party had to pick up the pieces, come together as much as possible, and refocus attention on the campaign against Richard Nixon. Yet even now, Johnson refused to let Humphrey run the campaign he wanted (or needed) to in order to maximize his chance to win in November. On August 31, 1968, Humphrey and LBJ spoke on the telephone immediately after the president had talked to Nixon. The president noted that he had suggested to Rusk "the possibility, when we could, of maybe getting a joint statement from Humphrey and Nixon to Harriman to say to Hanoi that you better get on with the business of making peace." Johnson wanted to ensure that the North Vietnamese knew that they "must not count on this political year division. We're going to be united at the water's edge, and I'm authorized by both the Vice President and Nixon to say to you that there's going to be no division that you can exploit between now and this election." Humphrey agreed that such a position would be "helpful" and suggested that "it'd do away with any kind of trepidation. I think that if somebody'd like to quietly take the initiative on it and get it done. . . . I think that would be very, very good for us."[61]

Of course, two days earlier, LBJ had told Humphrey in the wake of the latter's acceptance speech, "The best thing we can do together is try to get you peace before November. Now, you have laid the groundwork with the platform. Be careful, don't say anything, it runs away from it. But let us then go into Hanoi and say, 'Now, goddammit, you're not going to get anything better from Humphrey. He's going to be worse. Let's get peace.' You wrap that up, you'll have a landslide." Interestingly, the same day, Bill Moyers called Harriman in Paris and noted that "the Humphrey forces had decided [at the convention] that they were going to take their stand as close as they can to Nixon in the belief that no one can cut back from the Left. Nixon is not going to get any support from the Doves, so he thinks he is not going to make the war an issue but campaign as close as he can to the Nixon position."[62] Clearly, Humphrey's flexibility over the next three months would be constrained by LBJ's desperate desire to protect his legacy and achieve an historic, eleventh-hour peace settlement. Whether that would allow Humphrey to win the election, however, remained to be seen.

Irish playwright Oscar Wilde wrote in *An Ideal Husband*, "When the gods wish to punish us they answer our prayers."[63] Hubert Humphrey had worked earnestly his entire career to be in a position to win the White House. Yet just as it appeared that his dreams might become a reality, he faced the prospect of battling not just Richard Nixon during the general election but also Lyndon Johnson, whose obsession with Vietnam frustrated the vice president throughout most of 1968. Humphrey may have won the Democratic nomination, but he and the party never really recovered from the savage, debilitating, and divisive internecine conflict at the convention. Humphrey later complained, "I was a victim of the convention as much as a man getting the Hong Kong flu. Chicago was a catastrophe." Had the vice president asserted himself and broken with the administration, the outcome of the election in November might have been different. Michael Cohen's assessment of 1968 is correct: "Failing to stand up to Johnson on Vietnam would turn out to be Humphrey's greatest mistake." As Larry O'Brien noted at the end of the convention, "Hubert paid a high price for being a good boy."[64]

Chapter Five

"An Acceptable Risk for Peace"

Freedom is hammered out on the anvil of discussion, dissent, and debate.
—Hubert Humphrey

Men should be either treated generously or destroyed, because they take re-venge for slight injuries—for heavy ones they cannot.
—Niccolò Machiavelli

Hubert Humphrey may have emerged from the political rubble of the Democratic convention in Chicago as his party's presidential nominee, but that victory had come at a heavy price. With the myriad of problems he faced, he would not be mistaken for a phoenix rising from the ashes. His dual and contradictory efforts over the preceding summer to simultaneously distance himself from the war and pacify the McCarthy–RFK forces within the party while remaining loyal to Lyndon Johnson and avoiding the president's wrath placed him in a wholly untenable position going into the fall campaign against Richard Nixon. Humphrey later recalled, "In time, that year, I was to fall heir to virtually all the animosity directed toward the Johnson administration. . . . I found myself boxed in by . . . the conditioning of my first three years as Vice President, including my concept of loyalty and commitment to the President." He went on to lament that "In that complex world . . . LBJ's military problems became my political problems," and, as Humphrey claimed regretfully, "I had no simple answer for Vietnam." In retrospect, however, a simple answer rooted in both politics and principle did actually exist: Humphrey merely needed to break with the administration on the war. Yet the vice president conspicuously refused to consider that option seriously until too late in the presidential campaign.[1]

Since Humphrey deliberately chose not to repudiate the president and the administration's policies, he left himself open to attack by Nixon—regardless of the direction the vice president tacked on the war over the next three months—and faced mounting derision and condemnation from the antiwar movement and many of his former political allies. As Michael Cohen concludes, "Humphrey, perhaps more than any other political figure that year, found himself caught helplessly in the maelstrom of 1968."[2] But was he actually helpless? Certainly not. He would only be so if he allowed his allegiance to LBJ to override his principles and distract him from making the obvious political move. This chapter examines Humphrey's struggle to finally distance himself from Lyndon Johnson's policies during the campaign against Nixon in the fall of 1968, a race in which the Vietnam War played the central and decisive role.

Humphrey emerged from Chicago with a daunting twenty-two-point deficit in the polls, a hopelessly divided Democratic Party, and a campaign desperately short on funds and enthusiasm. Even worse, Humphrey's bifurcation on the war—both in his own mind and in his public statements—made it unlikely that the situation would improve any time soon. In a remarkably penetrating assessment of Humphrey's campaign in the first week after the convention, the *Washington Post* opined that "It is a safe guess that Vice President Humphrey's remarks on Vietnam during the first week of this campaign gave comfort to his political enemies and a case of the willies to his friends." Humphrey was "Impulsive, uncertain, [and] self-contradictory." Moreover, not only had the vice president "inherited much of the public hostility directed at President Johnson and plenty more, it appears, from the President himself, whose interests in the presidential campaign do not exactly coincide with Mr. Humphrey's," but he also faced dissent within his own campaign staff on the war and continuing pressure from disaffected liberals. What Humphrey needed to do, the *Post* concluded, was to explicitly assure the American public that he was "committed to ending the war in Vietnam and to taking giant steps to bring about a political settlement there," a task that would require the kind of "discipline" that the Democratic candidate had not yet demonstrated. Humphrey needed to exhibit the "self-confidence, toughness and clarity of purpose identified with the pre-vice-presidential Hubert Humphrey."[3]

Negative appraisals of the vice president's candidacy were not limited to the press. An internal campaign memorandum after the convention assessed the candidate's vulnerability on the Vietnam issue. It noted that there had been "a sizable decline" in Humphrey's popularity since June 1967 and that the "most important reason appears to be his close association with the Administration, clearly unpopular since the Tet offensive." The memorandum recommended that the campaign strategy on Vietnam be developed around three points: "Very firm, strong and positive emphasis on acting responsibly (even at the cost of foregoing statements that would be popular and emotionally appealing at home) in order to strengthen U.S. negotiating position in

Paris and thus protect our troops and hasten chances for peace"; focusing on "de-escalation and de-Americanization as rapidly as is consistent with the safety of American troops, sustaining American interests and honoring American commitments"; and making it clear that "peace is a goal."⁴ Humphrey's campaign staff identified the candidate's problems precisely. It would be up to the vice president to decide whether to act on their judicious counsel.

Unfortunately, none of those recommendations seemed likely to be implemented. As the campaign against Nixon began, Humphrey was tempted to embrace the antiwar position on the war in an effort to bring McCarthy–RFK voters back into the Democratic fold. But as usual, Johnson maneuvered to keep Humphrey in lockstep with the White House, telling him in early September that McCarthy was not his friend and was not supporting the vice president's campaign. "Hubert, somebody could knee you in the balls and you'd just come up giggling and saying 'Knee me again.' You're going to have to hang tough. Don't get off on a Vietnam issue." The president emphasized that if Humphrey just held his ground, "Nixon has a way of blowing it. He'll blow it. But you've got to stay tough and on a single path, not go jump[ing] all over the lot."⁵ Of course, the president was less interested in helping Humphrey win the election than he was in keeping the vice president from straying from the administration's policy on Vietnam while peace talks proceeded in Paris, albeit glacially. LBJ's support for Humphrey would be superficial at best over the next three months; indeed, the president's proclivity for favoring Nixon over Humphrey—both in word and in deed—would become one of the most intriguing aspects of the entire campaign.

Hamstrung by LBJ and dealing with crushing political pressure from all sides, the vice president attempted to walk a tightrope on Vietnam and try to please everyone as he launched his campaign, just as he had tried to do unsuccessfully at the convention. On September 2, Humphrey spoke about the influence of the presidential campaign on the negotiations in Paris, asserting, "I believe both candidates should make absolutely clear that they share a basic commitment to the success of the peace negotiations now taking place in Paris." What the government of North Vietnam should clearly understand, he argued, was that "it is not in its interest to continue the killing, and the accompanying psychological warfare, in the hope that partisan debate in America might create dissension here which would lead to a weakening of American determination either on the battlefield or at the negotiating table." At the end of the day, the vice president concluded, "North Vietnam must understand that a political campaign in the United States will not result in our granting to North Vietnam concessions which it cannot obtain through the legitimate processes of negotiation now underway in Paris. The time to negotiate is now, not later."⁶ Politics might influence Humphrey's decisions, but he hoped they would neither undermine the Paris talks nor give Nixon (or the hawkish third-party candidate, former Alabama governor George Wallace) an electoral advantage on the war issue.

Shortly thereafter, Humphrey flew back to Washington to attend a National Security Council meeting. This would be the last one that Johnson would allow him to attend during the campaign despite the vice president's statutory membership on the NSC. At the meeting, Dean Rusk informed the group that the North Vietnamese "have attacked the Vietnam policy statements of both U.S. political parties," and he revealed that the U.S. negotiators "have not presented our minimum position in Paris, because we want to keep the door open to almost any move" Hanoi might make. LBJ then made it clear that if the United States could "stay for a few weeks with our present posture in Vietnam, we can convince the North Vietnamese that they won't get a better deal if they wait" for the new administration. He also complained that some of Hanoi's work was "being done for them by people in the United States," noting sourly that "Some 1,000 votes at the convention went to a proposed platform plank which called for a change in our policy." This comment was clearly intended as a pointed warning to Humphrey. But even more problematic was the fact that the tenor of the discussion made it clear to the vice president that his presidential campaign was not going to get much help on the military front during the campaign. As the meeting concluded, Humphrey tried to speak directly with Johnson, but to no avail. The president did let the candidate know, however, that he would help in any way he could and that he would release the cabinet to assist the vice president's campaign as well. Humphrey doubted both statements.[7]

From Washington, Humphrey left to officially kick off his campaign with an appearance at John F. Kennedy Plaza in Philadelphia on September 9, where he faced opposition from "Dump the Hump" hecklers and repeated questions about his stance on the war. During a forum with students shortly after the speech, Humphrey downplayed the differences among the Democratic candidates at the convention and asserted that unless there were unusual developments in Vietnam, the United States might begin to withdraw troops while negotiations were underway—a statement that received enthusiastic applause from the audience. He also suggested that whether or not negotiations proved fruitful, the United States could conceivably start to "remove some of the American forces in early 1969 or late 1968." Humphrey said, "You have to take calculated risks," and claimed that he would "leave no matter untouched and no proposition unexplored that may lend itself to a more rapid success at the conference table in Paris." Regardless, he concluded, "No one wants peace in Vietnam more" than he did: "I want a cease fire. I want it now." Later the same day in Denver, Humphrey hinted at a bombing halt and observed that the two Vietnam planks proposed in Chicago were so mildly different that he would have no difficulty accepting and running on the minority plank.[8] Humphrey was obviously trying to minimize the differences between the Democratic platform on the war and the position of the antiwar left in an effort to mitigate the intraparty divisions that plagued his campaign. That strategy did not work well, however, and would quickly prove to be problematic for the vice president's already tenuous relationship with Lyndon Johnson.

The reaction to Humphrey's comments from the administration was swift. Rusk immediately told the press that a bombing halt would be unlikely to improve either the military situation or the stalled peace talks quickly and even falsely denied that he had approved the language of the dovish plank that Humphrey had vetted with him prior to the convention. According to Secretary of Agriculture Orville Freeman, Johnson "really went after Humphrey," calling him "a coward," accusing him of "trying to back off his family [the administration]," and charging him with "ogling McCarthy. . . . On and on he went. A lot of the language was four letter words." In a telephone conversation with Clark Clifford, Humphrey lamented that LBJ's aides had immediately reprimanded him for his statements. While sympathetic to the vice president's situation, Clifford later wrote, "I knew that, in fact, in his heart, Humphrey was against the war, but thought it was still *necessary* to stick with the President."[9] Rarely in U.S. history has a sitting vice president seeking the Oval Office experienced such open disdain from the president and from members of the administration with whom he served.

Johnson, anxious about the lack of progress in Paris, took out his frustration on Humphrey. After the vice president's speeches in Philadelphia and Denver, LBJ "called Humphrey and said the candidate had to decide whether he wanted the president's support or not." The next day, a furious Johnson made a last-minute, unscheduled trip to New Orleans, where he told the national American Legion convention that his Vietnam policy derived from those of his predecessors, who had intervened in small conflicts to ward off larger wars. Johnson likened Vietnam critics to 1930s isolationists and said that everyone yearned to bring home U.S. troops but "no man can predict when that day will come"—a clear shot at Humphrey. He also dismissed suggestions of invading North Vietnam, withdrawal of U.S. forces, or a bombing halt without concessions from Hanoi, essentially rebutting everything the vice president had said in his recent statements. The *Washington Post* noted that the president's "emphatic defense of his Vietnam policy and his vigorous argument against any bombing halt may have been designed as warnings to the major candidates." Humphrey characterized LBJ's remarks as "not an act of friendship," and presidential aide Harry McPherson said that everyone took Johnson's speech as "a real blast at Humphrey."[10]

What chance did Humphrey have of running his own campaign based on his own beliefs if he had to deal with negative and visceral reactions from the president whenever he apostatized? How could he convince the American public that he was more than just LBJ's vice president, especially with regard to the war? Indecision on those questions reigned in the campaign. The *New York Times* declared that on the Vietnam issue, Humphrey had "thrashed about inconclusively for a separate posture on the war in Vietnam that he had defended so ardently" in 1966 and 1967. "After fulsome obeisance to President Johnson, the Vice President did at last hold out tempting bait to those who want desperately to believe that he has the will and intention to declare his independence and strike out on a new path on that most divisive problem of all, Vietnam." Journalist William White put it succinctly: "For four years Humphrey, in public and in private, has spoken of the hard necessity to stand firm in Vietnam with an eloquence and a passion not exceeded, and indeed hardly even matched by any other member of the Johnson-Humphrey Administration." If the vice president abandoned that position now, White concluded, it "would be a recantation without ready example in politics."[11] But that is exactly what Humphrey needed to do. Whether he would actually take the leap, however, remained unclear.

While Humphrey scrambled to make sense of his own position on Vietnam and vacillated between continuing to support Johnson's policies and the political realities of the campaign, Richard Nixon continued to reap the benefits of the vice president's disinclination to break with the administration. From the beginning, the focus of Nixon's campaign was entirely defensive. He intended to run in place on Vietnam and protect his sizable lead in the polls until election day. This strategy ceded the initiative to Humphrey, who would have to detail his differences with Johnson on Vietnam eventually if he had any hope of overtaking the Republican candidate. Unfortunately for the vice president, such a move would at once allow Nixon to attack him for inconsistency when it finally came and obviate the need for specifics that could jeopardize Nixon's election. Nixon aide Patrick Buchanan summarized the campaign's strategy in a memorandum to the GOP candidate: "If HHH shifts on Vietnam now, then he has spent four years deceiving the American people and he is unfit for any job in public life, let alone the Presidency."[12]

Thus Nixon could focus on his other campaign themes, most notably law and order, while waiting to counterattack if and when Humphrey finally disavowed the administration's policies. That worked extraordinarily well for Nixon since he did not, in fact, have a "secret plan" to end the war, nor did he have any desire to get into a debate on the details of his intentions *vis-à-vis* Vietnam. Indeed, the GOP candidate had managed the issue of the war extraordinarily well through the Republican primaries, allowing the other challengers for the nomination—George Romney, Nelson Rockefeller, and Ronald Reagan—to grapple with and stumble on the war issue for months while Nixon coasted to the nomination. Nixon expected that strategy to work in the general election campaign as well. What Nixon understood with absolute clarity was that Humphrey—like Romney before him—could not afford to ignore the war if he hoped to win the election. But the vice president remained torn on exactly what direction to take in the campaign, so Nixon would be waiting in the political wings to pounce once Humphrey committed himself to any specific course of action. [13]

Of course, had it been up to the two candidates, both Nixon and Humphrey would have gladly agreed to a moratorium on discussing the war for the entire campaign. The issue held too much volatility and risk for both candidates. But the American people felt otherwise. A Gallup poll in early September confirmed what most politicians and pundits already knew: Vietnam was, by an overwhelming margin, the most important problem facing the United States by a 51 percent to 21 percent margin over the next most pressing issue: crime. [14] Nevertheless, Nixon fervently clung to his public position that he would not specifically discuss his plan to end the war during the campaign to avoid undermining the negotiations in Paris. While this had been his posture for several months, it left a sour taste in the mouths of some of his GOP colleagues. For example, Senator Mark Hatfield (R-OR), an opponent of the war, made a little-noticed but telling comment about Vietnam in the forthcoming election. "In the democratic process, voters should not be forced to go to the polls with their fingers crossed," he asserted; "they should not be forced to rely on blind faith that the men they vote for will share their views on the most important issue of the election." Hatfield's skepticism, shared by many in both parties, did not change Nixon's strategy of silence. Meanwhile, Humphrey's advisers believed that their candidate had to make one announcement on Vietnam and then stay away from the issue. The thinking was that "the war is irreparably viewed as a Democratic war; the less said about it the better." [15]

The likelihood of that happening was remote, however. As the campaign progressed, Humphrey faced ridicule and scorn from antiwar protesters. In Seattle, for example, Humphrey talked about de-Americanization and troop withdrawals while defending the Democratic platform, which "points the way to peace in Vietnam and a negotiated settlement." He also asserted that if a peace had not been achieved by the time LBJ left office, "I pledge to you that my first priority as President shall be to honorably end the war" and excoriated Nixon for not actually having a plan for peace in Vietnam. Yet his speech was constantly interrupted by protestors, one of whom yelled, "You are being accused now of complicity in the deaths of tens of thousands of Americans and hundreds of thousands of Vietnamese." At Stanford University, Humphrey's car was attacked by a mob enraged by his position on the war. At a piano recital in Vermont, a woman screamed "Warmonger!" at him and spit in his face. [16] Clearly, his efforts to straddle the divide between the administration and the antiwar movement failed to resonate with the liberal wing of his own party. In addition, the fact that Eugene McCarthy had decided to not endorse Humphrey after the convention certainly did not help the vice president with this cohort of Democratic voters. Humphrey needed to do something substantive on Vietnam or risk losing the election.

That reality had become clear to Humphrey's campaign staff. Two weeks removed from Chicago, the candidate's top advisers sent him a strategy memorandum focusing on the "Humphrey image," with specific suggestions on how to recast the vice president's public persona and rejuvenate his candidacy. According to his staff, Humphrey's image was "at its lowest point," due largely to his position on the war in Vietnam, and "What appeared to be vacillations and contradictions during the past week did not help." In an effort to improve his image, the campaign needed to emphasize the vice president's "qualities of wholesomeness, vigor, integrity, leadership and sincere dedication to the public interest that have a basic appeal to the American people."

To achieve this, they suggested several general steps. First, they argued that Humphrey should "keep on being the underdog . . . to get the greatest possible benefit from the American tradition of <u>sympathy for the underdog</u> and support for a good fighter against heavy odds." Second, they stressed the importance of portraying Humphrey as independent and strong through positive means. This should not be done "at the expense of a repudiation of LBJ policies, or by conflict or confrontation with LBJ. . . . Humphrey must support the achievements of the past 8 years without glossing over the last 5 years and without making an exception of Vietnam." Finally, they suggested the obvious tactic: a "vigorous attack on Nixon."

The memorandum then went on to address approaches to specific campaign issues. On Vietnam, the advisers recommended that Humphrey "take firm, positive, strong (and unwavering) stand on the basic principles (as expressed in platform and acceptance speech), emphasizing (a) dedication to seeking end of war by negotiated, honorable peace; (b) concern for security of American troops and American Nation." But they also counseled "flexibility" to respond to "changing conditions that *may* occur." They concluded that "A basic speech on Vietnam will probably be necessary—or it can possibly begin with Vietnam and turn to a basic foreign policy initiative highlighting H's proposal to strengthen peacemaking through the UN (approved by 87 percent of the people). Vietnam part should be formulated in consultation with the President." Many of his advisers had pleaded with the vice president to break with the administration on the war for months, and given the desperate straits the campaign found itself in at such an early stage of the race, they believed that the time for that change was now, although the language in the memorandum reflected a certain degree of caution—unsurprising given the familiarity many of the staffers had with Johnson's attitude toward the vice president.[17]

The president's disapproval of Humphrey was problematic to be sure. But the fact that by the middle of September the Democratic ticket appeared to be "coming apart at the seams," as Orville Freeman later wrote, caused even more consternation. Humphrey preferred to focus on domestic issues; all things being equal, he might have attempted to make them the fulcrum of the race. But he could not escape his problems with the war. Yet the struggle with Vietnam represented only the tip of the iceberg. The campaign had serious financial difficulties, a product of the lack of enthusiasm for the vice president's candidacy among many Democrats; the ticket continued to experience widespread defections from the left, especially among antiwar liberals and university students; and Humphrey faced dismal and ominous poll numbers—he trailed Nixon by a substantial margin in every major survey, and the polls indicated that his connection with the administration's Vietnam policy had crippled the vice president's candidacy. Indeed, pollster Elmo Roper announced in early September that he was not going to bother to publish any more surveys because Nixon was "almost as good as elected."[18]

The dire *status quo* disturbed the vice president and his advisers, and it was readily apparent that the failure to come out strongly against the war was subverting Humphrey's campaign. The vice president's liberal supporters kept urging him to do three things to kick start his candidacy: swing toward the doves to "pick up the disaffected left," break with the administration to "prove his independence," and "move dramatically to dispel Richard Nixon's aura of invincibility."[19] Those recommendations mirrored the counsel that the candidate had been getting from his closest advisers. Most of Humphrey's staff believed that the only way to salvage his campaign from annihilation in November would be for the vice president to dissociate himself from the administration's policies on Vietnam as soon as possible. These voices included Senator Fred Harris (D-OK), cochair of the campaign; Larry O'Brien, the Democratic National Committee chairman; and U.S. ambassador to the United Nations George Ball, who would become "the decisive figure" due to his close relationship with the candidate.[20]

A tipping point came on September 16, when O'Brien bluntly told Humphrey, "Let's face it, as of now we've lost. It's on every newsman's lips. You're not your own man. Unless you change direction on this Vietnam thing, and become your own man, you're finished." Humphrey agreed. He blamed himself for his statements in Philadelphia and Denver that had led to Johnson "undercutting me" in the New Orleans speech. The vice president told O'Brien that he needed something "positive" with which he could attack both Nixon and Wallace, suggesting that he tell the American people that "we have to start pulling our ground forces out as soon as the Vietnamese are ready—de-Americanization." O'Brien quickly pointed out that this would mean a break with Johnson: "A clean break this week or never. Do it now— even a white paper."

Yet even with his campaign hanging by a thread, Humphrey could not bring himself to take the last step and breach his loyalty to the president, reluctantly telling the DNC chairman, "I don't know." But Humphrey did float some trial balloons in an effort to change tactics and revive his faltering campaign in the weeks that followed. On the campaign trail in Columbus, Ohio, on September 21, he declared, "I'm going to seek peace in every way possible, but only the President can do it now. Come January, it's a new ball game. Then I will make peace." Humphrey promised that as president he would "stop the bombing of North Vietnam as an acceptable risk for peace," although he hedged his bets by saying that he expected Hanoi to restore the demilitarized zone prior to any bombing halt.[21] Statements like this created some distance from the president's policies, but only marginally. Moreover, they did not move the needle with public opinion.

Dissatisfaction over Humphrey's position on the war found expression in the media as well. The *Baltimore Sun* editorialized that the "quality of the discussion this week has been appallingly poor" on the issue of the war. They were specifically critical of the vice president, who "has got himself so entangled in his own words"—which they called "empty, even shopworn"— that "even he seems uncertain as to what he meant to say." They concluded that if Humphrey "proposed to cut himself loose from the Administration's war policy and urge a greater effort toward peace . . . it would be well for him to say so much more explicitly than he has thus far."[22] Similarly, the *Washington Star* recognized that the Democratic candidate was in a difficult position: "He can hardly take the political risk of breaking with the policies and the position of the Johnson administration, in which he has been an active participant. . . . Humphrey obviously feels the need to stake out some sort of position that is all his own. Unfortunately for him, he cannot hope to do this by being all things to all men. Yet this apparently is what he has been trying to do." The "waffling by Humphrey looks ridiculous."[23]

With the press, the antiwar left, and his own campaign team constantly demanding that the vice president finally break with the administration, pressure mounted on Humphrey to take decisive action. Journalist Crosby Noyes reported in the *Washington Evening Star* on September 24 that liberal critics who had been urging Humphrey to declare his independence from Johnson's Vietnam policy were "losing hope" and believed that it was too late "for a change of tune which could have a significant effect on the outcome of the election. It has always been too late." Given Humphrey's failure to make a break at the convention or resign the vice presidency, Crosby continued, "the whole problem of establishing his independence as a candidate has become almost insoluble . . . any drastic reversal of Humphrey's posture . . . would be universally interpreted as an act of desperation. It would betray inconsistencies too great to be explained away and an indecision which would cast the most serious doubt on his qualifications for leadership." Moreover, "it would also not help to win the election. If Humphrey is defeated in November, it will not be because most people in the country are against the war in Vietnam. . . . It will be because most people who are against the war are Democrats who may well stay home on election day." Those fissures would be the vice president's Achilles' heel, Noyes wrote, because "Humphrey is being deserted by a segment of left-wing dissidents who have lost faith in the party leadership. . . . The demand of the liberals for an abrupt about-face on Vietnam and a break with the administration would be, at this point, the surest prescription for disaster."[24]

Even though his political instincts had been largely repressed in recent months, Humphrey clearly recognized his dilemma. On September 25, in a radio appearance on KHJ in Los Angeles, Humphrey stated categorically that he would not advocate a bombing halt and added that some of his friends would be "quite unhappy because I won't say some of the things they want me to say." He did leave himself an out, however, stating that "if I had any reason to believe that stopping the bombing this afternoon could lend itself to bringing about better discussions in Paris . . . I would recommend it tomorrow morning." Humphrey also tried to convince his audience that the president was not pressuring him to hold back on supporting a bombing halt, stating that LBJ "is not screening my speeches. . . . The President has not made me his slave and I am not his humble servant. I am his partner and I am Vice President of these United States."[25] It is fascinating to witness the depths of Humphrey's loyalty to Johnson despite all of the harsh statements, lack of reciprocation, and the political realities of the campaign.

By the end of September, Gallup polls showed Nixon leading Humphrey by 43 percent to 28 percent, with independent candidate George Wallace registering an uncomfortably close 21 percent and actually leading the vice president in electoral votes according to some assessments. Tom Wicker of the *New York Times* noted that this problematic situation led many Democratic leaders to demand that their candidate "demonstrate his independence from President Johnson as the only means of salvaging a campaign dangerously close to disaster." Only a "positive demonstration that the Vice President has the vision and the will and the courage to define his problems and meet them effectively" would give Humphrey a chance against Nixon.[26]

Increasingly desperate for anything that could help to close the seemingly insurmountable gap with Nixon, Humphrey repeatedly challenged the GOP candidate to debate him. At a rally in Seattle, Humphrey challenged Nixon to "face the people" and reveal his "secret plan to end the war in Vietnam," asserting that if Nixon had such a plan, he should "let President Johnson in on it." If he did not do so, Humphrey concluded, Nixon should "stop playing games with the American people."[27] Despite the vice president's constant criticisms and repeated references to "Richard the Silent" and "Richard the Chickenhearted," Nixon refused—probably a wise decision on his part, given Humphrey's intellect and engaging personality. Nixon had clearly learned his lesson from the debacle of the 1960 presidential debates with John Kennedy. Meanwhile, Eugene McCarthy returned to the United States on September 27 after visiting France. Reports suggested that McCarthy had told some of his key supporters that he might openly support Humphrey's candidacy "at an appropriate time before the election." Yet when asked specifically by the press whether he intended to change his mind and endorse Humphrey, McCarthy declined to do so, saying that the vice president had not changed his basic views on Vietnam.[28]

Without debates or an infusion of support from the antiwar forces, Humphrey's travails continued. Fortunately for the vice president, he had a number of supporters within the administration who recognized that Johnson's treatment of Humphrey was undermining the Democratic campaign by keeping the candidate uninformed about the Paris negotiations. Undersecretary of State Nicholas Katzenbach and State Department official Benjamin Read began drafting a statement for Humphrey, explaining what he might do about Vietnam if elected. This included giving the Saigon government a schedule for de-Americanization of the war. When Humphrey received the draft statement, he was thrilled, saying, "My God, this is what I need." Additional help came when George Ball resigned his post as U.S. ambassador to the United Nations on September 26 to assist the "sagging fortunes" of his "poor friend." Ball played two roles in Humphrey's campaign. His first task was to assist the vice president in establishing an independent position on the war and a plan for a negotiated settlement, a "decidedly delicate" task since it had to be "sufficiently distinguishable from Johnson's to satisfy the more reasonable antiwar factions, without, at the same time, driving the president into outright opposition." Ball also sent his Lehman Brothers partner, George Fitzgibbon, and other aides to Paris to clear a proposed statement with U.S. negotiators Averell Harriman and Cyrus Vance.[29] This back channel to the peace talks would prove significant to the campaign going forward.

At the same time, Ball told Humphrey that the Paris talks had stalled and that Humphrey needed to help himself by speaking out on the war. Indeed, Ball was determined to break Johnson's "psychological grip" on the vice president. Humphrey admitted to Ball that he had "loused up the situation" by failing to stand firm on troop withdrawals and a bombing halt at the convention. Ball agreed that the vice president should have "stuck to your guns" but optimistically believed that Humphrey could still win. Arthur Goldberg, who like Ball had resigned as UN ambassador the previous April due to disagreement with the administration's policy on Vietnam, announced the formation of a "National Citizens Committee for Humphrey-Muskie" and called for a complete bombing halt. With so much pressure and support from his advisers, Humphrey finally decided to make the leap. He committed $100,000 of the campaign's dwindling funds to buy a half-hour block on NBC for the evening of September 30 with the intention of declaring a substantive change on his position on the war.[30]

The speech became the priority for the campaign. It became a true collaborative effort, with Ball, Ted Van Dyk, Averell Harriman, Fred Harris, Bill Moyers, and other key advisers helping to shape the new policy. Ball assured the vice president that the speech would not be a total break with Johnson; rather, it would only refer to actions Humphrey would take *after* he was elected president. At one point in the process, Harris asked Humphrey if he would seek LBJ's approval for the content of the speech. Humphrey replied, "Hell no. I'm not going to ask. I did that once." There was some dissent on the contours of the speech. O'Brien, Harris, and Van Dyk favored the inclusion of an unconditional bombing halt as the best way to win over the McCarthy–RFK voters and get the North Vietnamese to agree to serious negotiations, a view also supported by Goldberg and Governor Richard Hughes (D-NJ). Humphrey's chief of staff William Connell, who remained hawkish on the war, wanted to avoid offending Johnson and resisted any significant move toward a completely independent position. Ball and others—including Harriman and Cyrus Vance, who weighed in from Paris—sought a compromise: a bombing halt that would continue based on Hanoi's respect for the DMZ, a proposal that Humphrey had already suggested the previous week in Columbus. Humphrey worried about Johnson's reaction, but he also did not want to say anything that might have negative ramifications for the Paris talks. Thus, once the writing group gave him a draft, the vice president finished the final language of the speech himself, working until 5:45 a.m. on September 30. He told his advisers that he would inform LBJ of the main points just before the speech aired and would call the president to "get him down off the ceiling."[31]

As preparations for the speech continued at a frantic pace, observers continued to hammer away at the vice president's campaign. Writing in the *Boston Globe*, Mary McGrory compared the Humphrey campaign to "an overnight camping trip for which someone has forgotten the tents." McGrory criticized Humphrey for saying "little for fear of contradiction from his chief heckler, Lyndon B. Johnson." While she credited Nixon's campaign as being "a continuous show of virtuoso professionalism," Humphrey had "lost all credibility" and had "carried optimism into the realm of self-delusion, if indeed he believes what he says." McGrory's comments mirrored the sentiments of many Humphrey friends and supporters, particularly her conclusion that Humphrey was "running a potato race, tied to his benefactor and tormentor."[32] The venerable Walter Lippman referred to the vice president as "a man who is inextricably bogged in the failures of the Johnson administration" and argued that it was "painfully clear that the Democratic party is too disorganized to run the country."[33] Similar unflattering commentary appeared in scores of newspapers across the country; clearly, Humphrey's imminent announcement could not come soon enough if the vice president were to have any hope of changing public perceptions and salvaging his campaign.

On the day of the televised address, Humphrey met with Utah Democrats, including Hugh B. Brown, an apostle of the Church of Jesus Christ of Latter-day Saints who was a friend and political supporter. Brown had arranged for Humphrey to speak at the Mormon Tabernacle, a site that Humphrey later described as "a special, soothing break from partisan audiences" that left him "rather relaxed" as he prepared to tape his speech for broadcast later that evening. The speech at the Tabernacle seemed like the old Humphrey—energetic, optimistic, and hopeful. While the vice president did not address the war specifically in his remarks, he did take the opportunity to place his campaign in historical perspective and spoke about broad themes of liberty and democracy, including an appeal to "the silent majority of Americans," asking them to "speak their belief in the decency of our democracy" by going to the polls in November "in the spirit of faith, not fear."[34]

Meanwhile, rumors circulated about what the vice president might say in the speech that evening. Unsurprisingly, the potential of a change in Humphrey's position on the war concerned Richard Nixon deeply. At 6:45 p.m., Nixon called Johnson seeking assurance that the speech would not reveal a dramatic change in current administration policy. The president told the GOP candidate that he had not read Humphrey's remarks, so he could not directly speak to the issue. Johnson did say, however, that General Creighton Abrams, the U.S. commander in Vietnam, had written a memorandum contending that a bombing halt would greatly increase North Vietnam's military threat, the implication being that if Humphrey did make such a proposal, Nixon would have ammunition to use against the vice president in response. Johnson told Nixon that he had not shared Abrams's memorandum with Humphrey so as not to be accused of "coaching" him. LBJ opined that the best thing Nixon could say publicly was that the president was solely responsible for making U.S. foreign policy. Rostow, who was also on the call, assured Nixon that the administration was not changing its policy and would insist on three points: in return for a bombing halt, North Vietnam had to respect the DMZ, that Hanoi would not shell South Vietnamese cities, and that the North would accept the Saigon government at the negotiating table. Nixon pledged his continued support for the current policy.[35] The LBJ–Nixon conversation represented only the latest in a series of regular contacts between the two politicians throughout the campaign. These discussions make it clear that suggestions regarding Johnson's preference for the GOP candidate over his own vice president are not the fevered dreams of conspiracy theorists.

A mere fifteen minutes before the taped speech aired on NBC, Humphrey called the president to give him a preview of his remarks. The vice president emphasized that the speech outlined what he would do if elected but that he would not undermine the administration's negotiating position. He also assured Johnson that he did not intend to propose unilateral withdrawal; rather, he wanted to de-escalate the conflict and take a "risk for peace" by ordering a bombing halt if he had prior evidence that North Vietnam would respect the DMZ and enter into good-faith negotiations. Johnson blandly responded, "Okay," and promised to watch the speech but failed to mention his earlier conversation with Nixon. When the Democratic candidate finished his brief comments, the president said, "I gather you're not asking my advice." Humphrey said that was true but once again assured LBJ that there was nothing in the speech that would embarrass the president or jeopardize the peace talks in Paris. Johnson replied curtly, "Well, you're going to give the speech anyway. Thanks for calling, Hubert," and hung up. Interestingly, the previous week, Johnson had told Clifford that he would respect Humphrey more if he "showed he had some balls." Now that Humphrey actually intended to stake out an independent position on the war, however, a bitter and resentful LBJ did not like what he was hearing.[36]

Undaunted by Johnson's abrupt dismissal, the vice president moved ahead with the speech. The address aired in prime time in an effort to maximize the exposure of his message. Humphrey appeared without the vice presidential seal or an American flag behind him; he wanted to speak as a "citizen" who was merely a candidate for the presidency. Humphrey began by saying, "For the past several weeks, I have tried to tell you what was in my heart and on my mind. But sometimes that message has been drowned out by the voices of protestors and demonstrators. . . . I have paid for this television time this evening to tell you my story uninterrupted by noise . . . by protest . . . or by second-hand interpretation" then reiterated his central rhetorical message from the convention and from the previous month on the campaign trail: "My first priority as President shall be to end the war and obtain an honorable peace."

Humphrey then established for the audience his role in making, implementing, and advocating for the administration's policy on the war. He stated, "For the past four years I have spoken my mind about Vietnam, frankly and without reservation, in the Cabinet and in the National Security Council—and directly to the President. When the President has made his decisions, I have supported them." While certainly an exaggeration—the vice president's self-censorship on Vietnam was at the root of most of his current political problems—his loyal support of LBJ and his policies cannot be denied. Humphrey noted that Johnson would be president until January 20, 1969, and repeated his oft-stated position that the "voice at the negotiating table must be his. I shall not compete with that voice. I shall cooperate and help." Yet he also made it clear that he would not feel limited in his responses to the war if elected: "As I said in my acceptance speech: The politics of tomorrow need not be limited by the policies of yesterday," a signal to his audience that he would not be bound by Johnson's policies after the inauguration.

The vice president proceeded to outline his new position on the war. While he "would not undertake a unilateral withdrawal" or "escalate the level of violence in either North or South Vietnam," Humphrey did commit to a specific course of action. "We must seek to de-escalate," the vice president said, and he expressed a willingness "to stop the bombing of the North as an acceptable risk for peace because I believe it could lead to success in the negotiations and a shorter war. This would be the best protection for our troops. . . . If the Government of North Vietnam were to show bad faith, I would reserve the right to resume the bombing." This was the money line for Humphrey, the long-awaited break with the administration for which his advisers and political allies had lobbied for months. But the vice president did not stop there. Instead, he committed to moving toward "de-Americanization of the war. . . . That would be an immediate objective of the Humphrey-Muskie Administration as it sought to end the war."

Moreover, he "would propose once more an immediate cease-fire . . . free elections in South Vietnam—with all people, including members of the National Liberation Front and other dissident groups, able to participate . . . [and would] accept their judgment, whatever it is." According to Humphrey, none of these decisions represented a risk or "would jeopardize our security or be contrary to our national interest." He concluded, "Let me be clear: I do not counsel withdrawal from the world. I do not swerve from international responsibility. I only say that, as President, I would undertake a new strategy for peace in this world, based not on American omnipotence, but on American leadership—not only military and economic, but moral. . . . In a troubled and dangerous world," he concluded, "we should seek not to march alone, but to lead in such a way that others will wish to join us."[37] The die was cast. Humphrey's speech—based on both principle and political realities—represented his last, best hope to win the election regardless of what that meant for his relationship with the president he had loyally served for four years.

That did not mean, however, that the vice president was unconcerned with LBJ's reaction, which he knew could be unpredictable and potentially damaging to Humphrey's campaign. That is exactly what happened, as the president blasted the speech and the candidate to his advisers and with the Nixon campaign. In his memoirs, Johnson made the highly dubious claim that Humphrey's pivot on the war effectively cost the vice president the election because it made the South Vietnamese government "extremely nervous and distrustful" of the administration and the entire Democratic Party. As a result, he argued, it encouraged Saigon to "thwart the negotiations in Paris in the decisive phase that was about to begin."[38] Whether Johnson's analysis after the fact was accurate is open to debate. But one thing is certain: whatever the effect the speech had on the race for the presidency or the trajectory of the fighting and peace talks, it undeniably had a negative impact on the already anemic relationship between Humphrey and Johnson. The vice president's remarks angered LBJ and reinforced the president's obvious reluctance to help Humphrey in the race against Nixon.[39]

The friendship between Johnson and Humphrey had always been based in politics; as convivial as they may have appeared to outsiders—and as close as they may have actually been while serving in the Senate—the fundamental nature of their relationship was transactional. With Humphrey's overt break with the administration, any lingering value that the vice president had for LBJ evaporated, leaving him as a liability to Johnson—politically, diplomatically, and in terms of his legacy. For the remainder of the campaign, Johnson consistently went out of his way to deride and belittle Humphrey. Even Orville Freeman, who usually gave LBJ the benefit of the doubt, was "appalled" by the president's "petulance and pettiness," which had cost him his "personal popularity" and the "affection of the people." Freeman could not believe that Johnson was "so mean and petty" toward Humphrey. But Johnson would be even more upset when the Paris negotiations started to see some movement, perhaps partially due to the proposed bombing halt in Humphrey's speech, with the Soviets and North Vietnamese conceding the admission of the Saigon government to the talks in exchange for a bombing halt. All of LBJ's insecurities resurfaced, and he blamed Humphrey for threatening his place in history. Any prospect of electoral support from Johnson was now obliterated. Of course, up to this point in the campaign, the president had done precious little in support of Humphrey's candidacy anyway, and given Humphrey's rise in the polls following the address, it is probable that the vice president did not want any additional "assistance" from the Oval Office at this critical juncture.

So Johnson raged at Humphrey and took both covert and overt actions in favor of Nixon in the weeks that followed. He told Senate Minority Leader Everett Dirksen (R-IL), who was a conduit to the Nixon campaign, that Humphrey was trying to gain the support of McCarthy voters and that Nixon would do well to say that the current administration was responsible for running the war. Two days later, LBJ spoke to Rusk to express his frustration with Harriman (whom he called "a damned fool") and Vance for collaborating with Ball in drafting Humphrey's speech. Johnson also told Rusk he was considering recalling Harriman and said that if he were Hanoi, he would ask himself, "Can I get a better deal out of Humphrey than I can Johnson?"[40] Hoping to calm the president, Clifford, Rusk, and Rostow suggested that "the speech need not give us trouble." According to the three national security officials, reporters should be told that the address should not be seen as a departure from current administration policy, and they advised Johnson to remain quiet publicly.[41]

Other administration assessments of Humphrey's speech reflected more-nuanced thinking. William Bundy suggested to Walt Rostow that Humphrey "would in practice be prepared to stop the bombing on the basis of almost any indication that Hanoi would respect the DMZ. In short, although the wording of the speech is certainly not clear, I would not read it as a categorical statement that he would stop the bombing without anything whatever from North Vietnam."[42] Nicholas Katzenbach opined to LBJ, "I would conclude that [Humphrey] has said that, as President, he would order a cessation of bombing if he believed the North Vietnamese would respect the DMZ and would enter into serious negotiations. . . . I would guess that Hanoi would read what he had to say as being different in tone, but not in substance" from the president's position.[43] But what other choice did Hubert Humphrey really have? Had he continued to balance precariously between Johnson and the doves, his electoral prospects would have looked bleak at best.

Aside from LBJ and his top advisers, however, the national reaction to the Salt Lake City address was overwhelmingly positive. Humphrey's speech brought accolades from Senator Edward Kennedy (D-MA), who told the vice president, "To all who look for peace in Vietnam, you have given great encouragement and hope. . . . I applaud the courage of your statement, its clarity and strength of purpose . . . you deserve the support of all who have worked and prayed for peace."[44] The *Washington Post* reported that Humphrey's speech "may help him to win back some of the dissident members of his own Party who left the fold after Chicago and may help him to improve his position with Republicans and Independent doves."[45] That optimistic assessment would be realized three days after the speech, as the Americans for Democratic Action endorsed Humphrey by a 71–16 vote, a solid indication that antiwar liberals believed in and embraced the vice president's new position on the war. But perhaps most notably, Humphrey's political allies were relieved, as Arthur Schlesinger wrote, that the Democratic candidate had "come out for himself, or rather as himself."[46] In terms of perception, Humphrey's speech distanced him from Johnson's public statements and, for the first time, established an independent position on the war. In domestic political terms, the vice president's statement was a "resounding success."[47] It would not be overstating the case to assert that it was the critical turning point in the presidential race.

Humphrey's remarks paid immediate tangible dividends for the campaign as well. Antiwar protestors dialed back their attacks on the vice president at public appearances, with some even apologizing for their previous animosity toward the candidate. The campaign, desperately low on funds, received a huge infusion of cash over the week that followed the televised address. The speech provided the campaign with a much-needed surge in the polls, a trend that would continue until election day. Even more crucially, Humphrey was endorsed by the *New York Times* on October 6, 1968. The editors suggested that "Humphrey has given unmistakable signals that he intends, if elected, to move away from the errors of the past." The editorial went on to paint the candidate's quandary in a positive light, noting that as vice president, he was forced into a position of "defending the President's policies in public and trying to influence them in private" and suggested that "it is significant that the former members of the Johnson Administration who are rallying to Mr. Humphrey's support include its best-known doves."[48] All of these developments foreshadowed a revived campaign and, for the first time, real hope for victory in November. About the only thing that did not happen was the long-anticipated McCarthy endorsement; the Minnesota senator asserted that "Humphrey first had to call for a new government in South Vietnam that included the NLF and a revamped U.S. draft law."[49]

From the candidate's perspective, the break with LBJ was a relief. After the speech, Humphrey commented, "I feel good inside for the first time."[50] While the Salt Lake City speech did not represent a radical departure from the administration's position, it did call for a bombing halt with qualifications. Humphrey later recalled, "It was just enough to give a little light between the president's position and mine, but without jeopardizing his." But perception frequently drives politics, and as Albert Eisele commented, "for the beleaguered candidate, it was the Magna Charta and Declaration of Independence rolled into one." Ted Van Dyk, one of the speech's architects, stated, "It was the turning point of the campaign, not because of what he said, but because saying it liberated him internally. The American voter watching the screen that night finally saw that Humphrey was for peace, that he was sincere, and that he meant it. On that night, the onus of the war shifted to Nixon."[51] For the next five weeks, Humphrey would inch closer to Nixon—passing him in some polls by the end of October—and would force Nixon to address the Vietnam issue he absolutely preferred to avoid. Victory, considered a near impossibility by pundits just days earlier, now seemed to be within Humphrey's grasp.

For his part, Nixon responded predictably to the Salt Lake speech. He accused Humphrey of vacillating on his position on the war, deriding the call for a bombing halt as "his fourth different position" on the issue. "He first indicated that he opposed the Minority plank submitted at the Democratic Convention which called for a bombing halt. He then indicated that he could support that plank. Then he shifted his position and indicated that he could not support that position." Nixon reiterated his stance that "we can have only one President at a time" and argued that by calling for a bombing halt, Humphrey was depriving the administration's negotiators in Paris of their "trump card." He also attempted to undermine Humphrey by quoting the vice president's statement from the previous week in which Humphrey stated, "North Vietnam must understand that a political campaign in the United States will not result in our granting to North Vietnam concessions which it cannot obtain through the legitimate process of negotiation now underway in Paris."[52] The desperation and concern from the Nixon camp was palpable.

Humphrey had done the one thing that could force the GOP candidate to engage the war directly and potentially threaten Nixon's lead in the polls.

Hoping to regain the momentum and fend off the surging Democratic campaign, Nixon and his supporters doubled-down on the strategy of linking Humphrey to what they characterized as a failed Johnson-Humphrey administration approach in Vietnam. Appearing on CBS's *Face the Nation* on October 13, 1968, GOP vice presidential candidate Spiro Agnew (R-MD) was asked, "Governor, I get the feeling listening to both you and Mr. Nixon, that you're really much closer to defending the Johnson record on Vietnam than Vice President Humphrey is. Is that a fair conclusion?" Agnew replied, "Well, that's not what the Vice President says. He says he defends it wholeheartedly because, after all, it's his record too." Agnew was also critical of the bombing halt, especially without any reciprocal action on the part of Hanoi.[53] Despite having a clear advantage financially and the implicit support of LBJ himself, the Republican ticket found itself in an undeniably defensive posture in the wake of the Salt Lake City speech.

That sense of foreboding would only increase as the administration began to contemplate a major change to its negotiating position—due at least in part to the positive reaction garnered by Humphrey's address. In a series of meetings with national security officials on October 14, Johnson discussed the possibility of a bombing halt and a cease-fire. Of course, domestic political calculations factored into the decision; LBJ feared that this would be considered as a ploy to aid the Humphrey campaign—both in terms of public perception and in his *sub rosa* relationship with Nixon. The president explicitly wondered what the reaction of the Senate and the country would be if the administration took these steps. Senator Richard Russell (D-GA) noted that since the country was in the midst of a presidential election campaign, "Reactions will vary. The press will hail this. You will be charged with politics. What everybody wants is an end to the war." Rusk jumped in and asserted, "No decision has been made in relationship to domestic politics." Press secretary George Christian observed, "The reaction will be good from the press and media. Political charges of helping Vice President Humphrey will be made." LBJ responded, "I will be charged with doing this to influence the election. Nixon will be disappointed. The doves will criticize us for not doing it before now."

Later that day, LBJ told Rusk and Clifford that conservative Senator George Smathers (D-FL) had informed the president, "The word is out that we are trying to throw the election to Humphrey," and said that Nixon told him "he did not want the President to be pulled into this, that wrong results could flow," and that Nixon "is afraid we could be misled." Clifford said that he doubted that the proposed actions "would have any effect on the campaign," but Johnson retorted, "Both sides think it will." The secretary of state then told the president, "Nixon has been honorable on Vietnam. We must give him a chance to roll with this. . . . He has been more responsible on this than our own candidate." Clifford, however, insisted that most people had already made up their minds about the election and asked, "What's the matter with rocking the boat?"[54] The problem was that the resentful and petulant LBJ did not want to cede any credit to the vice president or give him any additional advantage in the campaign.

The president's frustrations colored all of his conversations and decisions over the final weeks of the presidential race. On October 16, Johnson called Mike Mansfield to complain about Humphrey's position on the war and about former national security adviser McGeorge Bundy's call for a bombing halt and the start of U.S. troop withdrawals. Later that morning, LBJ told Humphrey, Nixon, and Wallace "in absolute confidence"—without advance notice to his vice president—of the U.S. proposal being sent to the Paris negotiating team. He stressed that it was consistent with past policy, that it would not be changed until he left office, and that he wanted silence on the matter from the candidates because anything they might say would be "injurious to your country." In an obvious negative reference to Humphrey's September 30 speech, he said, "We're not going to get peace through speeches, and we're not going to get peace through the newspapers." While Humphrey remained quiet, Wallace endorsed a "strong" position on Vietnam, and Nixon—lying, as the White House would soon discover—assured LBJ that he would not say anything to "undercut" negotiations.[55] The vice president must have realized that he would have to sprint to the finish with Johnson actively impeding his progress.

Yet Humphrey and Johnson would surprisingly find themselves on the same side once again as a result of the Nixon campaign's covert machinations with the Saigon government. On October 22, Nixon ordered his closest aide, H. R. Haldeman, to "monkey wrench" the peace talks by having Anna Chennault, a GOP fundraiser who had a close relationship with the Saigon regime, continue to pressure the regime to not accept any deal in Paris before the U.S. election.[56] Nixon also told Haldeman to have Rose Mary Woods, the candidate's personal secretary, to have her friend, Chinese businessman Louis Kung, put pressure on South Vietnamese president Thieu and "Tell him hold firm." In a conversation with Dirksen about Nixon's conspiratorial efforts, LBJ confided in his former Senate colleague and friend, "I'm reading their hand Everett. This is treason." Dirksen responded, "I know." But even with the wiretaps and other intelligence—the FBI had been tracking Chennault's movements and recorded her meeting with South Vietnamese ambassador Bui Diem, for example—the administration was reluctant to go public because they lacked "absolute proof," as Clark Clifford asserted, of Nixon's direct involvement.[57]

Johnson faced both a moral and a political dilemma. As furious as he was with Nixon for the intrigue and chicanery with Chennault, Diem, and Thieu, he did not want to be responsible for the chaos—in terms of both the presidential election and the peace talks in Paris—that would inevitably ensue if the GOP–RVN contacts were made public. Thus he left the decision to expose the scheme up to Humphrey. Most of the vice president's campaign staff and key administration officials with whom he consulted—including Clifford and Rusk—advised Humphrey to keep the plot undisclosed because the revelation of the secret deal between the Republicans and the Thieu regime could hurt the administration's attempts to get Saigon back to the negotiating table, not to mention potentially producing a backlash against the Democratic candidate by voters who might perceive this to be an electoral ploy on the part of the Humphrey campaign.

Moreover, the legality of the methods used to obtain the information would have been called into question and could backfire in such a close race. Walt Rostow alluded to this in a memo to Johnson, stating, "the materials are so explosive that they could gravely damage the country whether Mr. Nixon is elected or not. If they get out in their present form, they could be the subject of one of the most acrimonious debates we have ever witnessed."[58] Some aides did try to convince Humphrey to publicize the story as a way of gaining ground on Nixon in the last hours of the campaign, but lacking a smoking gun, the vice president demurred. In a move that Theodore White has called one of the most decent and moral acts in American political history, Humphrey decided to not drop the bombshell that could have at once provoked a national crisis and won him the election. Humphrey aide Ted Van Dyk later commented, "Ninety-nine out of a hundred men with the presidency at stake would have had no inhibitions; they would have demagogued it." With the country already divided over so many issues, Humphrey concluded that discretion was the better part of valor. His decision, according to Jules Witcover, "was either one of the noblest in American political history or one of the great tactical blunders. Possibly it was both."[59]

Should Humphrey have exposed Nixon's reckless and selfish attempt to interfere with and influence the presidential election by undermining the negotiations in Paris? A good argument can be made that the U.S. public should have been informed. In the U.S. constitutional system, voting is sacrosanct, and any effort to manipulate the electorate for political gain that might compromise the democratic process or threaten national security should be disclosed as expeditiously as possible—especially one that involves intrigue with a foreign government. Yet such an explosive and potentially destabilizing revelation could have easily sparked a political backlash, undermined the public's faith in the results of the election, and perhaps even precipitated a constitutional crisis. Thus, lacking absolute proof—and unsure that the administration would actually provide the crucial evidence that it had gathered on the GOP campaign's activities—Humphrey did the only reasonable thing he could do from both an ethical and a political standpoint.

Even without the potentially incendiary revelations about Nixon being exposed, the campaign was trending in a positive direction, and Humphrey would receive more good news on October 26. Courts in New York denied a petition by McCarthy's supporters to get the senator's name on the presidential ballot at the last minute. Three days later, McCarthy finally endorsed Humphrey despite lingering reservations about his Vietnam statements. The momentum that Humphrey had gained since Salt Lake City now received an additional boost; indeed, so sharply had the vice president cut into Nixon's lead in the polls that some Democrats began talking openly about the realistic possibility of a Humphrey victory in November—an unthinkable notion just a few weeks earlier. In response, Nixon accused Humphrey of vacillating on Vietnam, suggesting that Humphrey had first favored an unconditional, and then a conditional, bombing halt, which confused the enemy about U.S. intentions, which led them to escalate the fighting. Nixon claimed to have been told of a "cynical, last minute attempt" by the administration to salvage Humphrey's candidacy "through a bombing halt and perhaps a ceasefire," adding self-righteously, "This I do not believe." While even Johnson attacked Nixon's "ugly and unfair charges," Nixon instructed Mitchell to call Chennault again on his behalf and have her say, "It's very important that our Vietnamese friends understand our Republican position and I hope you have made that clear to them."[60] Nixon appeared ready to do anything necessary to win the election, even if it meant conspiring with a foreign power and prolonging a war that most Americans wanted to end.

On October 31, Johnson and Humphrey spoke on the phone to discuss Nixon's dissembling, the GOP's attempt to influence the election, and the president's decision to make a radical change to the U.S. negotiating position in Paris. The always calculating and self-aggrandizing LBJ described the statement he would make that evening—which Johnson and his closest advisers had discussed for several weeks—and pressed Humphrey to "let all the laurels come to me," to say that everyone supported the administration and that the bombing halt followed Johnson's "San Antonio Formula," which promised a halt if "productive" talks promptly followed. Humphrey, as he typically did, acquiesced to the president's demands. The vice president was aware that if he made any public statements about Nixon's tactics without citing proof of his actions—which he would not have, as Johnson refused to provide the surveillance tapes to the campaign—any charge he might make about Nixon's treasonous activities would be dismissed as a desperate campaign ploy.[61] Thus, Humphrey found himself once again taking a backseat to the president, this time on a policy change that the vice president had initially proposed but that LBJ was now going to appropriate.

In his address to the nation that night, Johnson rehearsed the explanation of the administration's efforts to end the war over the past six months, with an emphasis on his personal and granular involvement in the process. He

then announced that he had "ordered that all air, naval, and artillery bombardment of North Vietnam cease as of 8 a.m. Washington time, Friday
morning," based on the developments in the Paris negotiations. Serious peace
talks would subsequently begin on November 6—the day after the presidential election. Johnson noted that he had informed all three of the candidates of
his decision and that this did not represent a departure from administration
policy, as it "very closely conforms to the statements that I have made in the
past concerning a bombing cessation." LBJ assured the country that, based
on his consultations with the Joint Chiefs of Staff and General Abrams, "this
action would not result in any increase in American casualties." In addition,
the president announced that when talks resumed on November 6, representatives of the NLF would be present, and representatives of the Saigon
government would be "free to participate." All of this meant that the United
States expected "prompt, productive, serious, and intensive negotiations in
an atmosphere that is conducive to progress" toward "an early peace." Johnson concluded by claiming that he had "devoted every resource of the Presidency to the search for peace in Southeast Asia" but had not allowed politics
to enter into the process: "I have kept all of the presidential candidates fully
briefed on developments in Paris as well as in Vietnam. I have made it
abundantly clear that no one candidate would have the advantage over others."[62]

It was an amazing turn of events, to be sure. LBJ not only positioned
himself as the peacemaker but also had managed to undermine Nixon's efforts with the South Vietnamese and undercut Humphrey's status as the
peace candidate at the same time. The Nixon campaign was predictably
enraged, framing the announcement as a blatant attempt to throw the election
to the vice president. For his part, Humphrey realized that he had been
outmaneuvered and hoped to make the best of the situation in the waning
days of the race. The day after the speech, Humphrey spoke to supporters in
Chicago. He noted that the campaign had "come a long way" since the
Democratic convention in August, speaking graciously about Eugene
McCarthy's "courage to speak out from his conscience on Vietnam" and
attacking Nixon vigorously. He then talked about Johnson's announcement,
calling it "a wise, a firm, and a courageous step toward ending the cruel war
in Vietnam—a step that a united Democratic Party can support." But at this
late date, the vice president largely avoided the subject of the war, preferring
instead to focus on less mercurial domestic issues and more popular international issues like nuclear nonproliferation. He sounded much more like the
pre-1964 Happy Warrior, full of optimism, joy, and eagerness to improve the
lives of his fellow citizens. Had Humphrey given speeches like this more
frequently—and spoken out on Vietnam earlier—perhaps his electoral fate
would have turned out differently.[63]

Yet, for all the problems Vietnam had caused for Hubert Humphrey, in the final days of the 1968 presidential campaign, the war nearly won the White House for him. While Humphrey and Nixon had avoided the conflict as much as possible, in the aftermath of the Salt Lake City speech and Johnson's dramatic announcement of the bombing halt, Humphrey had closed the gap with Nixon in the polls, thanks to the return of previously disaffected Democratic voters. Even before LBJ's statement, Humphrey had been rallying. A Harris poll taken just before the president spoke showed the Democratic candidate within three points of Nixon, only one point outside of the margin of error. As Warren Weaver Jr. wrote in the *New York Times*, "The fact that the late-blooming Vietnam question almost immediately over-shadowed most other political controversies of the fall gave some indication of how short of material issues the Nixon-Humphrey-Wallace contest had become."[64]

Moreover, in the week before the election, Stewart Alsop described Humphrey's campaign as "more genial" than Nixon's "in a disorganized, rather frantic sort of way." He also described it as "a bit sad," suggesting that Humphrey's candidacy likely marked "the swan song of the kind of liberalism that started more than 30 years ago with the New Deal" because "the plain fact seems to be that Hubert Humphrey and the rest of the liberal Democrats are fresh out of the kind of ideas that excite the interest and attract the adherence of the electorate."[65] But the bombing halt announcement did add to Humphrey's momentum as the campaign climaxed. By November 2, he had cut Nixon's once insurmountable Gallup poll lead to 42 to 40 percent; in the Harris poll, Humphrey had actually pulled ahead by 43 to 40 percent, with Wallace down to 13 percent.[66] It would be a sprint to the finish, and regardless of who ended up winning, it would be one of the closest presidential elections in U.S. history.

As the race entered its final hours, the long and complex relationship between Humphrey and Johnson would be encapsulated by the events of November 2 and 3. After campaigning in Maryland, the vice president arrived at the Oval Office a few minutes late for a meeting with LBJ. He was told that the president had already left for Texas. Humphrey, certain that LBJ was still in the White House, "said loudly that he had had enough of this stuff, and the president could 'cram it.'" The next morning, after rejecting a final opportunity to disclose Nixon's efforts to undermine the peace talks, Humphrey appeared on ABC's *Issues and Answers* to make a final pitch to the electorate and then flew to Texas to make his first joint campaign appearance with Johnson. At the rally, the president called Humphrey "my friend and co-worker for twenty years" and described him as a "healer and builder" who sought to inspire the American people. Later that night, Johnson told a national television audience that for "the sake of our American Union, Humphrey should and must become the 37th President of the United States."

Humphrey would later write that there was "no ambiguity about Lyndon Johnson that day. He strongly supported me. . . . That afternoon, at least, we seemed to have resolved whatever difficulties we had."[67] As much as the vice president may have desperately wished that to be true, it was an ephemeral hope that would evaporate over the next two days as Johnson and Nixon continued to consult behind the scenes without including Humphrey—more evidence for those who suggest that the president preferred the Republican candidate as his successor.

His deteriorating relationship with LBJ notwithstanding, Humphrey still held out hope that he would win. He told a rally at the Houston Astrodome on November 3, "I have sometimes set my face against the tide of public opinion—as I shall lead that opinion in the Presidency. For I believe that the Presidency is not worth winning, if winning it means compromising its integrity—or compromising the personal beliefs of the man who wins it." But that is exactly what he had done as vice president for four years, sublimating his integrity and principles to the demands of Lyndon Johnson. Indeed, as he said publicly to LBJ, who was in attendance at the rally,

> I shall enter the Presidency, Mr. President, because of your help knowing at least a little of what it means. I have served with a great President who has courageously borne the demanding and heavy burdens of his office, and I am proud, yes, very proud, to be the Vice President of the United States during the presidency of Lyndon Johnson. I have been, at least I have tried to be, and I will continue to be for all the years to come, his faithful friend, and during these months of his presidency, his loyal Vice President, and proud of it. [68]

Humphrey remained loyal to the end, despite Johnson's temporizing and lack of support in the campaign throughout the fall.

As the campaign reached its climax, Humphrey was cautiously optimistic about his chances, especially after the tremendous reception he received at a rally in Los Angeles the day before the election. On November 5, the morning of the election, Humphrey recalled that he woke up and thought to himself that if he prevailed in the balloting, he would "focus on getting the United States out of Vietnam. Fast. It's ripping the country apart." He planned to appoint Clark Clifford as secretary of state, Cyrus Vance as secretary of defense, and Henry Kissinger as a White House adviser—unaware that the Harvard professor had been secretly providing information to the Nixon campaign—all signs that he intended to make good on his promise to end the war as quickly as possible upon being elected. [69]

But neither Humphrey's plans for the war nor his hopes and dreams for the country would be realized. In one of the closest elections in U.S. history, Nixon won by a margin of only five hundred thousand votes out of over seventy-three million ballots cast. Humphrey was devastated by the defeat, but he accepted the verdict of the electorate. In his concession speech at 2:30

a.m. on November 6, Humphrey thanked his supporters and lamented that "We could have won it. We should have won it." Some bitterness did creep into his statement. He referred obliquely to some Democrats "who did not help"—undoubtedly a reference to Johnson as well as those McCarthy–RFK supporters who never embraced the vice president's campaign—but he concluded that he had "done my best. I have lost. Mr. Nixon has won. The democratic process has worked its will. So let us get on with the urgent task of uniting our country."[70] With that, Humphrey slipped away from the podium and went to bed—not as president-elect but as the lame duck vice president. One can only wonder what private regrets and second thoughts he had about his presidential campaign strategy, his abiding and often inexplicable loyalty to LBJ, and his inability to resolve his ambivalence on the war over the previous four years.

In a eulogy for Humphrey's campaign, the *New York Times* editorialized that Humphrey had "tortured himself visibly with his long effort simultaneously to defend President Johnson on Vietnam while establishing himself as a candidate with ideas of his own on how to end the war."[71] Did Vietnam cost Hubert Humphrey the presidency? Almost certainly. Pollster George Gallup opined that Humphrey "probably" would have won if the election had occurred a few days later, which suggests that had the vice president made the break with the administration earlier, he might have pulled off the upset.[72] Scholars and pundits could speculate endlessly on counterfactual scenarios that envision a prospective electoral victory and subsequent presidency for the Minnesotan. Yet the historical evidence is incontrovertible on one point: with regard to the war, Humphrey's choice to privilege loyalty to Lyndon Johnson over the political realities of the campaign and his own principles cost him the election. While his electoral defeat would not mark the end of his political career, his presidential ambitions had been fatally damaged by his failure to grapple successfully with the Vietnam conflict.

Conclusion

Humphrey's Faustian Bargain

Had I been elected, we would now be out of that war.
—Hubert Humphrey, January 1972

Politics have no relation to morals.
—Niccolò Machiavelli

Hubert Humphrey's political career did not come to an end after losing the presidential election to Richard Nixon. Instead, he quickly returned to public life, defeating former Nixon aide Clark MacGregor to fill Eugene McCarthy's seat in the U.S. Senate in the 1970 midterm election, a seat he would hold until his untimely death from bladder cancer in January 1978. Humphrey made it clear that he wanted to be a "harmonizer" within the Democratic Party going into the next presidential election cycle, hoping to help avoid the dissent and internecine attacks that had crippled the party in 1968.[1] Yet the former vice president's political ambitions simply would not fade away; he had come so close to the White House that he believed that he could defeat Nixon in a rematch. Thus, a little over a year later, Humphrey announced his candidacy for the 1972 Democratic presidential nomination in a speech in Philadelphia. The now-junior senator from Minnesota asserted that he was running for the White House on a platform of "reconciliation, rebuilding, and rebirth," which included revitalizing the U.S. economy, fixing the problems with U.S. cities and the environment, and renewing the country's faith in itself, among other issues.

But Humphrey focused the pivotal portions of his speech on attacking the "failures" of the Nixon administration—which he accused of exhibiting "sus-

131

tained indifference" toward the country's problems and suffering from "limited vision and understanding"—and on positioning himself as an opponent
of the war in Vietnam. While he admitted that he had served as vice president
during the period of the heaviest U.S. involvement there and attempted to
deflect responsibility for the conflict by pointing out that the war was the
product of "three Presidents who felt that our Vietnam involvement was
essential to our national security," he asserted that such a position was "no
longer valid." He reminded his audience that he had committed to "an end to
the bombing, a cease-fire, and an immediate troop withdrawal program" in
the 1968 campaign and insisted that he would have carried out those promises had he been elected. Meanwhile, he observed, Nixon had been unable or
unwilling to find a way out of the quagmire in Southeast Asia over the
previous three years. Therefore, Humphrey argued, "Our urgent immediate
need is to end the war and to do it now. . . . It is taking Mr. Nixon longer to
withdraw our troops than it took us to defeat Hitler. Had I been elected, we
would now be out of that war. I repeat that pledge."[2]

Yet simply stating his opposition to the conflict and confirming his intent
to end it would not be enough to overcome the lingering association with
Vietnam that hung like a millstone around Humphrey's neck. While he still
retained support from the constituencies within the Democratic Party that had
traditionally been in his corner—organized labor and minority groups, especially African Americans—the senator struggled with his lack of appeal
among young voters, which derived largely from his negative association
with the war in Vietnam. Moreover, Humphrey believed he could follow the
same path that he had in 1968, relying on the support of the party establishment and political maneuvering at the convention to obtain the requisite
support among Democratic delegates that he needed to secure the nomination. What he failed to appreciate, however, was the decisive role that the
primaries would play in the nominating process in 1972.[3] In the end, due to a
combination of his comparatively weak campaign organization, his impru-
dent strategic approach to the race, and his inescapable connection to the
war, Humphrey could not defeat Senator George McGovern (D-SD)—whose
antiwar credentials defined both his campaign and his career to a significant
degree—for the Democratic nomination.[4] Once again, the Vietnam conflict
played a crucial role in causing insurmountable and ultimately fatal problems
for Humphrey's presidential aspirations.

* * * * *

That Hubert Humphrey struggled so mightily and completely with the Vietnam War is one of the great ironies of twentieth-century U.S. political history. For Humphrey, Vietnam should have been an issue of absolute clarity
given the liberal principles he had championed and personified throughout

his career, from Minneapolis to the Senate to the vice presidency. Even factoring in his strident (bordering on militant) anticommunism in the 1940s and 1950s, his commitment to peace and social justice both at home and abroad should have definitively shaped his position on the conflict in Southeast Asia. Indeed, his presidential campaign in 1968 could have—and certainly should have—more directly reflected the principles that gave rise to his opposition to escalation and bombing and that elicited his February 1965 memorandum to LBJ. After all, this was the same man who forcefully, courageously, and successfully challenged the recalcitrant Democratic convention on civil rights in 1948.

Yet deciding where to stand on the Vietnam conflict had not been a facile or binary choice for Humphrey. He could not simply rely on his principles to guide him. Complicating the issue was the ambiguous and complex series of calculations he had to make based on a combination of loyalty, principle, and politics. To be sure, Humphrey rationalized his support for the war to a significant degree based on his support for the Great Society. But Humphrey first chose and then was forced to make choices based on his commitment to a shifting hierarchy of values, and that taxonomy came to privilege his relationship with Lyndon Johnson above all other factors. Loyalty—particularly allegiance to LBJ—came before politics, and both that fealty and political considerations overshadowed Humphrey's principles. Taken individually and collectively, these three factors underscore the critical—indeed, often decisive—nature of the overarching theme of this book: the intersection of domestic politics and U.S. foreign policy and their reciprocal influences on each other. The countervailing tensions created by Humphrey's devotion to these three frequently contradictory concepts placed the vice president in a nearly impossible situation as he grappled with the Vietnam conflict from 1964 through 1968.

Loyalty can be a virtue, but it can also lead to tragedy when taken too far. Classical literature teems with examples of that phenomenon, and one need only witness some of the sycophantic behavior exhibited by supporters of Richard Nixon or Donald Trump to understand that reality. As *Boston Globe* columnist Jeff Jacoby opined, "Loyalty in friends is a splendid trait, but loyalty above all? That isn't the mark of good character, it's a danger sign."[5] It was also a sign Humphrey failed to recognize. By accepting the terms of Lyndon Johnson's friendship, support, and largesse, the Minnesota senator ignored his own priorities and ceded control of his political destiny to a politician whose sole focus was his own success and who demanded absolute fidelity. LBJ once said of a prospective aide, "I don't want loyalty. I want *loyalty*. I want him to kiss my ass in Macy's window at high noon and tell me it smells like roses. I want his pecker in my pocket."[6] That is exactly what Johnson expected from Hubert Humphrey, and that is exactly what the president got.

The price of Humphrey's loyalty was privileging LBJ's perspective, principles, and politics over his own. By demonstrating a willingness to pay that price—no matter the ancillary costs to himself, his political ambitions, or the country—Humphrey not only lost the respect of his liberal friends and allies but also found himself trapped in an inextricable conundrum on the war, bearing a burden that cost him the presidency. There was nothing else that he could do, however, having accepted the fundamentally transactional nature of his political alliance with LBJ since their time together in the Senate in the 1950s. That relationship is absolutely crucial to understanding Humphrey's conflict over Vietnam. Humphrey wanted to be in the center of and influential in U.S. politics in the Senate, and he wanted to be president even more. Johnson dangled the prospect of both in exchange for Humphrey's loyalty, devotion, and support—not to mention as a valuable progressive aegis for his own political aspirations—and would never let his vice president forget the terms to which he agreed. It is perhaps too easy to cast Humphrey as Faust and LBJ as Mephistopheles in this tale, but it is also a brutally accurate description of their relationship.

One anecdote from the postelection period is quite revealing. Shortly after returning to Capitol Hill in 1971, Humphrey met with his long-time speechwriter Ted Van Dyk. The former vice president asked Van Dyk why they had lost the election in 1968. Van Dyk responded, "I thought we had lost, most of all, because voters had not gotten an early and clear picture of where he stood on the Vietnam War. 'For a long time you seemed weak and equivocal when voters wanted someone who was strong and unequivocal,' I said. 'Voters needed to know if you were with the antiwar forces or if you intended to just plain stick with Johnson.'" Humphrey considered Van Dyk's statement and replied, "You're right. . . . I've thought about it often. I should have stuck with Johnson."[7] It is an astonishing declaration, one that not only demonstrates an amazing level of residual loyalty to the former president but also utterly ignores the political realities and outcome of the 1968 campaign. For Humphrey, however, it was an indication of just how completely his Faustian bargain with LBJ had altered his perspective and determined his choices and responses.

But, in retrospect, Humphrey was not the only political or bureaucratic figure who found himself enmeshed in the web of loyalty spun by Lyndon Johnson. The historical record is replete with similar, if not as historically significant or damaging, examples. It is more of a challenge to discuss the existence and influence of principles in the realms of politics and foreign policy. To some, that may be a cynical view; to others, it is simply a realistic assessment of the vagaries of two arenas defined by conflict and compromise. Similarly, politics and political considerations, as we have seen, have driven decisions throughout the history of U.S. foreign relations. For Humphrey, the politics of the Great Society contributed to his willingness to support a war about which he had significant questions. But embracing LBJ as he did meant accepting the president's political agenda and priorities, and that meant advocating for the conflict regardless of the effect the fighting in Southeast Asia had on domestic reform programs or Humphrey's political fortunes.

The limits of loyalty, the influence of principle, and the power of politics appear in various guises throughout the history of U.S. foreign relations. In most cases, principle gives way to other considerations. Yet on occasion, personal or party loyalties and political expediency take a backseat to idealism, ethics, and morality. Two of the most prominent historical examples are William Jennings Bryan and Cyrus Vance, both of whom resigned as secretary of state over policy differences with their respective administrations— Bryan over Woodrow Wilson's Anglophilia during the period of nominal U.S. neutrality in 1914–1915, and Vance because Jimmy Carter disregarded the principles Vance supported when the president attempted the military rescue of the hostages in Iran in 1980.[8] But perhaps the best comparative case demonstrating that it was not inevitable that these three ideas would affect Humphrey's Vietnam conflict so profoundly is the crusade against the war waged by Representative Paul N. "Pete" McCloskey (R-CA) and his eventual challenge to Richard Nixon for the 1972 Republican presidential nomination.

McCloskey owed his political career to his opposition to the war, having defeated the hawkish Shirley Temple Black for the GOP nomination in a special election to the House of Representatives in 1967. While most Republicans demonstrated a willingness to give Nixon the benefit of the doubt on Vietnam at the beginning of his presidency, McCloskey did not display such patience. He stood virtually alone within the party in publicly opposing U.S. Vietnam policy from the beginning of Nixon's presidency and consistently berated the administration in public and private for its failure to take decisive steps to end the war. In late March 1969, for example, he wrote the first in a series of letters to Nixon in which he urged the president to act on his ambiguous campaign promises to bring a swift end to the conflict. McCloskey realized that the only way that U.S. policy would change would be to convince Nixon that it was in his best interest politically to do so, and he intended to accomplish this through reasoned argument—after all, McCloskey had been a successful attorney.

In the letter, McCloskey flatly stated, "In Viet Nam, we are wrong. We were wrong to seek to contain communism through massive victory force. . . . We were wrong in thinking we could win, or that we can yet win." Essentially, he asked Nixon to admit that Americanization of the war was wrong and that troop withdrawals would begin shortly, arguing that "Both you and the United States are big enough to admit past mistakes." Doing so would restore the credibility of the government in the eyes of the American people, "far more valuable than the credibility we will lose abroad and which Mr. Kissinger has urged as requiring our continued involvement in Viet Nam."[9] Attached to the letter was a more detailed memorandum from the congressman explaining his rationale. He argued that "our policy has been predicated upon the expectancy that with *enough* assistance, over a *reasonable* period of time, the Saigon government could achieve a sufficient degree of national cohesion to maintain its independence." For McCloskey, those assumptions were false, and no level of U.S. support for Vietnamization would change the fact that the conflict was "essentially a civil war." He urged Nixon to begin withdrawal of U.S. troops within ninety days, suggesting that the "success or failure of the Nixon administration will be determined by its ability to extricate the U.S. from its massive military commitment in Viet Nam . . . by the 1970 congressional elections."[10]

By appealing to Nixon using the logic of domestic political considerations, McCloskey hoped to prod the president to take action based on his overriding fixation with electoral success, both in the forthcoming midterms the following year and in Nixon's bid for a second term in 1972. McCloskey would "not support President Nixon so long as he continues his bombing policies. I think the policy of continued killing in Southeast Asia transcends any concept of loyalty or partisan politics."[11] Despite his best efforts, however, the California Republican failed to convince the administration to institute the policy changes he recommended. Rather than falling in line like so many others in the GOP, McCloskey continued to inundate Nixon with letters over the next three years, pleading with the president to end the war. Eventually, McCloskey had had enough. His absolute opposition to the war and the devastation it caused led him to make the decision to challenge Nixon for the 1972 Republican nomination despite his lack of presidential ambitions and the clear understanding that his candidacy was, at best, a quixotic quest that would almost inevitably end in defeat.

Though unsuccessful in both his efforts to persuade Nixon and his campaign for the nomination, Pete McCloskey acted on the courage of his convictions in opposing the Vietnam War. For the California congressman, Vietnam transcended politics; it was a moral issue on which he was willing to sacrifice his political career, if necessary, to bring the war to an end—much like the soldier he had once been, throwing himself on a grenade to save his comrades. Indeed, not only did McCloskey face intense opposition, isolation, and political backlash in California due to his breaking of the GOP's so-called "Eleventh Commandment," but the Nixon administration struck back fiercely at McCloskey for his disloyalty to both party and the president, supporting potential primary opponents and undermining his credibility and reputation.[12] Because of McCloskey's willingness to risk everything over a matter of principle, he had more in common with Bryan and Vance than most of the other antiwar politicians of the late 1960s and early 1970s in either the

Republican or the Democratic parties. For McCloskey, principle trumped party loyalty and any inherent political peril.

The contrast between McCloskey and Humphrey could not be more apparent or pronounced. Both attempted to sway a politically minded president to change his approach to the war in Vietnam using domestic political arguments at a moment of minimal political jeopardy. Yet when LBJ rejected Humphrey's memorandum and moved ahead with escalation, the vice president did not continue his efforts to change Johnson's position on the war. Instead, after suffering the humiliation of being banished from policy discussions relating to Vietnam, Humphrey enthusiastically embraced the conflict and became the administration's leading spokesman in support of the war. McCloskey, in the same position, continued his ferocious and relentless attacks on U.S. policy. When Humphrey ran for president in 1968, he refused—until far too late in the campaign—to break with the president despite the fact that the political wisdom of doing so was manifestly obvious to everyone around him. McCloskey, in the same position, ran a Sisyphean campaign doomed to failure for obvious political reasons, but he did so without hesitation or regret. To be sure, their respective roles informed how both responded to the president with whom they dealt. A member of Congress does not face the same constraints or considerations as the vice president. Yet one cannot help but wonder how differently the U.S. experience in Vietnam might have evolved had Hubert Humphrey possessed the intestinal fortitude and commitment to principle that Pete McCloskey exhibited.

There are, of course, other intriguing counterfactuals to consider as well. What if Humphrey had not accepted the vice presidency in 1964? Would he have remained committed to his principles and free from the self-imposed restrictions based on his loyalty to the president, and would he have been an outspoken skeptic of escalation in Southeast Asia from his seat on the Senate Foreign Relations Committee? Quite possibly. In fact, Humphrey suggested as much in his memoirs. Had that been the case, then perhaps Humphrey would have emerged as the leading antiwar candidate in 1968, one who would have been both palatable to the Democratic Party's establishment and appealing to the disenchanted antiwar forces, ADA liberals, and youth activists in the party. The tragedy of Humphrey's February 1965 memorandum to LBJ is that it represents one of the many key turning points where the disastrous Vietnam War could have been avoided or, at the very least, limited. It was an opportunity lost. It is also interesting to consider what might have happened had Humphrey broken with the administration earlier than his Salt Lake City speech—as his advisers had suggested repeatedly throughout 1968. Had he done so, would that have propelled him to defeat Nixon in November? If so, how differently (and rapidly) would the denouement of the war have played out? And how differently would the history of the 1970s have evolved without the shadow of Watergate? One thing is certain, however: Humphrey's inability to value his own principles over political considerations or his allegiance to LBJ would have serious ramifications for his own career and the future of the country.

In his impressive and detailed biography of Humphrey, Arnold Offner refers admiringly to the former vice president as the "conscience of the country."[13] That appellation may be accurate when considering domestic issues like civil rights and Medicare, or foreign policy issues such as nuclear weapons. Moreover, Humphrey should absolutely be recognized as one of the most influential legislators of the twentieth century. But when it came to Vietnam, the Minnesotan's conscience was obscured, confused, and overruled by his nearly inviolable Faustian allegiance to Lyndon Johnson and his own prioritization of politics over principle. For four years, he was an enigma, full of contradictions and cognitive dissonance on the war. The results can only be described as tragic for the country and devastating for Humphrey's political career and historical reputation. Like so many others of his generation, Hubert Humphrey's ambitions and legacy were sacrificed on the altar of the Vietnam conflict, a war that continues to reverberate and have significant ramifications for the country over five decades later.

Acknowledgments

One of my pet peeves in undergraduate papers is when they begin with something like "Since the beginning of time . . ." or "Throughout the history of the world . . ." You can almost hear Carl Sagan reading the essay. Sadly, those introductory phrases would almost describe how long this project has been gestating. I am reminded of the lyrics of the classic Pink Floyd song "Time" from the epic 1973 album, *Dark Side of the Moon*: "You are young, and life is long, and there is time to kill today, and then one day you find ten years have got behind you."

David Anderson, editor of the *Vietnam: America in the War Years* book series, a brilliant historian of the Vietnam conflict and a great friend and mentor to me for over two decades, has been *extraordinarily* patient (and that may be the understatement of those two decades!) waiting for this book to appear. Over the years since we first discussed this project, he gently prodded me at conferences and via e-mail, always graciously accepting my increasingly feeble excuses for the lengthening delay in completing the manuscript and never failing to provide generous support, encouragement, and understanding. More recently, he provided thoughtful comments and expert feedback on the entire manuscript when it finally materialized on his desk, hopefully not shocking him too much when it did arrive. I am deeply grateful for the opportunity to work with him on this project.

As with any book, plenty of others deserve recognition for helping to make it a reality. Jon Sisk, Dina Guilak, Elaine McGarraugh, and the entire publishing team at Rowman & Littlefield earned my thanks for their faith in the original proposal, lo those many years ago, for their tremendous patience and support over the years, and for bringing this book to publication so quickly. Jon, like David, always took the time to encourage me at conferences and never played the guilt card (despite having every right to do so);

instead, he invariably asked about my family and life in general, which I deeply appreciated. If you ever have the opportunity to work with Jon, do not hesitate; it will be a terrific experience.

I am grateful for the financial support over the years that made the research on the book possible, specifically for grants from the Minnesota Historical Society (Visiting Scholar Grant), the Lyndon Baines Johnson Foundation (Moody Research Grant), SunWest Endodontics, Brigham Young University (two Family, Home and Social Sciences research grants), and the David M. Kennedy Center for International Studies. On a related note, the archivists at the collections in which I conducted research for this book, especially those at the Minnesota Historical Society and the Lyndon Baines Johnson Presidential Library, are consummate professionals whose knowledge of their respective archives was invaluable to me during my long hours reading documents, taking notes, and making copies (I'm not competent enough with technology to use a digital camera for research . . . plus, the "old ways" are better).

I can trace the idea for a book on Hubert Humphrey and the Vietnam conflict to two *very* different sources. The first was a suggestion from Fred Logevall, who initially drew my attention to the significance of Humphrey's February 1965 memorandum to LBJ, that this could be a terrific book project. The second came from a series of conversations with my good friend Michael Alaimo during Monday night poker games. Michael, who has appeared in *The China Syndrome*, *Space Jam*, and *Mr. Mom*, among many other films and TV shows, was quite active in protesting against the Vietnam War in the 1960s, including his involvement with Jane Fonda and Donald Sutherland in their touring protest-cum-vaudeville show, *Free the Army*. We talked a lot about the war and about Humphrey's 1968 campaign, which sparked my interest even further. I definitely miss trading stories (and poker chips) with Michael every week.

I would also like to thank Michael Brenes, Mitch Lerner, Jason Parker, and David Schmitz for reading portions of the manuscript and providing excellent suggestions on how to improve the narrative and arguments. It really helps to have friends who are smarter than you are (insert joke about that being a low bar here). I appreciate the research assistance I received from Dan Combs, Russell Stevenson, and Andrew Skabelund; congratulations to all three for completing their respective graduate degrees, an MA for Dan (BYU), and PhDs for Russ (Michigan State) and Andrew (The Ohio State), in the years since they worked on this project.

My wife, Kayli, deserves boundless thanks (as always) for her nearly limitless patience as I grappled with the worst writer's block of my career (and complained about it endlessly to her) and then spent six months locked away in my office trying to finish an article, my PCB-AHA presidential address, and the Humphrey manuscript once my brain started working again.

After twenty-nine years of marriage (and counting), I should not be surprised by her love and support, but I do not know what I would do without it. I hope to be able to return the favor as she finishes her master's degree at BYU over the next couple of years. Thanks, too, to my adult children (Mitch, Matthew, and Jenna, along with Jenna's husband, Kade), my parents (Larry and Judy), and my dogs (Bentley and Bear) for their support along the way. And, last but not least, my granddaughter Rosie deserves recognition for keeping me grounded and focused on what is truly important in life.

Finally, thanks to the usual suspects—especially Molly Wood, Dustin Walcher, Ken Osgood, Jason Parker, Mitch Lerner, Lori Clune, Brian Etheridge, Kim Quinney, and Heather Dichter—for their frequent, merciless, and totally well-deserved ridicule over the years for not having the book done: it really did help motivate me, even if it took a couple of (okay, eighteen) years.

As always, whenever I complete an academic project, whether it is a book review or a book manuscript, my deepest gratitude and profound thanks go out to Kathryn Statler, who has read every word I have ever published, most of them at least twice. Kathryn provides brilliant insights and suggestions that make my writing and argumentation exponentially better, and she has been the best friend anyone could ask for over the past three decades since we started graduate school together. I owe her big time.

This book is dedicated to three teachers, without whom my life and career would look completely different. At Horizon High School from 1984 to 1986, Nanette Stark urged me to aim higher and achieve my potential rather than being satisfied with the easier path. At the University of Arizona during the 1987 spring semester, my honors sociology professor Michael Hechter first planted the seemingly ludicrous idea in my head that I might have a future in academia as a professor, which eventually helped to derail my nascent career as a lawyer after one semester of law school. Neil York has been a mentor, friend, confidant, and colleague at Brigham Young University for over thirty years and has inspired me, provided excellent advice, and pushed me to think more deeply and completely about what I was doing with my life and career (including his sage advice in October 1992: "You don't apply to graduate schools based on the success of their football teams!"). I cannot imagine where I would be today if not for their generosity, counsel, and influence. Thank you, sincerely.

Notes

INTRODUCTION

1. Andrew L. Johns, *Vietnam's Second Front: Domestic Politics, the Republican Party, and the War* (Lexington: University Press of Kentucky, 2010), 334. The list of prominent U.S. politicians whose career trajectories fell short of the White House or prematurely ended their tenure in the Oval Office owing to issues related to the Vietnam conflict includes Hubert Humphrey, Lyndon Johnson, George Romney, Eugene McCarthy, Richard Nixon, Nelson Rockefeller, George McGovern, Gerald Ford, Pete McCloskey, Barry Goldwater, John Kennedy (if one believes the conspiracy theorists who argue that his Vietnam policies led to his assassination), Jimmy Carter, and John Kerry.

2. Arnold A. Offner, *Hubert Humphrey: The Conscience of the Country* (New Haven, CT: Yale University Press, 2018).

3. See especially Robert Sherrill and Harry W. Ernst, *The Drugstore Liberal* (New York: Grossman Publishers, 1968). For example, Sherrill and Ernst refer to Humphrey's wavering on civil rights and shifting his position on labor as "his ambitions mounted. Nothing has made his beliefs so casual as the vice presidency." They also criticize him on Vietnam, opining that with Humphrey and the war issue, "fickleness comes first." See pages 12 and 174. Sherrill made similar comments about Lyndon Johnson, describing him as lacking any moral values whatsoever and characterizing him as "treacherous, dishonest, manic-aggressive, petty, spoiled." See Robert Sherrill, *The Accidental President* (New York: Grossman Publishers, 1967), 4.

4. Norman Ornstein, "Welcome to Another Golden Era of Liberal Senators," *The New Republic*, January 8, 2013, www.tnr.com/print/blog/plank/111731/liberal-wave-senate-pro-duces-third-golden-era-our-lifetime, accessed January 9, 2013.

5. David Halberstam, *The Unfinished Odyssey of Robert Kennedy* (New York: Random House, 1969), 165.

6. Edgar Berman, *Hubert: The Triumph and Tragedy of the Humphrey I Knew* (New York: G. P. Putnam's Sons, 1979), 101.

7. Hubert H. Humphrey, *Education of a Public Man: My Life and Politics* (Garden City, NY: Doubleday, 1976), 234.

8. Quoted in William E. Schmickle, *Preservation Politics: Keeping Historic Districts Vital* (Lanham, MD: Altamira Press, 2012), 93.

9. Quoted in "The President Giveth and Taketh," *Time*, November 14, 1969.

10. On the importance of domestic politics as a methodological approach in the history of U.S. foreign relations, see, for example, Ralph B. Levering, "Is Domestic Politics Being Slighted as an Interpretive Framework?" *SHAFR Newsletter* 25, no. 1 (March 1994): 17–35;

Jussi M. Hanhimäki, "Global Visions and Parochial Politics: The Persistent Dilemma of the 'American Century,'" *Diplomatic History* 27, no. 4 (September 2003): 423–47; Fredrik Logevall, "Domestic Politics," in Frank Costigliola and Michael J. Hogan, eds., *Explaining the History of American Foreign Relations*, 3rd ed. (New York: Cambridge University Press, 2016), 151–67; Jason Parker, "On Such a Full Sea Are We Now Afloat: Politics and U.S. Foreign Relations across the Water's Edge," *Perspectives*, May 2011, https://www.historians.org/publications-and-directories/perspectives-on-history/may-2011/political-history-today/on-such-a-full-sea-are-we-now-afloat; Thomas A. Schwartz, "'Henry, . . . Winning an Election Is Terribly Important': Partisan Politics in the History of U.S. Foreign Relations," *Diplomatic History* 33, no. 2 (April 2009): 173–90. Representative scholarship includes Melvin Small, *Democracy and Diplomacy: The Impact of Domestic Politics on U.S. Foreign Policy, 1789–1994* (Baltimore: Johns Hopkins University Press, 1996); Robert David Johnson, *Congress and the Cold War* (New York: Cambridge University Press, 2005); Andrew L. Johns and Mitchell B. Lerner, eds., *The Cold War at Home and Abroad: Domestic Politics and U.S. Foreign Policy since 1945* (Lexington: University Press of Kentucky, 2018); Julian E. Zelizer, *Arsenal of Democracy: The Politics of National Security—From World War II to the War on Terrorism* (New York: Basic Books, 2010); Johns, *Vietnam's Second Front*; Andrew Johnstone and Andrew Priest, eds., *U.S. Presidential Elections and Foreign Policy: Candidates, Campaigns, and Global Politics from FDR to Bill Clinton* (Lexington: University Press of Kentucky, 2017).

11. Dan Cohen, *Undefeated: The Life of Hubert H. Humphrey* (Minneapolis, MN: Lerner Publications, 1978); Carl Solberg, *Hubert Humphrey: A Biography* (New York: Norton, 1984); Offner, *Hubert Humphrey*. See also Sheldon Engelmayer, *Hubert Humphrey: The Man and His Dream* (London: Routledge, 1978); Paul Westman, *Hubert Humphrey: The Politics of Joy* (Minneapolis, MN: Dillon Press, 1978); Charles Lloyd Garrettson, *Hubert H. Humphrey: The Politics of Joy* (New Brunswick, NJ: Transaction Publishers, 1993).

12. Humphrey, *The Education of a Public Man*. On Humphrey's vision for the country as a U.S. senator, see Hubert H. Humphrey, *The Cause Is Mankind: A Liberal Program for Modern America* (New York: Praeger, 1964). For a compilation of Humphrey's public comments, see, for example, Jane C. Thompson, ed., *Wit & Wisdom of Hubert H. Humphrey* (Minneapolis, MN: Partners Press, Ltd., 1984). Most of the textual versions of Humphrey's public speeches (1941–1978) have been digitized by the Minnesota Historical Society and are available at http://www2.mnhs.org/library/findaids/00442.xml (accessed October 25, 2019). It should be noted, however, that Humphrey frequently went "off script" and spoke extemporaneously. In addition, many of his speeches on the Senate floor are not included in this digital collection.

13. Berman, *Hubert*; Ted Van Dyk, *Heroes, Hacks, and Fools: Memoirs from the Political Inside* (Seattle: University of Washington Press, 2007).

14. Timothy N. Thurber, *The Politics of Equality: Hubert H. Humphrey and the African American Freedom Struggle* (New York: Columbia University Press, 1999); Robert Mann, *The Walls of Jericho: Lyndon Johnson, Hubert Humphrey, Richard Russell, and the Struggle for Civil Rights* (New York: Harcourt Brace, 1996). See also Paula Wilson, ed., *The Civil Rights Rhetoric of Hubert H. Humphrey: 1948–1964* (Lanham, MD: University Press of America, 1996); Jennifer A. Delton, *Making Minnesota Liberal: Civil Rights and the Transformation of the Democratic Party* (Minneapolis: University of Minnesota Press, 2002).

15. See, for example, Clinton Anderson, *Outsider in the Senate* (New York: World Publishing Company, 1970); Michael Amrine, *This Is Humphrey: The Story of the Senator* (Garden City, NY: Doubleday & Co., 1960); Richard P. Jennett, *The Man from Minnesota* (Minneapolis, MN: Joyce Society, 1965); Winthrop Griffith, *Humphrey: A Candid Biography* (New York: Morrow, 1965); Gladys Zehnpfenning, *Hubert H. Humphrey: Champion of Human Rights* (Minneapolis, MN: T. S. Denison and Company, Inc., 1966).

16. The massive historiography on the 1968 presidential election includes Michael A. Cohen, *American Maelstrom: The 1968 Election and Politics of Division* (New York: Oxford University Press, 2016); Theodore White, *The Making of the President, 1968* (New York: Atheneum Publishers, 1969); Michael Nelson, *Resilient America: Electing Nixon in 1968, Channeling Dissent, and Dividing Government* (Lawrence: University Press of Kansas, 2014); Dan T. Carter, *The Politics of Rage: George Wallace, the Origins of the New Conservatism,*

and the Transformation of American Politics (New York: Simon & Schuster, 1995); Lawrence O'Donnell, *Playing with Fire: The 1968 Election and the Transformation of American Politics* (New York: Penguin, 2017); Michael Schumacher, *The Contest: The 1968 Election and the War for America's Soul* (Minneapolis: University of Minnesota Press, 2018); Lewis Chester, Godfrey Hodgson, and Bruce Page, *An American Melodrama: The Presidential Campaign of 1968* (New York: Viking Press, 1969); Lewis L. Gould, *1968: The Election That Changed America* (Chicago: Ivan R. Dee, 1993); Kyle Longley, *LBJ's 1968: Power, Politics, and the Presidency in America's Year of Upheaval* (New York: Cambridge University Press, 2018); Kent G. Sieg, "The 1968 Presidential Election and Peace in Vietnam," *Presidential Studies Quarterly* 16, no. 4 (Fall 1996): 1062–80; Walter LaFeber, *The Deadly Bet: LBJ, Vietnam, and the 1968 Election* (Lanham, MD: Rowman & Littlefield, 2005); Aram Goudsouzian, *The Men and the Moment: The Election of 1968 and the Rise of Partisan Politics in America* (Chapel Hill: University of North Carolina Press, 2019).

17. See, for example, Fredrik Logevall, *Choosing War: The Lost Chance for Peace and the Escalation of War in Vietnam* (Berkeley: University of California Press, 1999), 346–47; Humphrey, *The Education of a Public Man*, 236–42; Robert Mann, *A Grand Delusion: America's Descent into Vietnam* (New York: Basic Books, 2001), 401–8.

1. THE HAPPY (COLD) WARRIOR

1. Lewis Chester, Godfrey Hodgson, and Bruce Page, *An American Melodrama: The Presidential Campaign of 1968* (New York: Viking Press, 1969), 147.

2. *Newsweek*, November 9, 1964; Chester, Hodgson, and Page, *An American Melodrama*, 147.

3. *New York Times*, August 25, 1968.

4. Americans for Democratic Action was founded on January 3, 1947, by leading anticommunist liberals from academia, labor, and politics, including theologian Reinhold Niebuhr, historian Arthur Schlesinger Jr., Eleanor Roosevelt, labor organizer Walter Reuther, civil rights attorney Joseph Rauh, and Humphrey. It advocates progressive policies and social and economic justice. See Clifton Brock and Max Lerner, *Americans for Democratic Action: Its Role in National Politics*, rev. ed. (Whitefish, MT: Literary Licensing, 2012).

5. *Christian Science Monitor*, November 23, 1956; *Chicago Tribune*, April 6, 1958.

6. Humphrey's friend Bill Moyers, who had served as LBJ's press secretary from 1965 to 1967, recalled in a speech on June 23, 1998, that Humphrey earned the nickname "The Happy Warrior" because "he loved politics and because of his natural ebullience and resiliency." See Speech Transcript, June 23, 1998, https://billmoyers.com/1988/06/23/the-happy-warrior-june-23-1998/, accessed October 19, 2019.

7. *Chicago Tribune*, April 6, 1958; Charles Lloyd Garrettson III, *Hubert H. Humphrey: The Politics of Joy* (New Brunswick, NJ: Transaction Publishers, 1993), 276.

8. Robert Mann, *A Grand Delusion: America's Descent into Vietnam* (New York: Basic Books, 2001), 226; Arnold A. Offner, *Hubert Humphrey: The Conscience of the Country* (New Haven, CT: Yale University Press, 2018), 105–7. The McCarran Internal Security Act was enacted over Harry Truman's veto in 1950. See Public Law 81-831, 53 Stat. 987, September 23, 1950. The Communist Control Act of 1954 (Public Law 83-637, 68 Stat. 775) was passed by Congress on August 24, 1954. While the Supreme Court has never ruled on the constitutionality of the act, a federal district court in Arizona did hold that it was unconstitutional. See *Blawis, et. al.* v. *Bolin, et. al.*, 358 F. Supp. 349 (D. Ariz. 1973), May 8, 1973, https://law.justia.com/cases/federal/district-courts/FSupp/358/349/1412503/, accessed August 15, 2019. Humphrey's support of the CCA led left-wing journalist Murray Kempton to say in 1955 that the ADA should "unfrock" Humphrey as its vice chairman. In 1964, Humphrey would admit that the CCA was "not one of the things I'm proudest of." See Offner, *Hubert Humphrey*, 107.

9. Fredrik Logevall, "Lyndon Johnson and Vietnam," *Presidential Studies Quarterly* 34, no. 1 (March 2004): 108.

10. Carl Solberg, *Hubert Humphrey: A Biography* (New York: W. W. Norton & Company, 1984), 181. Because of this interest in international affairs, Humphrey was always sensitive to and cognizant of the domestic political implications of U.S. foreign policy—both for his own political prospects and in terms of how the two realms interacted.

11. For example, Dulles had written the 1952 GOP platform plank that referred to containment as a "futile, negative, and immoral" policy. Quoted in Offner, *Hubert Humphrey*, 107.

12. Transcript, Hubert Humphrey Oral History Interview, August 17, 1971, by Joe B. Frantz, p. 8, Lyndon Baines Johnson Presidential Library, Austin, TX (hereafter LBJL).

13. *Time*, September 4, 1964, 20. Humphrey's formal speeches were clocked at an astounding 250 words a minute. The Humphrey-Khrushchev conversation occurred after repeated requests by Humphrey to meet while he visited Moscow in the wake of Khrushchev's ultimatum to the Western powers that they transform Berlin into a demilitarized free city. See Offner, *Hubert Humphrey*, 138–42.

14. William Taubman, Sergei Khrushchev, and Abbot Gleason, *Nikita Khrushchev* (New Haven, CT: Yale University Press, 2000), 219.

15. Offner, *Hubert Humphrey*, 140–41. Herter and Dulles were so impressed with Humphrey's report and insights that they asked him to repeat the briefing to their subordinates, especially focusing on the success of Humphrey's "informal diplomacy" techniques.

16. The Point Four program was a technical assistance program announced by Harry Truman in his inaugural address on January 20, 1949, taking its name from the fact that it was the fourth foreign policy objective mentioned in the speech. It was the first U.S. plan for international economic development. See Thomas G. Paterson, "Foreign Aid under Wraps: The Point Four Program," *The Wisconsin Magazine of History* 56, no. 2 (Winter 1972–1973): 119–26. Public Law 480 (or Food for Peace) was the colloquial name for the Agricultural Trade Development and Assistance Act of 1954. It permitted the president to authorize the shipment of surplus commodities to "friendly" nations either on concessional or grant terms and established a broad basis for U.S. distribution of foreign food aid. See Thomas J. Knock, "Feeding the World and Thwarting the Communisists," in David F. Schmitz and T. Christopher Jespersen, eds., *Architects of the American Century: Individuals and Institutions in Twentieth-Century U.S. Foreign Policymaking* (Chicago: Imprint Publications, 2000). The Alliance for Progress was designed by the Kennedy administration to establish economic cooperation between the United States and Latin America in an effort to blunt the appeal of communism. It was a public relations success in the short term but is generally regarded as a failure. See, for example, Stephen G. Rabe, *The Most Dangerous Area in the World: John F. Kennedy Confronts Communist Revolution in Latin America* (Chapel Hill: University of North Carolina Press, 1999).

17. Speech, Humphrey at Yale University, December 7, 1959, 310.G.11.9B, Hubert H. Humphrey Papers, Minnesota Historical Society, St. Paul, MN (hereafter HHHP, MHS). In the speech, Humphrey discussed a wide range of topics related to disarmament, including the need for a test-ban treaty, regional arms control conferences, and the importance of inspections.

18. William Conrad Gibbons, *The U.S. Government and the Vietnam War: Part I, 1945–1960* (Princeton, NJ: Princeton University Press, 1986), 73; quoted in Mann, *A Grand Delusion*, 79–80.

19. Quoted in Mann, *A Grand Delusion*, 129.

20. Mann, *A Grand Delusion*, 158.

21. Gibbons, *The U.S. Government and the Vietnam War, Part I*, 166.

22. Statement, Humphrey on Indochina, April 19, 1954, 150.E.14.10F, HHHP, MHS.

23. On the transition from French to U.S. dominance in Vietnam in the 1950s, see especially Kathryn C. Statler, *Replacing France: The Origins of American Intervention in Vietnam* (Lexington: University Press of Kentucky, 2007); Fredrik Logevall, *Embers of War: The Fall of an Empire and the Making of America's Vietnam* (New York: Random House, 2012).

24. Hubert H. Humphrey, *The Education of a Public Man: My Life and Politics* (Minneapolis: University of Minnesota Press, 1991), 234.

25. William C. Berman, *William Fulbright and the Vietnam War: The Dissent of a Political Realist* (Kent, OH: Kent State University Press, 1988), 10.

26. William Conrad Gibbons, *The U.S. Government and the Vietnam War: Part II, 1961–1964* (Princeton, NJ: Princeton University Press, 1986), 126.

27. Humphrey, *The Education of a Public Man*, 235.

28. Albert Eisele, *Almost to the Presidency: A Biography of Two American Politicians* (Blue Earth, MN: Piper Co., 1972), 230.

29. Transcript, Hubert H. Humphrey Oral History Interview, August 17, 1971, by Joe B. Frantz, LBJL, 5; Transcript, Hubert H. Humphrey Oral History Interview III, June 21, 1977, by Michael L. Gillette, LBJL, 11.

30. Walter LaFeber, *The Deadly Bet: LBJ, Vietnam, and the 1968 Election* (Lanham, MD: Rowman & Littlefield, 2005), 121.

31. David Halberstam, *The Best and the Brightest* (New York: Ballantine Books, 1992), 433–35.

32. Mitchell Lerner makes a convincing argument that some of LBJ's ancillary duties as vice president—specifically his extensive international travel (eleven trips to thirty-three countries, covering 120,000 miles)—were "not nearly as unimportant as many believed (and as the Kennedy people often tried to suggest)." See Mitchell Lerner, "'A Big Tree of Peace and Justice': The Vice Presidential Travels of Lyndon Johnson," *Diplomatic History* 34, no. 2 (April 2010): 357–93 (quote from 359). On the role of the vice president in modern politics and foreign policy, see, for example, Joel K. Goldstein, *The Modern American Vice Presidency: The Transformation of a Political Institution* (Princeton, NJ: Princeton University Press, 1982); Paul Kengor, *Wreath Layer or Policy Player: The Vice President's Role in Foreign Policy* (Lanham, MD: Lexington Books, 2000).

33. Quoted in Erik van den Berg, "Supersalesman for the Great Society: Vice President Hubert H. Humphrey, 1965–1969," *American Studies International* 36, 3 (October 1998): 60.

34. Telephone conversation transcript, Hubert Humphrey and Lyndon Johnson, March 6, 1965, https://millercenter.org/the-presidency/secret-white-house-tapes/conversation-hubert-humphrey-march-6-1965-0, accessed October 7, 2019.

35. Halberstam, *The Best and the Brightest*, 531–35 (emphasis in original).

36. Lyndon Baines Johnson, *The Vantage Point: Perspectives of the Presidency, 1963–1969* (New York: Holt, Reinhart and Winston, 1971), 101.

37. Robert Dallek, *Flawed Giant: Lyndon Johnson and His Times, 1961–1973* (New York: Oxford University Press, 1998), 137.

38. *Newsweek*, April 13, 1964, 26.

39. Kenneth Crawford, "HHH Anonymous," *Newsweek*, January 11, 1965, 32.

40. Randall B. Woods, *LBJ: Architect of American Ambition* (New York: Free Press, 2006), 533; *Newsweek*, November 9, 1964, 30.

41. In social science, role theory suggests that each role or office has a set of expectations, behaviors, and responsibilities with which a person must grapple and fulfill, which influences the locus of possible options for rhetoric and decision-making.

42. Chester, Hodgson, and Page, *An American Melodrama*, 148.

43. Mann, *A Grand Delusion*, 339.

44. Memorandum, John Reilly to Hubert Humphrey, June 8, 1964, HHH Vice Presidential Files, 1965–1968, Foreign Affairs General Files, 150.E.14.1B, MHS.

45. Quoted in Gibbons, *The U.S. Government and the Vietnam War, Part II*, 278; Memorandum, Hubert Humphrey to Lyndon Johnson, June 8, 1964, 150.D.10.1B, HHHP, MHS. See also Van Dyk, *Heroes, Hacks, and Fools*, 29.

46. On the Gulf of Tonkin attacks, see especially Edwin E. Moïse, *Tonkin Gulf and the Escalation of the Vietnam War* (Chapel Hill: University of North Carolina Press, 1996).

47. Telephone conversation transcript, Lyndon Johnson and Robert Kennedy, May 28, 1964, quoted in Michael R. Beschloss, ed., *Taking Charge: The Johnson White House Tapes, 1963–1964* (New York: Simon & Schuster, 1997), 499 (emphasis in original).

48. Eisele, *Almost to the Presidency*, 229.

49. *Congressional Record* (Senate), August 6, 1964, 17836-17837.

50. On Vietnam and the 1964 presidential campaign, see, for example, Andrew L. Johns, "Mortgaging the Future: Barry Goldwater, Lyndon Johnson, and Vietnam in the 1964 Presidential Election," *Journal of Arizona History* 61, no. 1 (Spring 2020): 149–60.

51. Speech, Humphrey at Los Angeles town hall meeting, August 17, 1964, 310.G.12.4F, HHHP, MHS.

52. Robert David Johnson, *All the Way with LBJ: The 1964 Presidential Election* (New York: Cambridge University Press, 2009), 194.

53. *New York Times*, August 28, 1964.

54. Offner, *Hubert Humphrey*, 208.

55. "Humphrey and Rauh," *National Review Bulletin* 16, no. 37 (September 15, 1964): 1.

56. Johnson, *All the Way with LBJ*, 243.

57. Quoted in *Time*, September 4, 1964, 20.

58. Speech, Hubert Humphrey, October 26, 1964, Thomson Papers, box 12, John F. Kennedy Presidential Library, Boston, MA (hereafter JFKL).

59. Johnson, *All the Way with LBJ*, 16.

60. *U.S. News & World Report*, November 16, 1964, 58.

61. Solberg, *Hubert Humphrey*, 265.

62. Quoted in Fredrik Logevall, *Choosing War: The Lost Chance for Peace and the Escalation of the War in Vietnam* (Berkeley: University of California Press, 1999), 287.

63. Melvin Small, *Johnson, Nixon, and the Doves* (New Brunswick, NJ: Rutgers University Press, 1988), 29; quoted in David M. Barrett, *Uncertain Warriors: Lyndon Johnson and His Vietnam Advisers* (Lawrence: University Press of Kansas, 1993), 18.

64. Quoted in David M. Barrett, *Uncertain Warriors: Lyndon Johnson and His Vietnam Advisors* (Lawrence: University Press of Kansas, 1993), 19. Johnson's recollections about his relationship with Kennedy are supported by William Bundy, George Ball, and others. Interestingly, however, Humphrey's memoirs make no mention of Johnson's strong desire for Humphrey's "reticence in White House meetings."

65. There is a substantial literature on the planning that occurred within the administration throughout 1964, including Larry Berman, *Planning a Tragedy: The Americanization of the War in Vietnam* (New York: W. W. Norton & Company, 1983); Logevall, *Choosing War*; Mann, *A Grand Delusion*; and Brian VanDeMark, *Road to Disaster: A New History of America's Descent into Vietnam* (New York: Custom House, 2018).

2. NO GOOD DEED GOES UNPUNISHED

1. Quoted in *U.S. News & World Report*, July 1, 1968, 39.

2. Andrew L. Johns, *Vietnam's Second Front: Domestic Politics, the Republican Party, and the War* (Lexington: University of Kentucky Press, 2010), 80.

3. Telephone conversation transcript, McGeorge Bundy and Lyndon Johnson, March 2, 1964, https://millercenter.org/the-presidency/secret-white-house-tapes/conversation-mcgeorge-bundy-march-2-1964-1, accessed October 7, 2019.

4. Memorandum, John Rielly to Hubert Humphrey, November 16, 1964, 150.D.10.4F, HHHP, MHS.

5. Robert Mann, *A Grand Delusion: America's Descent into Vietnam* (New York: Basic Books, 2001), 401.

6. William Conrad Gibbons, *The U.S. Government and the Vietnam War: Executive and Legislative Roles and Relationships, Part III: January-July 1965* (Princeton, NJ: Princeton University Press, 1989), 37.

7. Fredrik Logevall, *Choosing War: The Lost Chance for Peace and the Escalation of the War in Vietnam* (Berkeley: University of California Press, 1999), 310.

8. Memorandum, January 27, 1965, Bundy to Johnson, NSF/Memos to the President, McGeorge Bundy, LBJL.

9. Quoted in Gibbons, *The U.S. Government and the Vietnam War, Part III*, 49.

10. Letter, Frank Church to Hubert Humphrey, January 29, 1965, 150.E.13.4F, HHHP, MHS.

11. Quoted in Gibbons, *The U.S. Government and the Vietnam War, Part III*, 61.

12. George W. Ball, *The Past Has Another Pattern: Memoirs* (New York: W. W. Norton & Company, 1983), 390; Hubert H. Humphrey, *The Education of a Public Man: My Life and Politics* (Minneapolis: University of Minnesota Press, 1991), 237. Llewellyn Thompson also

expressed reservations about the bombing strikes. See Gibbons, *The U.S. Government and the Vietnam War, Part III*, 78.

13. Humphrey, *Education of a Public Man*, 237; Carl Solberg, *Hubert Humphrey: A Biography* (New York: W. W. Norton & Company, 1984), 271.

14. Offner, *Hubert Humphrey*, 227; Solberg, *Hubert Humphrey*, 271–72; Logevall, *Choosing War*, 346.

15. Andrew Preston, *The War Council: McGeorge Bundy, the NSC, and Vietnam* (Cambridge, MA: Harvard University Press, 2006), 180–81.

16. Gibbons, *The U.S. Government and the Vietnam War, Part III*, 92.

17. Fredrik Logevall suggests that the "right-wing beast" Johnson feared did not exist in early 1965. See Logevall, "Comment on Francis M. Bator's 'No Good Choices: LBJ and the Vietnam/Great Society Connection,'" *Diplomatic History* 32, no. 3 (June 2008): 355–59. The counterargument for the existence of such a threat is made in Johns, *Vietnam's Second Front*, 328.

18. Memorandum, Hubert Humphrey to Lyndon Johnson, February 17, 1965, 150.D.10.1B, HHHP, MHS. The version of the memorandum given to the president (apparently through Bill Moyers) is found in U.S. Department of State, *Foreign Relations of the United States, 1964–1968*, vol. II: *Vietnam, January–June 1965* (Washington, DC: U.S. Government Printing Office, 1996), 309–10 (hereafter *FRUS*, volume information). An earlier version of the memorandum dated February 15, 1965, appears in Humphrey, *Education of a Public Man*, 238–41.

19. Quoted in Albert Eisele, *Almost to the Presidency: A Biography of Two American Politicians* (Blue Earth, MN: The Piper Company, 1972), 233; see also Ted Van Dyk, *Heroes, Hacks, and Fools: Memoirs from the Political Inside* (Seattle: University of Washington Press, 2007), 41.

20. Edgar Berman, *Hubert: The Triumph and Tragedy of the Humphrey I Knew* (New York: Putnam, 1979), 106.

21. Solberg, *Hubert Humphrey*, 272.

22. Logevall, *Choosing War*, 346.

23. Michael A. Cohen, *American Maelstrom: The 1968 Election and the Politics of Division* (New York: Oxford University Press, 2016), 71.

24. At this point in the conflict, Johnson received more support for escalating the conflict in Vietnam from Republicans, including key figures like former President Dwight D. Eisenhower and House Minority Leader Gerald Ford (R-MI) than he did from his own party. See Johns, *Vietnam's Second Front*, especially chapters 2–3. On the need to "sell" policy to the public, see, for example, Kenneth Osgood and Andrew K. Frank, eds., *Selling War in a Media Age: The Presidency and Public Opinion in the American Century* (Gainesville: University Press of Florida, 2010).

25. Offner, *Hubert Humphrey*, 228.

26. Mann, *A Grand Delusion*, 404, 407; Solberg, *Hubert Humphrey*, 273.

27. This argument is discussed in Francis M. Bator, "No Good Choices: LBJ and the Vietnam/Great Society Connection," *Diplomatic History* 32, no. 3 (June 2008): 309–40. The article is part of a forum that includes responses to Bator from Evan Thomas, Randall B. Woods, Marilyn B. Young, Mark Moyar, Fredrik Logveall, and Larry Berman.

28. Quoted in Mann, *A Grand Delusion*, 408. On Eisenhower's meeting with LBJ, see Johns, *Vietnam's Second Front*, 86–90.

29. Solberg, *Hubert Humphrey*, 274.

30. Barrett, *Uncertain Warriors*, 20; Offner, *Hubert Humphrey*, 229.

31. *Time*, February 12, 1965, 15.

32. Offner, *Hubert Humphrey*, 228.

33. Mann, *A Grand Delusion*, 405.

34. On how to most effectively engage in counterfactual historical analysis, see Phililp Nash, "The Use of Counterfactuals in History: A Look at the Literature," *The Society for Historians of American Foreign Relations Newsletter* 22, no. 1 (March 1991): 2–12; Fredrik Logevall, "Vietnam and the Question of What Might Have Been," in Mark J. White, ed., *Kennedy: The New Frontier Revisited* (London: Palgrave, 1998), 19–62; Niall Ferguson, ed., *Virtual History: Alternatives and Counterfactuals* (New York: Macmillan, 1997); and the four

essays that appear in "Counterfactual Analysis in Security Studies: A Symposium," in *Security Studies* 24, no. 3 (2015): 377–430.

35. Offner, *Hubert Humphrey*, 230.

36. David M. Barrett, *Uncertain Warriors: Lyndon Johnson and His Vietnam Advisors* (Lawrence: University Press of Kansas, 1993), 20.

37. Berman, *Hubert*, 92, 104; Van Dyk, *Heroes, Hacks, and Fools*, 43.

38. Humphrey, *Education of a Public Man*, 242; Mann, *A Grand Delusion*, 499.

39. Eisele, *Almost to the Presidency*, 234.

40. Eisele, *Almost to the Presidency*, 234–35.

41. Mann, *A Grand Delusion*, 414–15.

42. Humphrey, *Education of a Public Man*, 244.

43. David English, *Divided They Stand* (Englewood Cliffs, NJ: Prentice-Hall, Inc., 1969), 216. On the British perspective on U.S. involvement in Vietnam, see, for example, Eugenie M. Blang, *Allies at Odds: America, Europe, and Vietnam, 1961–1968* (Lanham, MD: Rowman & Littlefield, 2011), especially chapters 4 and 8.

44. For an example of the vice president's defense of US Vietnam policy, see Speech, Humphrey to NGO Foreign Policy Conference, March 16, 1965, 310.G.12.8F, HHHP, MHS.

45. Cohen, *American Maelstrom*, 74.

46. Memorandum, McGeorge Bundy to Lyndon Johnson, April 14, 1965, NSF Aides Files, McGeorge Bundy Memos to the President, LBJL.

47. Speeches, Humphrey at Norfolk, VA, April 22, 1965, and Humphrey at Duke University Convocation, April 24, 1965, 310.G.12.8F, HHHP, MHS.

48. Michael R. Beschloss, ed., *Reaching for Glory: Lyndon Johnson's Secret White House Tapes, 1964–1965* (New York: Touchstone, 2001), 183–85 (emphasis in original).

49. David L. DiLeo, *George Ball, Vietnam, and the Rethinking of Containment* (Chapel Hill: University of North Carolina Press, 1991), 116.

50. DiLeo, *George Ball, Vietnam, and the Rethinking of Containment*, 116–17. See also Halberstam, *The Best and the Brightest*, 534–35.

51. Beschloss, *Reaching for Glory*, 340.

52. Memorandum, Hubert Humphrey to Lyndon Johnson, May 4, 1965, 150.E.14.1B, HHHP, MHS.

53. Memorandum, Hubert Humphrey to Lyndon Johnson, May 10, 1965, Hubert H. Humphrey Vice Presidential Files, 1965–1968, Foreign Affairs General Files, 150.E.14.1B, MHS.

54. James Deakin, "Humphrey: Lyndon Johnson's John the Baptist," *The New Republic* 152, May 29, 1965, 10–12.

55. Speech, Humphrey at Michigan State University, June 1, 1965, NSF/Name File, box 4, LBJL.

56. Solberg, *Hubert Humphrey*, 282.

57. Mann, *A Grand Delusion*, 499; Tom Wells, *The War Within: America's Battle over Vietnam* (New York: Henry Holt and Company, 1994), 205.

58. Offner, *Hubert Humphrey*, 232.

59. Eisele, *Almost to the Presidency*, 242.

60. Mann, *A Grand Delusion*, 499–500.

61. "What's Ahead—Dissolving Consensus," *National Review Bulletin* 17, no. 25 (June 22, 1965): 4–5.

62. Offner, *Hubert Humphrey*, 233.

63. Solberg, *Hubert Humphrey*, 283.

64. Berman, *Hubert*, 106.

65. Humphrey, *Education of a Public Man*, 245.

66. Solberg, *Hubert Humphrey*, 283–84.

67. Memorandum, Hubert Humphrey to Lyndon Johnson, December 2, 1965, NSF/Name File, box 4, LBJL.

3. THE RECRUITING SERGEANT

1. Carl Solberg, *Hubert Humphrey: A Biography* (New York: W. W. Norton & Company, 1984), 285.

2. *New York Times*, March 23, 2018.

3. Arnold A. Offner, *Hubert Humphrey: The Conscience of the Country* (New Haven, CT: Yale University Press, 2018), 234. While such a challenge by Humphrey would have been highly unlikely, it is a testament to LBJ's insecurities that he considered it as even a remote possibility.

4. Hubert H. Humphrey, *The Education of a Public Man: My Life and Politics* (Minneapolis: University of Minnesota Press, 1991), 246–48.

5. Memorandum, Lyndon Johnson to Hubert Humphrey, February 12, 1966, NSF/International Meetings and Travel File, box 25, LBJL.

6. William Conrad Gibbons, *The U.S. Government and the Vietnam War: Executive and Legislative Roles and Relationships, Part IV: July 1965–January 1968* (Princeton, NJ: Princeton University Press, 1995), 129; Offner, *Hubert Humphrey*, 234.

7. Offner, *Hubert Humphrey*, 235; Meeting notes (Bromley Smith), 555th NSC Meeting, January 5, 1966, NSC Meeting File, LBJL.

8. Gibbons, *The U.S. Government and the Vietnam War, Part IV*, 171.

9. Robert Mann, *A Grand Delusion: America's Descent into Vietnam* (New York: Basic Books, 2011) 487–91; Andrew Johns, *Vietnam's Second Front: Domestic Politics, the Republican Party, and the War* (Lexington: University Press of Kentucky, 2010), 106. On the SFRC hearings, see *The Vietnam Hearings*, with an introduction by J. William Fulbright (New York: Vintage, 1966); Joseph A. Fry, *Debating Vietnam: Fulbright, Stennis, and Their Senate Hearings* (Lanham, MD: Rowman & Littlefield, 2006); Gary Stone, *Elites for Peace: The Senate and the Vietnam War, 1964–1968* (Knoxville: University of Tennessee Press, 2007), especially chapters 5–7.

10. Quoted in Offner, *Hubert Humphrey*, 236.

11. A. J. Langguth, *Our Vietnam/Nuóc Viêt Ta: The War, 1954–1975* (New York: Simon & Schuster, 2000), 421–22; Humphrey, *The Education of a Public Man*, 245–46.

12. Humphrey, *The Education of a Public Man*, 246.

13. Langguth, *Our Vietnam/Nuóc Viêt Ta*, 421–22.

14. *New York Times*, February 15, 1966.

15. *Newsweek*, February 28, 1966, 39.

16. *Newsweek*, February 28, 1966, 39.

17. Solberg, *Hubert Humphrey*, 288–89.

18. Kenneth Crawford, "Humphrey's Chickens," *Newsweek*, March 14, 1966, 38; Solberg, *Hubert Humphrey*, 290; Jeff Shesol, *Mutual Contempt: Lyndon Johnson, Robert Kennedy, and the Feud that Defined a Decade* (New York: W. W. Norton & Company, 1997), 290.

19. *New York Times*, February 24, 1966; Albert Eisele, *Almost to the Presidency: A Biography of Two American Politicians* (Blue Earth, MN: The Piper Company, 1972), 243–44; Offner, *Hubert Humphrey*, 239, 242; Mann, *A Grand Delusion*, 501.

20. Memorandum, Hubert Humphrey to Lyndon Johnson, March 3, 1966, Thompson Papers, box 12, John F. Kennedy Presidential Library, Boston, MA (hereafter JFKL). This version of Humphrey's report was written after his original fifty-page draft was edited down to seven pages on LBJ's instructions. The vice president believed that much of the detail in the longer version needed to be included; hence the creation of the revised document with a date of March 3.

21. Solberg, *Hubert Humphrey*, 291; quoted in Gibbons, *The U.S. Government and the Vietnam War, Part IV*, 234.

22. Mann, *A Grand Delusion*, 502.

23. Quoted in Gibbons, *The U.S. Government and the Vietnam War, Part IV*, 235.

24. Gibbons, *The U.S. Government and the Vietnam War, Part IV*, 236.

25. Arthur M. Schlesinger Jr., *Robert Kennedy and His Times* (New York: Ballantine Books, 1978), 738–39.

26. *Newsweek*, March 7, 1966, 25–26.

27. *New York Times*, March 23, 2018.

28. *Washington Post*, March 9, 1966.

29. Quoted in Eisele, *Almost to the Presidency*, 245–46.

30. "Old Hubert," *New Republic* 154 (March 12, 1966), 7.

31. Ted Van Dyk, *Heroes, Hacks, and Fools: Memoirs from the Political Inside* (Seattle: University of Washington Press, 2007), 46–47.

32. *U.S. News & World Report*, March 7, 1966, 20. On Nixon's hawkish rhetoric on the war during this period, see Andrew L. Johns, "A Voice from the Wilderness: Richard Nixon and the Vietnam War, 1964–1966," *Presidential Studies Quarterly* 29, no. 2 (Spring 1999): 317–35.

33. *New York Times*, April 27, 1966.

34. Quoted in Eisele, *Almost to the Presidency*, 246, 248; *Time*, March 4, 1966, 25–26; *New York Times*, February 20, 1966; quoted in Mann, *A Grand Delusion*, 503. Regarding his estrangement from liberals, Humphrey said in an interview with journalist Saul Pett, "Politics is unpredictable—there are even seasonal fluctuations. I've never left the liberals even though some are disappointed in me. Liberals have a great emotional commitment. They're volatile. If you do something to displease them, their respect becomes cynical." See *Baltimore Sun*, April 10, 1966.

35. Humphrey, *The Education of a Public Man*, 252.

36. Gibbons, *The U.S. Government and the Vietnam War, Part IV*, 234, 236–37.

37. Transcript, *Meet the Press*, March 13, 1966, 150.E.14.5B, HHHP, MHS.

38. Speech, Humphrey to AFL-CIO conference, March 24, 1966, 310.G.13.2F, HHHP, MHS.

39. Quoted in Eisele, *Almost to the Presidency*, 246–47.

40. *Time*, April 1, 1966, 21, 23; Offner, *Hubert Humphrey*, 243.

41. Transcript, Humphrey interview with CBS, April 19, 1966, 310.G.13.3B, HHHP, MHS.

42. Speech, Humphrey to Democratic National Committee luncheon, April 20, 1966, 310.G.13.3B, HHHP, MHS.

43. *New York Times*, April 29, 1966.

44. *National Review Bulletin* 18, no. 19 (May 10, 1966): 1, 4.

45. Letter, Richard Hudson to Hubert Humphrey, July 5, 1966; Letter, Hubert Humphrey to Richard Hudson, July 27, 1966, 150.E.14.5B, HHHP, MHS.

46. Memorandum, John Rielly to Hubert Humphrey, August 17, 1966, 150.E.13.6F, HHHP, MHS. On Lowenstein, see William H. Chafe, *Never Stop Running: Allard Lowenstein and the Struggle to Save American Liberalism* (New York: Basic Books, 1979).

47. Solberg, *Hubert Humphrey*, 292.

48. Eisele, *Almost to the Presidency*, 250; Offner, *Hubert Humphrey*, 247. Humphrey's penchant for speaking extemporaneously makes it challenging to identify specific instances of campaign rhetoric in support of U.S. Vietnam policy. Many of his formal, written remarks tend to be highly generalized and frequently ended up either being ignored or serving as a jumping-off point for his comments during his appearances.

49. Offner, *Hubert Humphrey*, 247; quotes from Johns, *Vietnam's Second Front*, 124. On Humphrey's perspective on LBJ's trip to Manila, see Memorandum, Hubert Humphrey to Lyndon Johnson, October 16, 1966, WHCF, FG 44, LBJL.

50. *New York Times*, November 13, 1966.

51. Memorandum, Walt Rostow to Lyndon Johnson, November 28, 1966, WHCF, CF, box 72, LBJL.

52. Offner, *Hubert Humphrey*, 247–48; Shesol, *Mutual Contempt*, 449.

53. Andrew Kopkind, "Humphrey's Old Pals: An Account of the ADA Convention," *New Republic* 154 (May 7, 1966), 19. In his keynote speech at the convention, Humphrey referred to the "inescapable agony and pain of Vietnam" and cited the "differences within this room as to just how we should meet our responsibilities in Asia, and particularly in Vietnam." He also criticized the NLF, called the task in South Vietnam a "social revolution," supported free elections in the South, and announced the administration's willingness to negotiate. See Speech, Humphrey keynote at the ADA, April 23, 1966, 310.G.13.3B, HHHP, MHS.

54. *U.S. News & World Report*, February 13, 1967, 42.

55. Solberg, *Hubert Humphrey*, 305–6. Humphrey visited Switzerland, the Netherlands, West Germany, Italy, Great Britain, France, and Belgium on the trip.

56. Offner, *Hubert Humphrey*, 255.

57. Eisele, *Almost to the Presidency*, 252.

58. *Washington Post*, April 26, 1967.

59. Eisele, *Almost to the Presidency*, 252–53.

60. Eisele, *Almost to the Presidency*, 253–55.

61. Schlesinger, *Robert Kennedy and His Times*, 775.

62. Humphrey, *The Education of a Public Man*, 259. On McNamara's doubts about the war, see, for example, Robert S. McNamara, with Brian VanDeMark, *In Retrospect: The Tragedy and Lessons of Vietnam* (New York: Times Books, 1995).

63. *Newsweek*, November 6, 1967, 25–26.

64. Quoted in *New York Times*, April 4, 2017.

65. Charles DeBenedetti, with Charles Chatfield, *An American Ordeal: The Antiwar Movement of the Vietnam Era* (Syracuse, NY: Syracuse University Press, 1990), 173–74; and *New York Times*, April 11, 1967.

66. *New York Times*, August 24, 1967.

67. Quoted in John Osborne, "Talk with Humphrey: The Dogged Loyalty that Dogs HHH," *New Republic* 158 (May 4, 1968), 13.

68. Speech, Humphrey to National Defense Reserve, October 23, 1967, 310.G.13.10F, HHHP, MHS; Solberg, *Hubert Humphrey*, 310–11.

69. Offner, *Hubert Humphrey*, 261. On McCarthy's presidential campaign, see Dominic Sandbrook, *Eugene McCarthy: The Rise and Fall of Postwar American Liberalism* (New York: Alfred A. Knopf, 2004), especially chapters 8–11.

70. Gibbons, *The U.S. Government and the Vietnam War, Part IV*, 894–95; Telegram, Hubert Humphrey to Lyndon Johnson, October 30, 1967, NSF/International Meetings and Travel File, LBJL.

71. Humphrey, *The Education of a Public Man*, 260.

72. Edgar Berman, *Hubert: The Triumph and Tragedy of the Humphrey I Knew* (New York: Putnam, 1979), 115–16. Humphrey's comments to Berman reflect the vice president's sentiments that he expressed during a briefing in Vietnam. He exclaimed at one point, "I'll be damned if I will be part of sending more American kids to die for these corrupt bastards! We've got to do something about this." Quoted in Van Dyk, *Heroes, Hacks, and Fools*, 55.

73. Summary notes (Bromley Smith) of 578th NSC Meeting, November 8, 1967, NSF/NSC Meetings, box 2, LBJL; Gibbons, *The U.S. Government and the Vietnam War, Part IV*, 895–96; Dallek, *Flawed Giant*, 497.

74. *Newsweek*, November 11, 1967.

75. Humphrey, *The Education of a Public Man*, 261–62.

76. Speech, Humphrey to Young Democrats' National Convention, November 18, 1967, 310.G.13.10F, HHHP, MHS.

77. Offner, *Hubert Humphrey*, 265–66.

78. Solberg, *Hubert Humphrey*, 313.

4. "WHEN THE GODS WISH TO PUNISH US . . ."

1. Arnold A. Offner, *Hubert Humphrey: The Conscience of the Country* (New Haven, CT: Yale University Press, 2019), 268.

2. Speech, Hubert Humphrey to California Democratic Campaign Committee, January 13, 1968, 310.G.14.1B, HHHP, MHS.

3. Humphrey notes, January 19, 1968, 150.E.13.4F, HHHP, MHS.

4. Quoted in Offner, *Hubert Humphrey*, 270. During a visit to Vietnam in December 1967, for example, Johnson told U.S. troops at Cam Ranh Bay, "All the challenges have been met.

The enemy is not beaten, but he knows that he has met his master in the field." Quoted in *Department of State Bulletin*, vol. 58, no. 1488, January 1, 1968 (Washington, DC: U.S. Government Printing Office, 1968), 76. On the Tet Offensive of 1968, see, for example, Don Oberdorfer, *Tet! The Turning Point in the Vietnam War*, rev. ed. (Baltimore: Johns Hopkins University Press, 2001); James H. Willbanks, *The Tet Offensive: A Concise History* (New York: Columbia University Press, 2006); Edwin E. Moïse, *The Myths of Tet: The Most Misunderstood Event of the Vietnam War* (Lawrence: University Press of Kansas, 2017); David F. Schmitz, *The Tet Offensive: Politics, War, and Public Opinion* (Lanham, MD: Rowman & Littlefield, 2005).

5. *New York Times*, February 18, 1968.

6. Hubert Humphrey, *Pageant Magazine*, February 22, 1968, 1968 Campaign Files, Candidate Files, 1949–1968, HHHP, MHS.

7. Draft memorandum, Hubert Humphrey to Lyndon Johnson, undated (c. late February 1968), William Connell Files, 150.F.18.6F, HHHP, MHS; Offner, *Hubert Humphrey*, 271.

8. During the Vietnam War, there were three such intraparty challenges: Senator Eugene McCarthy's (D-MN) stunning near-upset of Lyndon Johnson in the 1968 New Hampshire primary; Representative John M. Ashbrook's (R-OH) conservative challenge of Richard Nixon in 1972; and Representative Paul N. "Pete" McCloskey's (R-CA) antiwar campaign against Nixon that same year.

9. Speech, McCarthy to the National Conference of Concerned Democrats, December 3, 1967, 150.E.13.4F, HHHP, MHS; Offner, *Hubert Humphrey*, 269.

10. Offner, *Hubert Humphrey*, 271; Speech, Humphrey to Democratic Regional Conference, March 15, 1968, William Connell Files, 150.F.18.6F, HHHP, MHS.

11. Memorandum, Hubert Humphrey to Lyndon Johnson, March 20 and 21, 1968, Marvin Watson Files, box 31, LBJL; Carl Solberg, *Hubert Humphrey: A Biography* (New York: W. W. Norton & Company, 1984), 319–20; Offner, *Hubert Humphrey*, 268.

12. The so-called "Wise Men" were a group of U.S. government officials and members of the foreign policy establishment who provided counsel and advice to presidents from FDR to LBJ. Over the years, the group included Dean Acheson, Averell Harriman, George Kennan, John J. McCloy, Charles Bohlen, and General Omar Bradley. On the Wise Men, see Walter Isaacson and Evan Thomas, *The Wise Men: Six Friends and the World They Made* (New York: Simon and Schuster, 1986).

13. Offner, *Hubert Humphrey*, 272. On the changing attitudes within the administration prior to Tet, see, for example, Schmitz, *The Tet Offensive*.

14. Kyle Longley, *LBJ's 1968: Power, Politics, and the Presidency in America's Year of Upheaval* (New York: Cambridge University Press, 2018), 90; Solberg, *Hubert Humphrey*, 321–22.

15. Offner, *Hubert Humphrey*, 275.

16. Solberg, *Hubert Humphrey*, 323; *New York Times*, April 14, 1968; Kenneth Crawford, "Last Man In," *Newsweek*, April 15, 1968, 53.

17. Speech, Humphrey candidacy announcement, April 27, 1968, 310.G.14.3B, HHHP, MHS.

18. Chester L. Cooper, *The Lost Crusade: America in Vietnam* (New York: Dodd, Mead, & Company, 1970), 398; Crawford, "Last Man In," 53.

19. *Newsweek*, April 29, 1968, 24.

20. *Newsweek*, April 29, 1968, 30. See also *Baltimore Sun*, April 28, 1968.

21. Transcript, *Meet the Press*, April 28, 1968, 150.G.1.6F, HHHP, MHS.

22. John Osbourne, "Talk with Humphrey: The Dogged Loyalty that Dogs HHH," *New Republic* 158 (May 4, 1968): 11–12.

23. Ted Van Dyk, *Heroes, Hacks, and Fools: Memoirs from the Political Inside* (Seattle: University of Washington Press, 2007), 71; Offner, *Hubert Humphrey*, 282.

24. Quoted in "He'd Rather Be Wrong," *The New Republic* 158 (June 29, 1968), 6–7; Albert Eisele, *Almost to the Presidency: A Biography of Two American Politicians* (Blue Earth, MN: The Piper Company, 1972), 333; Lewis Chester, Godfrey Hodgson, and Bruce Page, *An American Melodrama: The Presidential Campaign of 1968* (New York: Viking Press, 1969),

154. Moyers had resigned from the White House in large measure due to his skepticism of administration policy on Vietnam.

25. Speech, Humphrey to National Press Club, June 20, 1968, 310.G.14.4F, HHHP, MHS. The majority of the speech focused on issues of civil order and civil justice.

26. *New York Times*, June 23, 1968.

27. Offner, *Hubert Humphrey*, 277; Solberg, *Hubert Humphrey*, 347; Marie D. Natoli, "The Humphrey Vice Presidency in Retrospect," *Presidential Studies Quarterly* 12, no. 4 (Fall 1982): 606–7. Among the Democrats who suggested Humphrey resign were Governor Harold Hughes (D-IA) and Governor Philip Hoff (D-VT).

28. Van Dyk, *Heroes, Hacks, and Fools*, 72–73.

29. Cooper, *The Lost Crusade*, 401–2.

30. Kyle Longley, *LBJ's 1968: Power, Politics, and the Presidency in America's Year of Upheaval* (New York: Cambridge University Press, 2018), 210–11. The "San Antonio Formula" dates to a speech given by Johnson on September 29, 1967, in San Antonio, Texas. LBJ offered to cease the bombing of North Vietnam if Ho Chi Minh would agree to initiate serious negotiations for a peaceful settlement to the conflict and if the North Vietnamese leader would promise not to use the bombing halt as an opportunity to increase the infiltration of troops and supplies into South Vietnam. Hanoi never responded positively to the offer.

31. Created by William E. Colby—an OSS officer during World War II who had been the CIA station chief in Saigon, head of the CIA's Far East Division, and later deputy MACV commander in charge of pacification—the Phoenix Program was designed to destroy the infrastructure of the Viet Cong. With the assistance of the CIA and Civil Operations and Revolutionary Development Support, Colby charged South Vietnam with eliminating the Viet Cong's leadership through arrest, conversion, or assassination. By 1972, as many as twenty thousand people had been killed. On the Phoenix Program, see, for example, Dale Andradé, *Ashes to Ashes: The Phoenix Program and the Vietnam War* (Lexington, MA: Lexington Books, 1990).

32. Transcript, *Issues and Answers*, July 7, 1968, 310.G.14.4F, box 33, HHHP, MHS.

33. Offner, *Hubert Humphrey*, 284–85.

34. Speech, Humphrey in San Francisco, CA, July 12, 1968, Personal Papers of Ramsey Clark, box 96, LBJL.

35. Solberg, *Hubert Humphrey*, 347–48.

36. Offner, *Hubert Humphrey*, 285; *New York Times*, July 23, 1968.

37. *Chicago Sun-Times*, July 21, 1968.

38. *Time*, July 26, 1968, 21.

39. Offner, *Hubert Humphrey*, 286.

40. Quoted in Melvin Small, *At the Water's Edge: American Politics and the Vietnam War* (Chicago: Ivan R. Dee, 2005), 112.

41. Clark Clifford, with Richard Holbrooke, *Counsel to the President: A Memoir* (New York: Random House, 1991), 563–64; Robert Dallek, *Flawed Giant: Lyndon Johnson and His Times, 1961–1973* (New York: Oxford University Press, 1998), 571.

42. Van Dyk, *Heroes, Hacks, and Fools*, 74.

43. Justin A. Nelson, "Drafting Lyndon Johnson: The President's Secret Role in the 1968 Democratic Convention," *Presidential Studies Quarterly* 30, no. 4 (December 2000): 690–91.

44. Transcript, *Issues and Answers*, August 11, 1968, 310.G.14.4F, box 33, HHHP, MHS.

45. Cooper, *The Lost Crusade*, 402; Offner, *Hubert Humphrey*, 288–89; Longley, *LBJ's 1968*, 212.

46. *Washington Post*, July 17, 1968.

47. Nelson, "Drafting Lyndon Johnson," 694; *New York Times*, August 11, 1968.

48. John Morton Blum, *Years of Discord: American Politics and Society, 1961–1974* (New York: W. W. Norton & Company, 1991), 305.

49. Nelson, "Drafting Lyndon Johnson," 703; Offner, *Hubert Humphrey*, 296; A. J. Langguth, *Our Vietnam/Nước Viêt Ta: The War, 1954–1975* (New York: Simon & Schuster, 2000), 514–15.

50. Longley, *LBJ's 1968*, 212–13.

51. Offner, *Hubert Humphrey*, 297; *New York Times*, August 30, 1968; Lewis L. Gould, *1968: The Election That Changed America* (Chicago: Ivan R. Dee, 1993), 119.

52. *Washington Post*, August 26, 1968.

53. Transcript, *Meet the Press*, August 25, 1968, 310.G.14.7B, box 35, HHHP, MHS.

54. *New York Times*, August 28, 1968.

55. Longley, *LBJ's 1968*, 225–27.

56. Telephone conversation transcript, August 28, 1968, *FRUS, 1964–1968*, vol. VI: *Vietnam, January–August 1968*, 978, n5.

57. Gould, *1968*, 129.

58. Quoted in Longley, *LBJ's 1968*, 226.

59. Longley, *LBJ's 1968*, 228.

60. Speech, Humphrey nomination acceptance, August 29, 1968, 310.G.14.7B, box 35, HHHP, MHS.

61. Telephone conversation transcript, Hubert Humphrey and Lyndon Johnson, August 31, 1968, *FRUS, 1964–1968*, vol. VI: *Vietnam, January–August 1968*, 989–90.

62. Telephone conversation transcript, Hubert Humphrey and Lyndon Johnson, August 31, 1968, *FRUS, 1964–1968*, vol. VI: *Vietnam, January–August 1968*, 990, n2.

63. Oscar Wilde, *An Ideal Husband* (1893), https://www.gutenberg.org/files/885/885-h/885-h.htm, accessed October 5, 2019.

64. Quoted in Small, *At the Water's Edge*, 115; Michael Cohen, *American Maelstrom: The 1968 Election and the Politics of Division* (New York: Oxford University Press, 2016), 163; David Halberstam, *The Best and the Brightest* (New York: Ballantine Books, 1992), 662.

5. "AN ACCEPTABLE RISK FOR PEACE"

1. Hubert H. Humphrey, *The Education of a Public Man: My Life and Politics* (Minneapolis: University of Minnesota Press, 1991*)*, 264–65.

2. Michael Cohen, *American Maelstrom: The 1968 Election and the Politics of Division* (New York: Oxford University Press, 2016), 12.

3. A. J. Langguth, *Our Vietnam/Nước Việt Ta: The War: 1954–1975* (New York: Simon and Shuster, 2000), 520; *Washington Post*, September 15, 1968. By way of comparison, Gallup polls showed Humphrey with 34 percent support in April before he announced his candidacy, 42 percent in June after RFK's death, and dropping to 29 percent in early August. More problematic, the vice president only saw his poll numbers rise a paltry two percentage points to 31 percent after Chicago—far below the typical postconvention bounce from which candidates have benefited historically—and fall to 28 percent by the end of September. See *New York Times*, April 21, 1968; June 12, 1968; August 21, 1968; and September 29, 1968, for poll results.

4. Memorandum, "Policy, Issues, and Approaches," undated (postconvention), 150.F.13.8F, HHHP, MHS (emphasis in original).

5. Randall Bennett Woods, *LBJ: Architect of Ambition* (New York: Free Press, 2006), 867.

6. Statement, September 2, 1968, 150.F.4.8.F, HHHP, MHS.

7. Summary Notes, 590th NSC Meeting, September 4, 1968, *FRUS, 1964–1968*, vol. VII, 11–12; Arnold Offner, *Hubert Humphrey: The Conscience of the Country* (New Haven, CT: Yale University Press, 2017), 307–8.

8. Speeches, Humphrey in Denver, CO, and Philadelphia, PA, September 9, 1968, 150.F.13.8F, HHHP, MHS.

9. Tom Wells, *The War Within: America's Battle over Vietnam* (New York: Henry Holt and Company, 1994), 286; Offner, *Hubert Humphrey*, 309; Clark Clifford, with Richard Holbrooke, *Counsel to the President: A Memoir* (New York: Random House, 1991), 570 (emphasis in original).

10. Speech, Lyndon Johnson to 50th Annual National Convention of the American Legion, September 10, 1968, *Public Papers of the Presidents of the United States: Lyndon Johnson, 1968–1969*, vol. 2 (Washington, DC: National Archives and Records Service, 1970), 936–43. See also Offner, *Hubert Humphrey*, 308–9; *Washington Post*, September 11, 1968; *New York Times*, September 10, 1968.

11. *New York Times*, August 25, 1968; *New York Times*, September 1, 1968; *Washington Post*, September 20, 1968.

12. Richard J. Whalen, *Catch the Falling Flag: A Republican's Challenge to His Party* (Boston: Houghton Mifflin, 1972), 217; David Halberstam, *The Best and the Brightest* (New York: Ballantine Books, 1992), 661. The Republican National Committee had extensive files on Humphrey's vacillations and cited "many contradictory and confused comments about the war" since he had become vice president. See "Humphrey Handbook for the 1968 Presidential Campaign," RNC Opposition Research series, Melvin Laird Papers, box A3, Gerald R. Ford Presidential Library, Ann Arbor, MI (hereafter GRFL).

13. On Nixon, the "secret plan," and the GOP presidential primaries in 1968, see Andrew L. Johns, *Vietnam's Second Front: Domestic Politics, the Republican Party, and the War* (Lexington: University Press of Kentucky, 2010), chapters 5–6. On Romney's 1968 presidential campaign, which foundered specifically on his failure to engage the Vietnam issue successfully, see Andrew L. Johns, "Achilles' Heel: The Vietnam War and George Romney's Bid for the Presidency, 1967 to 1968," *Michigan Historical Review* 26, no. 1 (Spring 2000): 1–29.

14. *New York Times*, September 8, 1968.

15. Quoted in Whalen, *Catch the Falling Flag*, 220; Memorandum, John Havelock to Hubert Humphrey, September 13, 1968, quoted in Kent G. Sieg, "The 1968 Presidential Election and Peace in Vietnam," *Presidential Studies Quarterly* 26, no. 4 (Fall 1966): 1066.

16. Speech, Humphrey to Seattle Civic Center rally, September 28, 1968, 310.G.14.8F, HHHP, MHS; Langguth, *Our Vietnam/Nuóc Viêt Ta: The War*, 520.

17. Memorandum, "Issues and Strategy," September 14, 1968, 150.F.20.2F, HHHP, MHS (emphasis in original).

18. *Newsweek*, October 7, 1968, 29.

19. *Newsweek*, October 14, 1968, 31.

20. Lewis Chester, Godfrey Hodgson, and Bruce Page, *An American Melodrama: The Presidential Campaign of 1968* (New York: Viking Press, 1969), 641–42.

21. Offner, *Hubert Humphrey*, 311; Speech, Humphrey in Columbus, OH, September 21, 1968, 310.G.14.8F, HHHP, MHS.

22. *Baltimore Sun*, September 12, 1968.

23. *Washington Star*, September 11, 1968.

24. *Washington Evening Star*, September 24, 1968.

25. Speech, Humphrey on KHJ (Los Angeles), September 25, 1968, 310.G.14.8F, HHHP, MHS; *Washington Post*, September 26, 1968.

26. *New York Times*, September 26, 1968.

27. Speech, Hubert Humphrey at Seattle Civic Center rally, September 28, 1968, 310.G.14.8F, HHHP, MNHS. Nixon, of course, did not have a "secret plan" or any other framework for dealing with Vietnam, a fact that became crystal clear once he took the oath of office on January 20, 1969, and immediately ordered the administration to conduct a comprehensive review of U.S. policy in order to figure out how to manage the war going forward.

28. Offner, *Hubert Humphrey*, 312–13; *Austin American Statesman*, September 29, 1968. Many Democrats, concerned about Humphrey's lack of support from the antiwar left, pressed McCarthy on this issue. Secretary of Labor W. Willard Wirtz, for example, told a press conference that he would have supported the minority plank at the convention and urged McCarthy to announce his endorsement of the vice president. See *New York Times*, September 28, 1968.

29. David L. DiLeo, *George Ball, Vietnam, and the Rethinking of Containment* (Chapel Hill: University of North Carolina Press, 1991), 174; *Los Angeles Times*, September 27, 1968. Harriman told a reporter during this period, "We're engaged in negotiations and in that capacity I'm taking no part in the campaign." Quoted in Brian VanDeMark, *Road to Disaster: A New History of America's Descent into Vietnam* (New York: Custom House, 2018), 512. When Ball resigned, Johnson commented dismissively that Ball's decision had "something to do with domestic politics." See *New York Times*, September 27, 1968.

30. Offner, *Hubert Humphrey*, 315. Journalist Ken Botwright wrote that many Democrats believed that the addition of Ball and Goldberg to the vice president's team "should help to revitalize his campaign, unite his and Sen. Eugene McCarthy's supporters, and speed efforts to end the Vietnam war." He quoted John Kenneth Galbraith as saying, "They're both on the right

side," while James MacGregor Burns considered it "a significant development. It ought to provide a bridge to help unite McCarthy and Humphrey supporters." Most interestingly, he quoted McCarthy's former Massachusetts campaign manager Paul Counihan as saying, "It is an indirect indication that Humphrey wants to change the administration's Vietnam policy." See *Boston Globe,* September 28, 1968.

31. Offner, *Hubert Humphrey,* 315–16.

32. *Boston Globe,* September 29, 1968.

33. *Baltimore Sun,* October 6, 1968. Lippmann wrote his column prior to Humphrey's speech in Salt Lake City.

34. Speech, Humphrey at Mormon Tabernacle, September 30, 1968, 310.G.14.9B, HHHP, MHS; Humphrey, *The Education of a Public Man,* 302. Humphrey's speech at the Mormon Tabernacle focused primarily on the law and order issue in the campaign.

35. Telephone conversation, Lyndon Johnson and Richard Nixon, September 30, 1968, *FRUS, 1964–1968,* vol. VII: *Vietnam, September 1968–January 1969,* 94–103.

36. Telephone conversation, Lyndon Johnson and Hubert Humphrey, September 30, 1968, *FRUS, 1964–1968,* vol. VII: *Vietnam, September 1968–January 1969,* 103–6; Langguth, *Our Vietnam/Nước Việt Ta: The War,* 521. Three years later, Humphrey recalled that LBJ said, "Hubert, you give that speech and you'll be screwed." See Albert Eisele, *Almost to the Presidency: A Biography of Two American Politicians* (Blue Earth, MN: The Piper Company, 1972), 377–78.

37. Speech, Hubert Humphrey in Salt Lake City, Utah (taped for broadcast), September 30, 1968, 310.G.14.9B, HHHP, MHS; *New York Times,* October 1, 1968.

38. Lyndon Baines Johnson, *The Vantage Point: Perspectives of the Presidency, 1963–1969* (New York: Holt, Reinhart and Winston, 1971), 548–49. Clark Clifford disputes LBJ's assessment in Clifford, *Counsel to the President,* 573.

39. Robert Dallek, *Flawed Giant: Lyndon Johnson and His Times, 1961–1973* (New York: Oxford University Press, 1998), 579.

40. Telephone conversation transcripts, Lyndon Johnson and Everett Dirksen, October 1, 1968; Lyndon Johnson and Dean Rusk, October 3, 1968, and October 6, 1968, *FRUS, 1964–1968,* vol. VII: *Vietnam, September 1968–January 1969,* 109–12, 130–37, 137–44.

41. Offner, *Hubert Humphrey,* 318.

42. Memorandum, William P. Bundy to Walt W. Rostow, October 1, 1968, NSF/CF/VN, box 248, LBJL (emphasis in original).

43. Memorandum, Nicholas deB. Katzenbach to Johnson, October 1, 1968, NSF/CF/VN, box 248, LBLJ.

44. Telegram, Edward Kennedy to Humphrey, September 30, 1968, 150.F.4.8F, HHHP, MHS.

45. *Washington Post,* October 6, 1968.

46. Offner, *Hubert Humphrey,* 318. Schlesinger termed the speech "half-assed" but meant that Humphrey would have done better to have supported the minority plank in Chicago or proposed a bombing halt earlier in the campaign. See Offner, *Hubert Humphrey,* 440n10.

47. McGeorge Bundy, *Tangled Web: The Making of Foreign Policy in the Nixon Presidency* (New York: Hill & Wang, 1998), 29.

48. *New York Times,* October 6, 1968. Polls indicated that in the wake of the speech, undecided voters were breaking for Humphrey. See VanDeMark, *Road to Disaster,* 511. Humphrey also received the endorsement of numerous other newspapers, including the *Denver Post.* While the paper noted a "lamentable clumsiness" at the start of the vice president's campaign— owing largely to being "entangled in a mesh of loyalties to the policies of Lyndon Johnson"—it opined that Humphrey had finally, with the Salt Lake City speech in particular, "staked out his own positions" and "is most clearly and forthrightly the peace candidate, the one most specifically dedicated to a plan to bring an end to the war in Vietnam and to achieve stability in our relations with the other world powers." See *Denver Post,* October 6, 1968.

49. Offner, *Hubert Humphrey,* 319.

50. Offner, *Hubert Humphrey,* 318.

51. Eisele, *Almost to the Presidency,* 379.

52. Statement, Richard Nixon, October 1, 1968, 1968 Campaign Files, Candidate Files, 1949–1968, 150.F.13.9B, HHHP, MHS.

53. Transcript, *Face the Nation*, October 13, 1968, Hubert Humphrey Papers, 150.F.13.8F, HHHP, MHS.

54. Meeting Notes, October 14, 1968 (two meetings), *FRUS, 1964–1968*, vol. VII: *Vietnam, September 1968–January 1969*, 194–95, 196–97; Offner, *Hubert Humphrey*, 321.

55. Telephone conversation transcripts, Lyndon Johnson and Mike Mansfield, October 16, 1968; Lyndon Johnson to George Wallace, Hubert Humphrey, and Richard Nixon, October 16, 1968, *FRUS, 1964–1968*, vol. VII: *Vietnam, September 1968–January 1969*, 213–16, 219, 226.

56. Anna Chennault was a prominent Republican fundraiser, a Washington, D.C., hostess, and a leading figure in the pro-Taiwan "China Lobby." She was also the widow of General Claire Chennault, the leader of the infamous "Flying Tigers," a group of U.S. pilots who had volunteered to fight against the Japanese in China prior to U.S. entry into World War II. Chennault maintained close contacts with the Saigon government and opposed peace negotiations with Hanoi because she feared the United States would abandon Thieu just as she believed it had abandoned Chiang Kai Shek in 1949. See VanDeMark, *Road to Disaster*, 513.

57. John A. Farrell, "Nixon's Vietnam Treachery," *New York Times Sunday Review*, December 31, 2016. In his interviews with David Frost in 1977, Nixon denied authorizing Chennault or others to contact the South Vietnamese government on his behalf. On Anna Chennault's involvement in the 1968 presidential campaign, see Catherine Forslund, *Anna Chennault: Informal Diplomacy and Asian Relations* (Wilmngton, DE: Scholarly Resources, 2002); Johns, *Vietnam's Second Front*, 221–31.

58. Sieg, "The 1968 Presidential Election," 1072; Memorandum, Walt Rostow to Lyndon Johnson, October 29, 1968, NSF, Files of Walt W. Rostow, box 5, LBJL.

59. Theodore H. White, *The Making of the President, 1968* (New York: Atheneum Publishers, 1969), 381; Dallek, *Flawed Giant*, 592; Jules Witcover, *The Resurrection of Richard Nixon* (New York: G. P. Putnam's Sons, 1970), 441. According to Brian VanDeMark, another factor in Humphrey's decision to not reveal Nixon's shenanigans to the electorate was that it might lead to the exposure of the Humphrey campaign's secret Ball-Fitzgibbon channel to Harriman and Vance in Paris. See VanDeMark, *Road to Disaster*, 515.

60. Offner, *Hubert Humphrey*, 322–23. Nixon's information about the Paris talks derived from back-channel communications from a White House source and from Henry Kissinger, who was secretly sending Nixon information from his contacts in Paris in the hope that it might lead to a position in the Nixon administration after the election.

61. Telephone conversation transcript, Lyndon Johnson and Hubert Humphrey, October 31, 1968, *FRUS, 1964–1968*, vol. VII: *Vietnam, September 1968–January 1969*, 485–93; Offner, *Hubert Humphrey*, 327.

62. Speech, Lyndon Johnson televised address, October 31, 1968, http://www.lbjlibrary.net/collections/selected-speeches/1968-january-1969/10-31-1968.html, accessed October 17, 2019.

63. Speech, Humphrey in Chicago, November 1, 1968, 310.G.15.1B, HHHP, MHS.

64. *New York Times*, November 3, 1968.

65. Stewart Alsop, "Why Humphrey Bomfogs," *Newsweek*, November 4, 1968, 120.

66. Offner, *Hubert Humphrey*, 329.

67. Offner, *Hubert Humphrey*, 329–30.

68. Speech, Humphrey in Houston, TX, November 3, 1968, 310.G.15.1B, HHHP, MHS.

69. Humphrey, *The Education of a Public Man*, xviii–xix; Offner, *Hubert Humphrey*, 332–33.

70. Speech, Humphrey concession remarks, November 6, 1968, 310.G.15.1B, HHHP, MHS.

71. *New York Times*, November 7, 1968.

72. *U.S. News & World Report*, November 18, 1968, 132. Scholarly assessments of voting patterns in the aftermath of the election were mixed. Political scientist Robert Smith, for example, commented that "most probably, a crucial element in Humphrey's defeat was the lack of support from antiwar Democrats who disliked his middle-of-the-road stance on Vietnam." But other experts agree with sociologist E. M. Schreiber, who argued that nonvoting doves did not constitute a large enough cohort to swing the election to Humphrey. See Robert B. Smith, "Disaffection, Delegitimation, and Consequences: Aggregate Trends for World War II, Korea,

and Vietnam," in Charles C. Moskos, ed., *Public Opinion and the Military Establishment* (Beverly Hills, CA: Sage Publications, 1971), 240–43; E. M. Schreiber, "Vietnam Policy Preferences and Withheld 1968 Presidential Votes," *The Public Opinion Quarterly* 37, no. 1 (Spring 1973): 91–98. Schreiber further contends that "'withheld' hawk votes made more of a difference in Mr. Humphrey's defeat than withheld dove votes."

CONCLUSION

1. *New York Times*, November 5, 1970.

2. Speech, Humphrey campaign announcement, January 1972, 310.G.10.7B, HHHP, MHS. Following Humphrey's speech, a Gallup poll showed him in second place among Democratic contenders behind Edmund Muskie. See *Austin American Statesman*, February 8, 1972.

3. In the wake of the 1968 debacle, the Democratic National Committee had created the Commission on Party Structure and Delegate Selection (more commonly referred to as the McGovern-Fraser Commission), cochaired by McGovern and Representative Donald Fraser (D-MN). The commission's mandate was to make recommendations to broaden participation in the nominating process, especially among minorities and women, and reduce the influence of party leaders. This had the effect of increasing the number and electoral importance of the party primaries in both parties. Ironically, these reforms gave McGovern a distinct advantage over Humphrey in the 1972 race for the Democratic presidential nomination given McGovern's more effective national campaign organization. On the role of the primaries in the Democratic nominating process in 1972, see, for example, Theodore H. White, *The Making of the President, 1972* (New York: Atheneum Publishers, 1973), especially chapter 4, and Elaine C. Kamarck, *Primary Politics: How Presidential Candidates Have Shaped the Modern Nominating System* (Washington, DC: Brookings Institution Press, 2009).

4. McGovern had been the first member of the Senate to challenge the escalating U.S. military involvement in Vietnam in a speech on the Senate floor on September 24, 1963, and he would remain a vocal advocate of disengagement throughout his career. On McGovern's opposition to the war, see especially Daryl Webb, "Crusade: George McGovern's Opposition to the Vietnam War," *South Dakota History* 28, no. 3 (Fall 1998): 161–90. McGovern frequently used Vietnam against Humphrey during the campaign. For example, he referred to Humphrey as unqualified to be president because he was one of the "architects" of U.S. war policy. See *Austin American Statesman*, February 6, 1972.

5. Jeff Jacoby, "In Politics, Patience Isn't Overrated, But Loyalty Often Is," *Pundicity*, October 22, 2014, http://www.jeffjacoby.com/15524/in-politics-patience-isnt-overrated-but-loyalty, accessed October 22, 2019. For more on the philosophy of loyalty, see, for example, John Kleinig, "Loyalty," *The Stanford Encyclopedia of Philosophy* (Winter 2017), Edward N. Zalta, ed., https://plato.standford.edu/archives/win2017/entries/loyalty/, accessed October 22, 2019.

6. Quoted in David Halberstam, *The Best and the Brightest* (New York: Ballantine Books, 1992), 434 (emphasis in original).

7. Ted Van Dyk, *Heroes, Hacks, and Fools: Memoirs from the Political Inside* (Seattle: University of Washington Press, 2007), 119.

8. On Bryan's resignation, see, for example, Michael Kazin, *A Godly Hero: The Life of William Jennings Bryan* (New York: Anchor Books, 2006), chapter 10. On Vance's resignation, see, for example, the profile by historian Douglas Brinkley in the *New York Times*, December 29, 2002, and *New York Times*, April 29, 1980.

9. Letter, Pete McCloskey to Richard Nixon, March 20, 1969, box 652, Paul N. 'Pete' McCloskey papers, Hoover Institution Archives, Stanford, CA.

10. Memorandum, Pete McCloskey to Richard Nixon, March 20, 1969, Robert Hartmann Files, Ford Congressional Papers, box R25, GRFL (emphasis in original).

11. *New York Times*, March 11, 1972.

12. For years, the Republican Party—especially although not exclusively in California—had committed itself to the "Eleventh Commandment": "Thou shalt not speak ill of any fellow

Republican." This doctrine derived from the experience of the 1964 presidential election, when many liberal Republicans (before that became an oxymoron) refused to campaign for or publicly support Barry Goldwater. Although Reagan had popularized the phrase during his gubernatorial campaign, it had originated with Gaylord Parkinson, chair of the California Republican Party, in the wake of Goldwater's defeat. In the ensuing elections in 1966 and 1968, Republicans made a concerted effort to restrict their criticisms to Democrats in an effort to build party unity and present a united front to the electorate, a strategy that helped the party make significant gains in the midterm elections and win the White House in 1968. See Andrew L. Johns, *Vietnam's Second Front: Domestic Politics, the Republican Party, and the War* (Lexington: University Press of Kentucky, 2010), 191–92.

13. To be fair, Offner does offer a pointed criticism of Humphrey's engagement with the Vietnam issue during his vice presidency and the 1968 presidential campaign. See Arnold A. Offner, *Hubert Humphrey: The Conscience of the Country* (New Haven, CT: Yale University Press, 2018), 335.

Bibliography

ARCHIVAL COLLECTIONS

Gerald R. Ford Presidential Library, Ann Arbor, MI
John F. Kennedy Presidential Library, Boston, MA
Hoover Institution Archives, Stanford, CA
Minnesota Historical Society, St. Paul, MN
Lyndon Baines Johnson Presidential Library, Austin, TX
Miller Center, Charlottesville, VA

PUBLISHED DOCUMENTS

Beschloss, Michael R., ed. *Reaching for Glory: Lyndon Johnson's Secret White House Tapes, 1964–1965*. New York: Touchstone, 2001.
———. *Taking Charge: The Johnson White House Tapes, 1963–1964*. New York: Simon & Schuster, 1997.
Congressional Record.
Executive Sessions of the Senate Foreign Relations Committee.
Foreign Relations of the United States.
George Gallup. *The Gallup Poll: Public Opinion, 1935–1971*. New York: Random House, 1972.
Public Papers of the Presidents.
The Vietnam Hearings. With an introduction by J. William Fulbright. New York: Vintage, 1966.

NEWSPAPERS & PERIODICALS

Austin American Statesman
Baltimore Sun
Boston Globe
Chicago Sun-Times
Chicago Tribune
Christian Science Monitor

Denver Post
Department of State Bulletin
Los Angeles Times
National Review
National Review Bulletin
New Republic
Newsweek
New York Times
New York Times Sunday Review
Time
U.S. News & World Report
Wall Street Journal
Washington Post
Washington Star

MEMOIRS

Ball, George W. *The Past Has Another Pattern: Memoirs*. New York: W. W. Norton & Company, 1983.
Berman, Edgar. *Hubert: The Triumph and Tragedy of the Humphrey I Knew*. New York: Putnam, 1979.
Clifford, Clark, with Richard Holbrooke. *Counsel to the President: A Memoir*. New York: Random House, 1991.
Humphrey, Hubert H. *The Education of a Public Man: My Life and Politics*. Minneapolis, MN: University of Minnesota Press, 1991.
Johnson, Lyndon Baines. *The Vantage Point: Perspectives of the Presidency, 1963–1969*. New York: Holt, Reinhart and Winston, 1971.
McNamara, Robert S., with Brian VanDeMark. *In Retrospect: The Tragedy and Lessons of Vietnam*. New York: Times Books, 1995.
Van Dyk, Ted. *Heroes, Hacks, and Fools: Memoirs from the Political Inside*. Seattle: University of Washington Press, 2007.

SECONDARY SOURCES

Alsop, Stewart. "Why Humphrey Bomfogs." *Newsweek*, November 4, 1968.
Amrine, Michael. *This Is Humphrey: The Story of the Senator*. Garden City, NY: Doubleday & Co., 1960.
Anderson, Clinton. *Outsider in the Senate*. New York: World Publishing Company, 1970.
Anderson, David L. *Vietnamization: Politics, Strategy, Legacy*. Lanham, MD: Rowman & Littlefield, 2019.
Andradé, Dale. *Ashes to Ashes: The Phoenix Program and the Vietnam War*. Lexington, MA: Lexington Books, 1990.
Barrett, David M. *Uncertain Warriors: Lyndon Johnson and His Vietnam Advisers*. Lawrence: University Press of Kansas, 1993.
Bator, Francis M. "No Good Choices: LBJ and the Vietnam/Great Society Connection." *Diplomatic History* 32, no. 3 (June 2008): 309–40.
Berman, Larry. *Lyndon Johnson's War: The Road to Stalemate in Vietnam*. New York: W. W. Norton, 1989.
———. *Planning a Tragedy: The Americanization of the War in Vietnam*. New York: W. W. Norton & Company, 1983.
Berman, William C. *William Fulbright and the Vietnam War: The Dissent of a Political Realist*. Kent, OH: Kent State University Press, 1988.

Bill, James A. *George Ball: Behind the Scenes in U.S. Foreign Policy*. New Haven, CT: Yale University Press, 1997.

Blang, Eugenie M. *Allies at Odds: America, Europe, and Vietnam, 1961–1968*. Lanham, MD: Rowman & Littlefield, 2011.

Bloodworth, Jeffrey. *Losing the Center: The Decline of American Liberalism, 1968–1992*. Lexington: University Press of Kentucky, 2013.

Blum, John Morton. *Years of Discord: American Politics and Society, 1961–1974*. New York: W. W. Norton & Company, 1991.

Brock, Clifton, and Max Lerner. *Americans for Democratic Action: Its Role in National Politics*. Rev. ed. Whitefish, MT: Literary Licensing, 2012.

Bundy, McGeorge. *Tangled Web: The Making of Foreign Policy in the Nixon Presidency*. New York: Hill and Wang, 1998.

Carter, Dan T. *The Politics of Rage: George Wallace, the Origins of the New Conservatism, and the Transformation of American Politics*. New York: Simon & Schuster, 1995.

Chafe, William H. *Never Stop Running: Allard Lowenstein and the Struggle to Save American Liberalism*. New York: Basic Books, 1979.

Chester, Lewis, Godfrey Hodgson, and Bruce Page. *An American Melodrama: The Presidential Campaign of 1968*. New York: Viking Press, 1969.

Cohen, Dan. *Undefeated: The Life of Hubert H. Humphrey*. Minneapolis, MN: Lerner Publications, 1978.

Cohen, Michael A. *American Maelstrom: The 1968 Election and Politics of Division*. New York: Oxford University Press, 2016.

Cooper, Chester L. *The Lost Crusade: America in Vietnam*. New York: Dodd, Mead & Company, 1970.

Crawford, Kenneth. "HHH Anonymous." *Newsweek*, January 11, 1965.

Crawford, Kenneth. "Humphrey's Chickens." *Newsweek*, March 14, 1966.

Crawford, Kenneth. "Last Man In." *Newsweek*, April 15, 1968.

Dallek, Robert. *Flawed Giant: Lyndon Johnson and His Times, 1961–1973*. New York: Oxford University Press, 1998.

Deakin, James."Humphrey: Lyndon Johnson's John the Baptist." *The New Republic* 152, May 29, 1965.

DeBenedetti, Charles, with Charles Chatfield. *An American Ordeal: The Antiwar Movement of the Vietnam Era*. Syracuse, NY: Syracuse University Press, 1990.

Delton, Jennifer A. *Making Minnesota Liberal: Civil Rights and the Transformation of the Democratic Party*. Minneapolis: University of Minnesota Press, 2002.

DiLeo, David L. *George Ball, Vietnam, and the Rethinking of Containment*. Chapel Hill: University of North Carolina Press, 1991.

Eisele, Albert. *Almost to the Presidency: A Biography of Two American Politicians*. Blue Earth, MN: The Piper Company, 1972.

Engelmayer, Sheldon. *Hubert Humphrey: The Man and His Dream*. London: Routledge, 1978.

English, David. *Divided They Stand*. Englewood Cliffs, NJ: Prentice-Hall, Inc., 1969.

Farrell, John A. "Nixon's Vietnam Treachery." *New York Times Sunday Review*, December 31, 2016.

Ferguson, Niall, ed. *Virtual History: Alternatives and Counterfactuals*. New York: Macmillan, 1997.

Forslund, Catherine. *Anna Chennault: Informal Diplomacy and Asian Relations*. Wilmington, DE: Scholarly Resources, 2002.

Fry, Joseph A. *Debating Vietnam: Fulbright, Stennis, and Their Senate Hearings*. Lanham, MD: Rowman & Littlefield, 2006.

Gaddis, John Lewis. *The Cold War: A New History*. New York: Penguin, 2005.

Garrettson, Charles Lloyd, III. *Hubert H. Humphrey: The Politics of Joy*. New Brunswick, NJ: Transaction Publishers, 1993.

Gibbons, William Conrad. *The U.S. Government and the Vietnam War: Executive and Legislative Roles and Relationships*. 4 vols. Princeton, NJ: Princeton University Press, 1986–1995.

Goldberg, Ronald Allen. *Bystanders to the Vietnam War: The Role of the United States Senate, 1950–1965*. Jefferson, NC: McFarland & Company, Inc., 2018.

Goldstein, Joel K. *The Modern American Vice Presidency: The Transformation of a Political Institution.* Princeton, NJ: Princeton University Press, 1982.

Gould, Lewis L. *1968: The Election That Changed America.* Chicago: Ivan R. Dee, 1993.

Griffith, Winthrop. *Humphrey: A Candid Biography.* New York: Morrow, 1965.

Halberstam, David. *The Best and the Brightest.* New York: Ballantine Books, 1992.

———. *The Unfinished Odyssey of Robert Kennedy.* New York: Random House, 1969.

Hanhimäki, Jussi M. "Global Visions and Parochial Politics: The Persistent Dilemma of the 'American Century.'" *Diplomatic History* 27, no. 4 (September 2003): 423–47.

Herring, George C. *America's Longest War: The United States and Vietnam, 1950–1975.* 5th ed. New York: McGraw-Hill, 2013.

———. *LBJ and Vietnam: A Different Kind of War.* Austin: University of Texas Press, 1994.

Hess, Gary R. *Presidential Decisions for War: Korea, Vietnam, and the Persian Gulf.* 2nd ed. Baltimore: Johns Hopkins University Press, 2009.

Humphrey, Hubert H. *The Cause Is Mankind: A Liberal Program for Modern America.* New York: Praeger, 1964.

Isaacson, Walter, and Evan Thomas. *The Wise Men: Six Friends and the World They Made.* New York: Simon and Schuster, 1986.

Jacoby, Jeff. "In Politics, Patience Isn't Overrated, But Loyalty Often Is." *Pundicity,* October 22, 2014. http://www.jeffjacoby.com/15524/in-politics-patience-isnt-overrated-but-loyalty.

Jennett, Richard P. *The Man from Minnesota.* Minneapolis, MN: Joyce Society, 1965.

Johns, Andrew L. "Achilles' Heel: The Vietnam War and George Romney's Bid for the Presidency, 1967 to 1968." *Michigan Historical Review* 26, no. 1 (Spring 2000): 1–29.

———. "Mortgaging the Future: Barry Goldwater, Lyndon Johnson, and Vietnam in the 1964 Presidential Election." *Journal of Arizona History* 61, no. 1 (Spring 2020): 149–60.

———. *Vietnam's Second Front: Domestic Politics, the Republican Party, and the War.* Lexington: University Press of Kentucky, 2010.

———. "A Voice from the Wilderness: Richard Nixon and the Vietnam War, 1964–1966." *Presidential Studies Quarterly* 29, no. 2 (Spring 1999): 317–35.

Johns, Andrew L., and Mitchell B. Lerner, eds. *The Cold War at Home and Abroad: Domestic Politics and U.S. Foreign Policy since 1945.* Lexington: University Press of Kentucky, 2018.

Johnson, Robert David. *All the Way with LBJ: The 1964 Presidential Election.* New York: Cambridge University Press, 2009.

———. *Congress and the Cold War.* New York: Cambridge University Press, 2005.

Johnstone, Andrew, and Andrew Priest, eds. *U.S. Presidential Elections and Foreign Policy: Candidates, Campaigns, and Global Politics from FDR to Bill Clinton.* Lexington: University Press of Kentucky, 2017.

Kamarck, Elaine C. *Primary Politics: How Presidential Candidates Have Shaped the Modern Nominating System.* Washington, DC: Brookings Institution Press, 2009.

Kazin, Michael. *A Godly Hero: The Life of William Jennings Bryan.* New York: Anchor Books, 2006.

Kengor, Paul. *Wreath Layer or Policy Player: The Vice President's Role in Foreign Policy.* Lanham, MD: Lexington Books, 2000.

LaFeber, Walter. *The Deadly Bet: LBJ, Vietnam, and the 1968 Election.* Lanham, MD: Rowman & Littlefield, 2005.

Langguth, A. J. *Our Vietnam/Nước Việt Ta: The War, 1954–1975.* New York: Simon & Schuster, 2000.

Lerner, Mitchell. "'A Big Tree of Peace and Justice': The Vice Presidential Travels of Lyndon Johnson." *Diplomatic History* 34, no. 2 (April 2010): 357–93.

Lerner, Mitchell B., ed. *Looking Back at LBJ: White House Politics in a New Light.* Lawrence: University Press of Kansas, 2005.

Levering, Ralph B. "Is Domestic Politics Being Slighted as an Interpretive Framework?" *SHAFR Newsletter* 25, no. 1 (March 1994): 17–35.

Logevall, Fredrik. *Choosing War: The Lost Chance for Peace and the Escalation of War in Vietnam.* Berkeley: University of California Press, 1999.

————. "Comment on Francis M. Bator's 'No Good Choices: LBJ and the Vietnam/Great Society Connection.'" *Diplomatic History* 32, no. 3 (June 2008): 355–59.

————. "Domestic Politics." In *Explaining the History of American Foreign Relations*, 3rd ed., edited by Frank Costigliola and Michael J. Hogan, 151–67. New York: Cambridge University Press, 2016.

————. *Embers of War: The Fall of an Empire and the Making of America's Vietnam*. New York: Random House, 2012.

————. "Lyndon Johnson and Vietnam." *Presidential Studies Quarterly* 34, no. 1 (March 2004): 100–112.

————. "Vietnam and the Question of What Might Have Been." In *The New Frontier Revisited*, edited by Mark J. White, 19–62. London: Palgrave, 1998.

Longley, Kyle. *LBJ's 1968: Power, Politics, and the Presidency in America's Year of Upheaval*. New York: Cambridge University Press, 2018.

Mann, Robert. *A Grand Delusion: America's Descent into Vietnam*. New York: Basic Books, 2001.

————. *The Walls of Jericho: Lyndon Johnson, Hubert Humphrey, Richard Russell, and the Struggle for Civil Rights*. New York: Harcourt Brace & Co., 1996.

Martin, Ralph G. *A Man for All People: Hubert Humphrey*. New York: Grosset & Dunlap, 1968.

McQuaid, Kim. *The Anxious Years: America in the Vietnam-Watergate Era*. New York: Basic Books, 1989.

Moïse, Edwin E. *The Myths of Tet: The Most Misunderstood Event of the Vietnam War*. Lawrence: University Press of Kansas, 2017.

————. *Tonkin Gulf and the Escalation of the Vietnam War*. Chapel Hill: University of North Carolina Press, 1996.

Nash, Philip. "The Use of Counterfactuals in History: A Look at the Literature." *The Society for Historians of American Foreign Relations Newsletter* 22, no. 1 (March 1991): 2–12.

Natoli, Marie D. "The Humphrey Vice Presidency in Retrospect." *Presidential Studies Quarterly* 12, no. 4 (Fall 1982): 603–9.

Nelson, Justin A. "Drafting Lyndon Johnson: The President's Secret Role in the 1968 Democratic Convention." *Presidential Studies Quarterly* 30, no. 4 (December 2000): 688–713.

Nelson, Michael. *Resilient America: Electing Nixon in 1968, Channeling Dissent, and Dividing Government*. Lawrence: University Press of Kansas, 2014.

Oberdorfer, Don. *Tet! The Turning Point in the Vietnam War*. Rev. ed. Baltimore: Johns Hopkins University Press, 2001.

O'Donnell, Lawrence. *Playing with Fire: The 1968 Election and the Transformation of American Politics*. New York: Penguin, 2017.

Offner, Arnold A. *Hubert Humphrey: The Conscience of the Country*. New Haven, CT: Yale University Press, 2018.

Ornstein, Norman. "Welcome to Another Golden Era of Liberal Senators." *The New Republic*, January 8, 2013. www.tnr.com/print/blog/plank/111731/liberal-wave-senate-produces-third-golden-era-our-lifetime.

Osborne, John. "Talk with Humphrey: The Dogged Loyalty that Dogs HHH." *The New Republic* 158, May 4, 1968.

Osgood, Kenneth, and Andrew K. Frank, eds. *Selling War in a Media Age: The Presidency and Public Opinion in the American Century*. Gainesville: University Press of Florida, 2010.

Parker, Jason. "'On Such a Full Sea Are We Now Afloat': Politics and U.S. Foreign Relations across the Water's Edge." *Perspectives*, May 2011. https://www.historians.org/publications-and-directories/perspectives-on-history/may-2011/political-history-today/on-such-a-full-sea-are-we-now-afloat.

Paterson, Thomas G. "Foreign Aid under Wraps: The Point Four Program." *The Wisconsin Magazine of History* 56, no. 2 (Winter 1972–1973): 119–26.

Prados, John. *Vietnam: The History of an Unwinnable War, 1945–1975*. Lawrence: University Press of Kansas, 2009.

Preston, Andrew. *The War Council: McGeorge Bundy, the NSC, and Vietnam*. Cambridge, MA: Harvard University Press, 2006.

Rabe, Stephen G. *The Most Dangerous Area in the World: John F. Kennedy Confronts Communist Revolution in Latin America*. Chapel Hill: University of North Carolina Press, 1999.

Ryskind, Allan H. *Hubert: An Unauthorized Biography of the Vice President*. New Rochelle, NY: Arlington House, 1968.

Sandbrook, Dominic. *Eugene McCarthy: The Rise and Fall of Postwar American Liberalism*. New York: Alfred A. Knopf, 2004.

Schlesinger, Jr., Arthur M. *Robert Kennedy and His Times*. New York: Ballantine Books, 1978.

Schmickle, William E. *Preservation Politics: Keeping Historic Districts Vital*. Lanham, MD: Altamira Press, 2012.

Schmitz, David F. *The Tet Offensive: Politics, War, and Public Opinion*. Lanham, MD: Rowman & Littlefield, 2005.

Schmitz, David F., and T. Christopher Jespersen, eds. *Architects of the American Century: Individuals and Institutions in Twentieth-Century U.S. Foreign Policymaking*. Chicago: Imprint Publications, 2000.

Schreiber, E. M. "Vietnam Policy Preferences and Withheld 1968 Presidential Votes." *The Public Opinion Quarterly* 37, no. 1 (Spring 1973): 91–98.

Schulzinger, Robert D. *A Time for War: The United States and Vietnam, 1941–1975*. New York: Oxford University Press, 1997.

Schumacher, Michael. *The Contest: The 1968 Election and the War for America's Soul*. Minneapolis: University of Minnesota Press, 2018.

Schwartz, Thomas A. "'Henry, . . . Winning an Election Is Terribly Important': Partisan Politics in the History of U.S. Foreign Relations." *Diplomatic History* 33, no. 2 (April 2009): 173–90.

Sherrill, Robert. *The Accidental President*. New York: Grossman Publishers, 1967.

Sherrill, Robert, and Harry W. Ernst. *The Drugstore Liberal*. New York: Grossman Publishers, 1968.

Shesol, Jeff. *Mutual Contempt: Lyndon Johnson, Robert Kennedy, and the Feud That Defined a Decade*. New York: W. W. Norton & Company, 1997.

Sieg, Kent G. "The 1968 Presidential Election and Peace in Vietnam." *Presidential Studies Quarterly* 26, no. 4 (Fall 1996): 1062–80.

Small, Melvin. *Antiwarriors: The Vietnam War and the Battle for America's Hearts and Minds*. Wilmington, DE: Scholarly Resources, 2002.

———. *At the Water's Edge: American Politics and the Vietnam War*. Chicago: Ivan R. Dee, 2005.

———. *Democracy and Diplomacy: The Impact of Domestic Politics on U.S. Foreign Policy, 1789–1994*. Baltimore: Johns Hopkins University Press, 1996.

———. *Johnson, Nixon, and the Doves*. New Brunswick, NJ: Rutgers University Press, 1989.

Smith, Robert B. "Disaffection, Delegitimation, and Consequences: Aggregate Trends for World War II, Korea, and Vietnam." In *Public Opinion and the Military Establishment*, edited by Charles C. Moskos, 240–43. Beverly Hills, CA: Sage Publications, 1971.

Solberg, Carl. *Hubert Humphrey: A Biography*. New York: W. W. Norton & Company, 1984.

Statler, Kathryn C. *Replacing France: The Origins of American Intervention in Vietnam*. Lexington: University Press of Kentucky, 2007.

Stone, Gary. *Elites for Peace: The Senate and the Vietnam War, 1964–1968*. Knoxville: University of Tennessee Press, 2007.

Taubman, William, Sergei Khrushchev, and Abbot Gleason. *Nikita Khrushchev*. New Haven, CT: Yale University Press, 2000.

Thompson, Jane C., ed. *Wit & Wisdom of Hubert H. Humphrey*. Minneapolis, MN: Partners Press, Ltd., 1984.

Thurber, Timothy N. *The Politics of Equality: Hubert H. Humphrey and the African American Freedom Struggle*. New York: Columbia University Press, 1999.

VanDeMark, Brian. *Road to Disaster: A New History of America's Descent into Vietnam*. New York: Custom House, 2018.

van den Berg, Erik. "Supersalesman for the Great Society: Vice President Hubert H. Humphrey, 1965–1969." *American Studies International* 36, no. 3 (October 1998): 59–72.

Webb, Daryl. "Crusade: George McGovern's Opposition to the Vietnam War." *South Dakota History* 28, no. 3 (Fall 1998): 161–90.

Wells, Tom. *The War Within: America's Battle over Vietnam*. New York: Henry Holt and Company, 1994.

Westman, Paul. *Hubert Humphrey: The Politics of Joy*. Minneapolis, MN: Dillon Press, 1978.

Whalen, Richard J. *Catch the Falling Flag: A Republican's Challenge to His Party*. Boston: Houghton Mifflin, 1972.

White, Theodore H. *The Making of the President, 1964*. New York: Atheneum Publishers, 1965.

———. *The Making of the President, 1968*. New York: Atheneum Publishers, 1969.

———. *The Making of the President, 1972*. New York: Atheneum Publishers, 1973.

Wicker, Tom. *JFK and LBJ: The Influence of Personality upon Politics*. New York: William Morrow, 1968.

Wilde, Oscar. *An Ideal Husband* (1893). https://www.gutenberg.org/files/885/885-h/885-h.htm.

Willbanks, James H. *The Tet Offensive: A Concise History*. New York: Columbia University Press, 2006.

Wilson, Paula, ed. *The Civil Rights Rhetoric of Hubert H. Humphrey: 1948–1964*. Lanham, MD: University Press of America, 1996.

Witcover, Jules. *The Resurrection of Richard Nixon*. New York: G. P. Putnam's Sons, 1970.

Woods, Randall Bennett. *J. William Fulbright, Vietnam, and the Search for a Cold War Foreign Policy*. New York: Cambridge University Press, 1998.

———. *LBJ: Architect of Ambition*. New York: Free Press, 2006.

Woods, Randall B., ed. *Vietnam and the American Political Tradition: The Politics of Dissent*. New York: Cambridge University Press, 2003.

Zehnpfenning, Gladys. *Hubert H. Humphrey: Champion of Human Rights*. Minneapolis, MN: T. S. Denison and Company, Inc., 1966.

Zelizer, Julian E. *Arsenal of Democracy: The Politics of National Security—From World War II to the War on Terrorism*. New York: Basic Books, 2010.

———. *The Fierce Urgency of Now: Lyndon Johnson, Congress, and the Battle for the Great Society*. New York: Penguin, 2015.

Index

Democratic Party platform plank on, 90, 94–100; division in, 93–94; as domestic policy in disguise, 9; duality approach to, 12–13; interest in, 11; leadership capacity in, 51; McCarthy concerns with, 78; recommendations, 56; reputation, 23; skepticism of, 14, 32, 42, 43; speech on changes to, 116–120, 158n48; Wise Men advising on, 80, 154n12. *See also specific policy*
fortune, 9
France, 13–14. *See also* Paris peace talks
freedom: defense of, 21, 44; Humphrey on, 103
free elections, 97, 152n53
Freeman, Orville, 107, 119
free spirit, 84
friendship, 15–16
Fulbright, J. William: disagreements with, 60; Lansdale meeting with Sparkman and, 29; SFRC public hearings launched by, 52

Gallup polls: on foreign policy approval ratings, 77; on Humphrey popularity, 50; on presidential campaign 1968, 113, 127, 156n3; on Vietnam conflict, 109
Ginsburg, David: advice from, 90; on policy statement, 94; Schlesinger writing to, 89
Goldwater, Barry, 160n12; campaign against, 22–23; LBJ criticism from, 64
Great Society programs: advocacy for, 5; ideas for, 10; threat to, 35
The Green Berets, 88
Greene, Wallace, 44
Gulf of Tonkin Resolution, 21–22, 44

Halberstam, David: on generation of liberals, 3; on LBJ, 16–17
Haldeman, H. R., 123
Happy Warrior nickname, 10, 145n6
Harris poll, 127
Hatfield, Mark, 109
hawkishness, 58, 62
Honolulu summit, 52–53, 61
House of Commons debate, 4
Hudson, Richard, 62–63
Hughes, Thomas L., 32–33, 58

Humphrey, Hubert. *See specific topics*

An Ideal Husband (Wilde), 101
Indochina, 13–14
informal diplomacy techniques, 146n15
Issues and Answers, 57, 88–89, 92, 127

JCS. *See* Joint Chiefs of Staff
JFK. *See* Kennedy, John F.
Johnson, Lyndon (LBJ): advice rejected by, 80; Bundy, M., suggestions to, 41; cease-fire from, 125–126; on character and reputation, 10; on Cronkite, 77; Democratic Party concerns of, 44–45; on discussion of differences, 25; on Dulles, 12; Eisenhower meeting with, 36; Eisenhower supporting, 149n24; FBI phone taps ordered by, 98; Ford and Goldwater critical of, 64; Ford supporting, 149n24; foreign policy draft statement rejected by, 94–95; friendship with, 15–16; independence from, 112–113; loyalty to, 2, 4–6; manipulation by, 16; marginalization by, 23–24; McCarthy on policy of, 78; memorandum response from, 35–36; Nixon conversations with, 116; Nixon favored by, 105, 119; Nixon undermined by, 126; paranoia of, 38–39, 90; on Paris peace talks, 107; on peace, 123, 126; personality of, 16–17; pettiness of, 119; policy alternatives for, 30; praise from, 50; resignation from re-election campaign, 80–81; respect from, lack of, 87–88, 107; San Antonio Formula of, 87, 125, 155n30; shadow of, 84; support from, lack of, 2; Thieu and Ky meeting with, 52–53; travel by, 147n32; trust from, lack of, 16, 44, 53–54; Veterans of Foreign Wars speech from, 92–93; as vice president, 17, 24–25, 147n32; vice president candidate selected by, 17–19, 22; Vietnam concerns of, 28; warning from, 18–19; Wise Men gathering with, 80
Joint Chiefs of Staff (JCS), 77

Kennedy, Edward, 120

Index

About the Author

Andrew L. Johns is associate professor of history at Brigham Young University and the David M. Kennedy Center for International Studies. He is author or editor of *The Cold War at Home and Abroad: Domestic Politics and U.S. Foreign Policy since 1945* (coedited with Mitchell B. Lerner, 2018); *A Companion to Ronald Reagan* (2015); *Diplomatic Games: Sport, Statecraft, and International Relations since 1945* (coedited with Heather L. Dichter, 2014); *Vietnam's Second Front: Domestic Politics, the Republican Party, and the War* (2010); and *The Eisenhower Administration, the Third World, and the Globalization of the Cold War* (coedited with Kathryn C. Statler, 2006).

A specialist in the history of U.S. foreign relations and presidential history in the twentieth century, he teaches courses on U.S. foreign relations, the Cold War, the U.S. presidency, the United States in Vietnam, and the United States since 1877. Professor Johns is past president of the Pacific Coast Branch of the American Historical Association (2018–2019) and has served as editor of *Passport: The Society for Historians of American Foreign Relations Review* since 2011.